Magic of the Runes

Magic of the Runes

Samael Aun Weor

GLORIAN

Magic of the Runes
A Glorian Book / 2014

Originally published in Spanish as "Mensaje de Navidad 1968-
1969" (1969) and later named by students "La Magia de las
Runas."

This Edition © 2014 Glorian Publishing

Print ISBN 978-1-934206-29-4
Ebook ISBN 978-1-934206-96-6

Glorian Publishing is a non-profit organization delivering to
humanity the teachings of Samael Aun Weor. All proceeds go to
further the distribution of these books. For more information,
visit our website.

gnosticteachings.org

Contents

Dedication...1

Chapter 1: The Divine Mother and the Holy Gods 3

Chapter 2: Parallel Universes 7

Chapter 3: Rune Fah (Feoh, Fehu) 11

Chapter 4: Pennate Gods 15

Chapter 5: The Puncta..19

Chapter 6: Return and Transmigration 23

Chapter 7: Rune Is (Isa)..27

Chapter 8: The Cosmic Egg..31

Chapter 9: The Oracle of Apollo 35

Chapter 10: Rune Ar...39

Chapter 11: Proton and Antiproton 43

Chapter 12: The Harpies 47

Chapter 13: Rune Sig (Sigel, Sowelu)...................................51

Chapter 14: The Ain Soph...55

Chapter 15: The King Helenus 59

Chapter 16: Rune Tyr (Teiwaz)..63

Chapter 17: Meditation...67

Chapter 18: The Deformed Giant Polyphemus 71

Chapter 19: Rune Bar (Beor, Berkana) 77

Chapter 20: The Ten Rules for Meditation 81

Chapter 21: The Tragedy of Queen Dido 85

Chapter 22: Rune Ur (Uruz)..89

Chapter 23: The Story of Master Meng Shan........................93

Chapter 24: The Country of the Dead....................................97

Chapter 25: Runes Dorn and Thorn (Thurisaz).....................101

Chapter 26: The "I" 105

Chapter 27: The Cruel Enchantress Circe 109

Chapter 28: Rune Os (Othila) 115

Chapter 29: Origin of the Pluralized "I" 119

Chapter 30: The Three Furies 125

Chapter 31: Rune Rita (Raido) 129

Chapter 32: The Divine Mother Kundalini 135

Chapter 33: The Forge of the Cyclops 141

Chapter 34: Rune Kaum 145

Chapter 35: The Purgatorial Region 151

Chapter 36: The Temple of Hercules 155

Chapter 37: Rune Hagal 159

Chapter 38: The River Lethe 165

Chapter 39: The Pines — The Nymphs 169

Chapter 40: Rune Not (Nauthiz) 173

Chapter 41: Parsifal 183

Chapter 42: The Sacred Fire 189

Chapter 43: Rune Laf (Lagu, Laguz) 193

Chapter 44: The Final Liberation 197

Chapter 45: The Dream of the Consciousness 201

Chapter 46: Rune Gibur (Gebo, Gyfur) 205

Final Salutations 211

Glossary 213

Index 241

Illustrations

The Divine Mother and the Christ-child 2

Neptune 5

Disguised Venus Directing Aeneas and Achates to Carthage 6

Rune Fah in Egypt 10

Rune Fah 14

Aeneas, Anchises and Ascanius Fleeing Troy 18

Centaurs in the Inferno 22

Swami Sivananda and Disciples 29

Rune Is 30

Parallel Universes (Dimensions) on the Tree of Life 32

Rune Ar 42

Harpies as Seen by Dante in the Inferno 46

Ain Soph and Four Bodies on the Tree of Life 58

Aeneas and the Sibyl of Cumae 61

Rune Tyr 66

The Triumphal Entry into Jerusalem 68

"Caves of Bameen" 72

The Seven Root Races 73

Stones of Carnac (Brittany) 74

Abraham and the Three Angels 76

Rune Tyr Bar 80

The Meeting of Dido and Aeneas 86

Rune Ur 92

The Tree of Life (Kabbalah) Superimposed over the Body 102

Rune Thorn 104

Circe 110

Arcanum Six 111

Padmasambhava and Yeshe Tsogyal 114

Rune Os 117

Krishna atop Kaliya 123

The Three Furies 124

Rune Rita...133

From Venus and Anchises..134

The Centers of the Human Machine 136

Forge of the Cyclops...140

Venus Gives Aeneas his Arms and Armor..................................143

Romulus and Remus...144

The Celestial Eagle...150

Pranayama...180

Rune Not...181

Parsifal Tempted in the Enchanted Garden...............................182

The Spinal Column 188

Rune Laf 196

Swastika on a Buddhist Temple in Korea...................................206

Dedication

In memory, honor, and glory of the Latin American Ecumenical Gnostic Congress, I write this 1968-1969 Christmas Message.

I write the fifth gospel. I teach the synthesis religion, which was the primeval religion of humanity, the doctrine of **Janus** or the doctrine of the **Jinns**. This is the religion of wisdom of the ancient sacerdotal colleges, of the Gymnosophists or solitary **Jinns** from Central Asia, of the Iohanes, Samoans, Egyptian ascetics, ancient Pythagoreans, medieval Rosicrucians, Templars, primeval Masons, and other more or less known esoteric brotherhoods, whose list would occupy a dozen pages. This is the secret doctrine of the knights of the Holy Grail. This is the living stone of Jacob, the Lapiz-Electrix (magnes), dialectically explained.

Without the fifth gospel, the four former gospels remain veiled. Therefore, I write the fifth in order to tear the veil of **Isis**.

It is urgent to unveil in order to teach. It is necessary to preach the gospel of the kingdom in all the nations of the world. To preach without unveiling is equivalent to not teaching. Therefore, we need to explain the four Gospels with the fifth one.

The gospel of the kingdom has never been preached, because it has never been explained. The four gospels are in code. This is why no one could ever essentially explain them. Therefore, with the fifth gospel, the light shines in the darkness.

Behold then, here is another book of the fifth gospel.

> "To whosoever knows, the Word gives power. No one has uttered it, no one will utter it, except the one who has the Word incarnated."

Mexico, March 14, 1968, the seventh year of Aquarius.

Inverential peace,

Samael Aun Weor

THE DIVINE MOTHER AND THE CHRIST-CHILD
"O Virgin Mother, Daughter of your Son..."

Chapter 1
The Divine Mother and the Holy Gods

"Virgin mother, daughter of your Son,
more humble and sublime than any creature,
fixed goal decreed from all eternity,
you are the one who gave to human nature
so much nobility that its Creator
did not disdain His being made its creature.
That love whose warmth allowed this flower to bloom
within the everlasting peace was love
rekindled in your womb; for us above,
you are the noonday torch of charity,
and there below, on earth, among the mortals,
you are a living spring of hope. Lady,
you are so high, you can so intercede,
that he who would have grace but does not seek
your aid, may long to fly but has no wings.
Your loving-kindness does not only answer
the one who asks, but it is often ready
to answer freely long before the asking.
In you compassion is, in you is pity,
in you is generosity, in you
is every goodness found in any creature.
This man who from the deepest hollow in
the universe, up to this height, has seen
the lives of spirits, one by one now pleads
with you, through grace, to grant him so much virtue
that he may lift his vision higher still
may lift it toward the ultimate salvation.
And I, who never burned for my own vision
more than I burn for his, do offer you
all of my prayers and pray that they may not
fall short that, with your prayers, you may disperse
all of the clouds of his mortality
so that the Highest Joy be his to see.
This, too, o Queen, who can do what you would,
I ask of you: that after such a vision,
his sentiments preserve their perseverance.

May your protection curb his mortal passions."
— The Divine Comedy, Paradise, Canto 33:1-37, by Dante Alighieri

"Oh Isis, mother of the cosmos, root of love, trunk, bud, leaf, flower and seed of all that exists, we conjure Thee, naturalizing force. We call the Queen of the space and of the night, and kissing Her loving eyes, drinking the dew of Her lips, inhaling the sweet aroma of Her body, we exclaim: Oh Nut! Thou eternal seity of heaven Who art the primordial soul, Who art what was and what shalt be, whose veil no mortal has lifted, when You are beneath the irradiating stars of the nocturnal and profound sky of the desert, with purity of heart and in the flame of the serpent, we call Thee." — Gnostic Ritual

"Glory, glory unto the Mother Kundalini who leads the sadhaka from chakra to chakra and illuminates his intellect, identifying him with the supreme Brahman, by means of Her infinite grace and power. May Her benedictions reach us!" — Sivananda

Was not Aeneas the son of the hero Anchises and of the goddess Venus?

How many times had the Divine Mother favorably assisted the Trojans, even inclining the will of Jupiter (the Solar Logos), father of gods and men, on their behalf?

Oh Aeolus! Lord of the wind, you who have the power of calming and raising the waves of the immense sea. You who submerged part of the Trojan fleet within the boisterous waves, tell me: what will become of thee without thy Divine Mother Kundalini? From whence will you get such great potency?

Oh Neptune! Lord of the sublime marine profundities. Oh thou, great god who makes the winds flee and who appeases the furious elements before thy divine sight, can you perhaps deny that You have a Mother? Oh lord of the profundities! You know very well that without Her, you cannot grasp in your dexterous hand that formidable trident that grants you power over the frightful, deepest pools of the abyss.

Oh Neptune! Venerable master of humanity, you who gave such wise precepts unto the populace of submerged Atlantis, remember us as well, the ones who love thee, oh great lord.

When the north wind raises
the waves towards heaven,
and some castaways see
themselves rising with
the waves to the stars,
while for others the
waters open, and in
the troughs they see
themselves submerg-
ing into the abysses,
then there is no other
hope than your mercy.

The south wind strikes
the ships against reefs hidden
in mid-ocean; the southeasterly

NEPTUNE

wind casts them helplessly from the high sea onto the sand-
banks, running them aground, blocking them in with walls
of sand, or striking them against the cliffs. But you, oh Lord
Neptune, save many people who swim. Then all the crashing of
the sea falls silent.

The marine grottos, home to the sea nymphs, are mysterious sites that conserve the memory of your works, oh great
god!

You who have known the dangers of the boisterous ocean
of life, the terrible anger of Scylla of the howling reefs, the
rocks thrown by the vigilant Cyclops, the hard path that leads
to Nirvana, and the battles with the tempter Mara and his
three furies, do not commit the crime of ingratitude: never ever
forget your Divine Mother.

Blessed be those who comprehend the mystery of their own
Divine Mother. She is the root of their own Monad. She carries
in Her arms our Innermost Buddha, the child who is gestated
within her immaculate bosom.

Descending from the high summits, Venus disguised
Herself as a Spartan girl out hunting in order to visit Her son
Aeneas, the Trojan hero. This was for the good purpose of
guiding him towards Carthage where Queen Dido—the one

DISGUISED VENUS DIRECTING AENEAS AND ACHATES TO CARTHAGE

who killed herself for passion after having sworn loyalty to Sychaeus' ashes—was reigning with flourish.

The Beloved One has the power of making Herself visible and tangible in the physical world when this is what she wishes.

Oh god of mine! How many times, oh ignorant mortals, have you been visited by your Divine Mother, and nonetheless you did not recognize her?

How fortunate you were, oh illustrious citizen of proud Ilium, when your beloved Mother covered you with her protective cloud in order to make you invisible!

Behold, all of you who covet magical powers: do you ignore perchance that your sacred Mother is omnipotent?

Oh lady of mine! Only the long-haired bard Iopas with his cithara of gold could sing your goodness.

Chapter 2
Parallel Universes

There is a bold hypothesis that suggests the existence of a phantom universe similar to our own: "Only a very weak interaction between these two universes exists, therefore we do not see this other world that is mixed with our own."

Revolutionary, scientific Gnosticism goes much further into this question, emphatically affirming the harmonious coexistence of an infinitude of parallel universes.

The radical exclusion of this transcendental, scientific concept would leave a considerable number of unclassified events without a logical explanation, such as mysterious disappearances, etc.

On the perfumed and delectable shores of a river, that joyfully and happily sings while gliding within the profound jungles of a tropical region of South America, a group of innocent children watched in horror as their own beloved mother disappeared. She floated in the air for a few moments, then apparently submerged herself into another dimension.

> "On a summer day of 1809, Benjamin Bathurst, Ambassador of England in the court of Austria, was in a small city of Germany. His chariot stopped before an inn. The Ambassador got off the chariot and walked a few steps — the horses hid his figure for a moment. The innkeeper, the Ambassador's servants, and some travelers who were present there did not see him again. He never reappeared."

In these unlucky days of life, the mysterious disappearances of men, women, children, ships, airplanes, etc., are scandalously multiplying, in spite of the secret intelligence services and the marvelous radar and radio equipment that theoretically should not permit such mysteries to exist in their domain.

The concept of parallel universes is by all means more exact and more scientific than the famous, subjective "planes" of the reactionary pseudo-occultism.

A deep analysis would take us to the logical conclusion that such universes exist not only in the superior dimensions of space, but also within the submerged infra-dimensions.

It is in no way an absurdity to affirm with complete clarity that within each parallel universe exists a series of universes. Let us refer to these as atoms, molecules, particles, cells, organisms, etc.

Please, dear reader, be so kind as to reflect and comprehend. We are not speaking of universes of anti-matter, which are something totally different. Anti-matter obeys the exact same laws as our matter, but each one of the particles by which it is compounded has an inverted electrical charge in relation with the matter that we know.

MIliums of galaxies constituted of anti-matter exist within the profound bosom of Mother Space, but they also have their own parallel universes.

No physicist ignores that this universe in which we live, move, and die, exists thanks to certain constants: speed of light, Planck's constant, Avogadro's number, elementary charge, electron-volt, and rest energy of a body of one kilogram of mass, etc.

When a universe possesses radically different constants, then it becomes totally strange and unimaginable for us. However, if the differences are not so great, interactions with our world become possible.

The modern wise men have invented an astonishing magical mirror: the accelerator of protons.

The scenes of our neighboring parallel universe, situated in the fourth dimension, certainly are astonishing.

The extraordinary behavior of a certain mysterious particle named K-meson causes perplexity, indecision, uncertainty.

Three Chinese scientists, Lee, Yang, and Mrs. Wu, who live and work in the United States, discovered with surprise and amazement that the Law of the Conservation of Parity is not upheld by the K-meson particles.

This admirable, stupendous, and portentous discovery came to demonstrate that the K-meson behaves in a strange manner because it is disturbed by the marvelous and extraordinary forces of a parallel universe.

Modern scientists are dangerously approaching the fourth dimension, and they even intend to pierce it with the help of the neutrino.

The neutrino is prodigious, portentous, and astonishing. It possesses the capacity of crossing through an infinite thickness of matter without any appreciable reaction.

Photons or grains of light can come from the unalterable infinite, but only a delicate sheet of paper is needed in order to stop them. Nonetheless, the neutrino can pass through the planet Earth in its totality, as if it were a void. The neutrino is by all means the primary agent capable of penetrating into the neighboring parallel universe.

It has been a long time since the famous Italian scientist Bruno Pontecorvo proposed the construction of a neutrino telescope. His idea was astonishing and momentous. Penetration into the neighboring parallel universe could be possible with such a revolutionary optical instrument.

Certainly, it is remarkable to know that the K-meson particles, whose strange activity permitted the Chinese scientists to establish the hypothesis of parallel universes, are obtained via the disintegrating effects of neutrino emissions.

The parallel universes interpenetrate each other without confusion. Each one possesses its own space, which is not of our circuit.

Revolutionary, scientific Gnosticism goes much further than simple hypotheses and suppositions, and solemnly affirms the existence of parallel universes.

Students of esotericism need a spiritual cultural revolution. This matter of "planes and sub-planes" is a matter or theme that has never been clear and objective, and has only succeeded in leading us into confusion. It is urgent to modify the esotericist's lexicon. A new occult vocabulary is needed, a revolutionary special language that can exactly serve the Aquarian ideology.

Instead of the aforesaid metaphysical planes and many pompous theories, it is better to talk of parallel universes.

RUNE FAH IN EGYPT

Chapter 3
Rune Fah (Feoh, Fehu)

Beloved reader, we have stated very solemnly in our former Christmas messages that the poor intellectual animal is only a chrysalid, and that which is called **man** must be formed and developed within it.

Certainly, the Solar Fire is necessary for the possibility of becoming human to be created and developed within each one of us.

Fohat is the generative force, the central, living, and philosophical fire that can originate the authentic and legitimate mutant, the real and true human within the cosmo-biology of the rational animal.

Many types of fire exist; let us remember the Lights of Saint Elmo seen during tempests.

It is good for us to remember the mysterious column of fire that guided the Israelites in the wilderness.

It is worthwhile to remember the strange meteors of fire that appear in cemeteries, that physics in its own way has qualified under the name of "ignis fatuus."

Many phenomena reminiscent of lightning exist in the form of balls, cat-meteors, etc.

In her monumental work entitled *The Secret Doctrine*, H. P. Blavatsky refers to the sacred fire of Zoroaster, or the **Atash-behram** of the Parsis.

How ineffable are the words of H.P.B. when she speaks of the fire of Hermes!

The explanations of this great martyr from the last century are notable when she brings to our memory the fire of Hermes of the ancient Germans, the flashing lightning of Cybele, the torch of Apollo, the flame of the altar of Pan, the shining sparks on the hats of the Dioscuri, on the head of the Gorgons, on the helmet of Pallas, and on the Caduceus of Mercury.

How sublime was the imperishable fire in the Temple of Apollo, and in the Temple of Vesta!

How sublime was the Egyptian **Ptah-Ra**! During the night of the centuries, how magnificently shone the fire of the Greek Cataibates Zeus, which according to Pausanias descended from heaven to earth.

Certainly, the Pentecostal tongues of fire and the flaming bush of Moses are very similar to the burning tunal that brought about the founding of Mexico.

The imperishable lamp of Abraham still shines, refulgent and terribly divine.

The eternal fire of the bottomless abyss or the pleroma of the Gnostics is something that can never be forgotten.

When referring to the sacred fire, it is convenient to mention the fulgent vapors of the Oracle of Delphi, the Sidereal Light of the Rosicrucian-Gnostics, the Akasha of the Hindustani adepts, the Astral Light of Eliphas Levi, etc.

The initiatic books are written with characters of fire. We need to fecundate our intimate nature if we truly want the Solar Man to be born within us.

I.N.R.I.
IGNIS NATURA RENOVATUR INTEGRA
The fire renews nature integrally

Among the multiple fires that crackle in the divine eagle, the one that glows, glitters, and shines in the pineal gland (the superior part of the brain) is always the troubadour of the Holy Spirit who carries the Ark from city to city, in other words, from chakra to chakra along the dorsal spine.

Indeed, we need to awaken consciousness with intensely accelerated urgency if we want to know ourselves in depth. Only the human being who is conscious of Self can enter into the parallel universes at will.

The Hindustani Hatha yogis talk at length about Devi Kundalini, the igneous serpent of our magical powers, and they even suppose that they can awaken it based on respiratory exercises and many other complicated and difficult physical practices.

We, the Gnostics, know that the brazen serpent that healed the Israelites in the wilderness, the divine princess of love, only awakens and rises along the dorsal spine by means of the

Maithuna. Nonetheless, it is not advantageous to undervalue pranayama.

It is worth knowing that this magical science of breath (pranayama), when wisely combined with scientific meditation, allows us to utilize certain sparks, flashes, flames of Kundalini, for the healthy purpose of attaining the awakening of the consciousness.

To consciously work within the distinct parallel universes, to travel by will in a lucid, clear, and brilliant way through all of those supra-sensible regions, is only possible by transforming the sub-consciousness into consciousness.

A judo of the Spirit exists; we are referring to the runic exercises. These are formidable in order to attain the awakening of the consciousness.

Whosoever wants to work with this judo must begin to work with the rune of Mercury, which has a violet color that originates extraordinary cosmic forces.

Therefore, it is necessary to know that this aforesaid Nordic rune encloses within itself all of the potency and impulse of fecundity.

We need the Fohat's breath, the Pentecostal sparks, in order to fecundate our own psyche, in order for us to become conscious of Self.

If we analyze the practice of the Rune **Fah**, we can affirm that pranayama, prayer, meditation, and a specific sacred posture all exist within it.

Practice

When we get out of bed, with immense happiness we must salute each new day by raising our arms towards our Lord, the Sun Christ. The arms must be placed in such a way that the left arm is a little more elevated than the right one, and the palms of our hands must face the light in an ineffable and sublime attitude of one who truly longs to receive the solar rays.

This is the sacred posture of the Rune **Fah**. Thus, this is also a method to work with pranayama, by inhaling the air through the nose and exhaling it through the mouth in a rhythmical way and with much faith.

Let us imagine in those instants that the light of the Sun Christ enters within us through the fingers of our hands, then circulates through our arms, inundates the whole of our organism, and finally reaches the consciousness in order to stimulate it, to awaken it, and to call it into activity.

You must also practice this runic judo in the mysterious and divine nights, before the starry sky of Urania, with the same posture, and praying like this:

Marvelous forces of love, revive my sacred fires so that my consciousness will awaken.

Fah...*

Feh...

Fih...

Foh...

Fuh...

This short yet great prayer can and must be prayed with all of our heart, as many times as we want.

RUNE FAH

* Editor's Note: Throughout this book, mantra vowels are pronounced with these sounds: Fah as in "ma," Feh as in "weigh," Fih as in "tea," Foh as in "toe," and Fuh as in "too."

Chapter 4

Penate Gods

Four times the horse of Troy bumped violently against the threshold of the unconquerable gate, and four times the clanging of armor echoed within its monstrous metallic womb. However, the Trojans paid no heed and pressed on blindly, accursed by a god's will.

Then the prophetess Cassandra, possessed by the Divine Spirit, convulsively agitated, and with her hair in disorder, opened her lips to foretell their tremendous doom. But Apollo had willed that these would be lips that the Trojans would never believe.

Oh Cassandra! You of marvelous prophesies, how horrible was your karma. With hair streaming, you were dragged in a cruel, pitiless, inhuman, and barbaric way, while in Priam's palace the ferocious and sanguinary Achaeans tore down the august towers, dismantled the venerable walls, and profaned everything with their homicidal bronze.

The sumptuous and splendid rooms of the royal house of the old king were inundated with cruel and pitiless soldiers.

Hecuba and her hundred women (wives of her sons) desperately ran as madwomen through the halls and corridors, and the elder King Priam's blood polluted the sacred altar of the holy gods with a frightful purplish red.

It is written that when the gods want to punish men, first they confuse them.

Useless was the damnation of the venerable monarch against Pyrrhus, for Pyrrhus then made his reply by lunging his cruel weapon at the respectable elder. While winding King Priam's hair in his left hand, he slaughtered him next to the altar of Jupiter, father of gods and men.

The fate of the beautiful Helen could have been horrendous if Venus, the Divine Mother Kundalini of Aeneas, had not stopped the right hand of her son.

She made herself visible and tangible before the Trojan hero, and filled with pain told him:

"O my son, what bitterness can have been enough to stir this wild anger in you? Why this raging passion? Where is all the love you used to have for me? Will you not first go and see where you have left your father, crippled with age, and find whether your wife Creusa is still alive, and your son Ascanius? The whole Greek army is prowling all around them and they would have been carried off by the flames or slashed by the swords of the enemy if my loving care were not defending them.

"It is not the hated beauty of the Spartan woman, the daughter of Tyndareus, that is overthrowing all this wealth and laying low the topmost towers of Troy, nor is it Paris although you all blame him; it is the gods, the cruelty of the gods. Look, for I shall tear away from all around you the dank cloud that veils your eyes and dulls your mortal vision."

After the uttering of these words by his Divine Mother Kundalini, She then passed Her beloved hand before the magnificent eyes of her son, Aeneas, the Trojan hero. Then before his rebel eagle sight, everything was transformed.

The warriors, the spears, the overthrowing weapons, generals and counselors, everything disappeared as if by magic, and replacing all of this, he saw something terribly divine: the dreadful vision of the bleeding gods in all of their might, beating with their awful aegis the unconquerable walls of proud Ilium, and the walls falling with a great thundering, crash and roar.

Old traditions tell us that from the side of the sea the Trojan warrior could see the god Neptune loosening the foundations, making an enormous and profound gap with his great steel trident.

Everything before the eyes of the warrior was dreadful: thundering Jupiter himself throwing lighting bolts from Olympus, and Minerva, the goddess of wisdom, killing thousands of Trojan warriors with her implacable sceptre.

The beloved Divine Mother Kundalini of the Trojan Aeneas then said:

"Behold, it is Jupiter himself who is rousing us the gods against the armies of Troy; everything is lost, such is the

heavenly decree. Escape, my son, escape, with all haste.
Put an end to your struggle; I shall not leave your side
till I see you safely standing on the threshold of your
father's door."

It is stated that this Trojan paladin immediately obeyed his
Divine Mother Kundalini and left his home, abandoning the
royal doom.

When arriving at his home, he found a true apocalyptic
drama: great weeping and lamentation. The head of the family, his elderly father, was complaining bitterly and refusing to
leave his home in exile. Aeneas, in complete despair, rushed to
take up his arms and once again rejoin the battle, in spite of
the gentle, anguished request of his wife.

Fortunately, divine Jupiter, the Cosmic Christ, intervened
by sending an extraordinary prodigy, bringing to him new
hopes.

The sacred fire of the altar jumped, and a light began to
stream from the top of the pointed cap of his son Iulus. The
flame seemed to lick his soft hair and feed round his forehead
without harming him, and when he wanted to quench the holy
fire with lustral water, the grandfather of the child, the father
of Aeneas, supreme head of the family, recognized the will of
God, and raising his palms upward, lifted his voice in prayer.
Then, a sudden peal of thunder rang out on the left. A star fell
from the sky gliding over the topmost pinnacles of the house
and buried itself, still bright, in the woods of Mount Ida.

The whole prodigy was definitive, so at last his old father
— who refused to abandon his home (where he saw himself lin-
gering for many long years) — was truly convinced and willing
to go with the illustrious warrior, his grandson, and the whole
family.

The legend of the centuries states that before abandoning
Troy, the respectable father of Aeneas had to enter into the
Temple of Ceres (the Cosmic Mother) in order to take with pro-
found devotion and divine terror his penate [household] gods.

The heroic General Aeneas could not personally touch
the sacred sculptures of the holy venerated gods, since he had
fought and killed many men. Only by purifying himself with

the pure waters of life could he have the right to touch these terribly divine effigies.

A lethargy of innumerable centuries weigh upon the ancient mysteries. Nonetheless, the penate gods continue to exist within the parallel universes.

The hierophants can converse with these penate gods, who are regents of cities, countries, towns, and homes, while in the supra-sensible worlds of the superior dimensions of space.

The blessed protector of a town is a penate god or holy guardian angel. The secret rector of any city is its special deity. The protector spirit of any family is its spiritual director.

All of these genii or mysterious "Jinns" of family, race, nation, tribe, or clan, certainly are the penate gods of ancient times, who continue to exist in the superior worlds.

We have conversed many times with these penate gods, regents of ancient classical cities. Some of them are suffering the unspeakable, paying terrible karmic debts.

Ulysses, who had been chosen to keep watch, was guarding the loot of bowls of solid gold, all the robes and treasures of Troy, etc., which they pillaged and were going to distribute among themselves. He could not see Aeneas the Trojan who shouted in the darkness of that tragic night, calling to his wife Creusa.

The will of the holy beings was fulfilled. Troy burned in a great holocaust, and Creusa died, but Aeneas, together with his elderly father, his son, and many people, escaped towards the lands of Lazio, carrying the penate gods.

AENEAS, ANCHISES AND ASCANIUS FLEEING TROY. 1827. ANNE LOUIS GIRODET DE ROUSSY TRIOSON. FRENCH 1767-1824.

Chapter 5
The Puncta

Very profound scientific analysis has come to impressively, convincingly, and decisively demonstrate that the atom is in no way the most infinitesimal particle of matter.

Atomic physicists have created the dogma of the atom, and they firmly and irrevocably proceed to unappealably excommunicate, accurse, and throw their imprecations and anathemas against any and all attempts to delve further.

We, the Gnostics, emphatically and solemnly affirm that matter is a compound of specific objects that are correctly defined and known by the name of puncta.

Our scientific theory will factually create a schism, a discord among academic people, but the truth must be uttered. We need to be frank and sincere and to once and for all put the cards upon the table.

The notion of space within the puncta is something that should not even be given the least bit of importance.

Even though the following seems to be incredible, the fact is that within these objects, the radius of one of the last seven points is without any doubt the smallest existing longitude.

A certain great wise man whose name I will not mention here said, "The puncta are attracted to each other when they are found very distant from one another; they repel each other when they are very close. Then, when they are at a certain distance, a new repulsion is executed again."

Deep investigations with my spatial sense, which I have fully and integrally developed, have permitted me to verify that the puncta have a very beautiful golden color.

Direct mystical experience has permitted me to clearly verify that the interacting movements of the puncta are developed in accordance with the modern theory of undulatory mechanics. Wise Gnostics could profoundly comprehend through rigorous scientific observations that the puncta are not atoms, nucleons, nor particles of any type.

Beyond any doubt, and without fear of being mistaken, we can and must categorically affirm that the puncta are absolutely unknown to contemporary physics.

To a mind that is accustomed to the heavy disciplines of thought, saying that the puncta occupy space appears to be an absurdity. To affirm that such objects possess some type of mass seems illogical and nonsensical.

It becomes clear by all means to understand that the puncta do not have electric or magnetic properties, even though these forces and principles govern and direct them.

Diverse aggregates of puncta under the intelligent impulse of the Creator Logos come to constitute all of that which we have called neutrinos, particles, nuclei, atoms, molecules, stars, galaxies, universes, etc.

Direct mystical experience in the parallel universe of the seventh dimension, or region of Atman the Ineffable, has permitted me to comprehend that everything that exists in any of the seven cosmos, beginning with the most insignificant atom up to the most complicated organism, in its last synthesis is reduced to numbers.

What quantity of puncta is indispensable for the construction of an electron?

What capital of puncta is required in order to restructure an atom of hydrogen?

What exact sum of puncta is urgent for the existence of an atom of carbon?

How many puncta are necessary for the creation of an atom of oxygen?

Which is the precise compendium of basic and cardinal puncta for the formation of an atom of nitrogen?

All of this is something that we unfortunately ignore. We must search for the secret of the universe and of each and all of the seven cosmoses, not in illusory formulae, but in numbers, in mathematics.

After rigorous observations and deep analytical studies, we have arrived at the conclusion that the undulatory mechanical movement of the puncta are processed in series that pass through one dimension into another, and then another.

The seven orders of worlds have their *causa causorum*, origin, and root in seven series of puncta.

By all means it is clear that the first series originated the second, and the second originated the third, and likewise successively.

By analyzing and examining this matter of the puncta and their development in series, which are multi-dimensionally processed, we find the very foundation of parallel universes.

Analysis, experience, and superior logic permit us to comprehend that there exist universes that travel in time in a distinct manner from our own, are constructed in a strange way, and are submitted to different laws.

Worlds that are located in other times, that are strange and mysterious for us, travel throughout starry space.

Nature plays multiple games in infinite space, but the puncta are the living foundation of any type of matter.

The last treatise of physics has never been written in any corner of the universe, and if, perchance, Einstein were to reincarnate in some galaxy of antimatter, he would astonishingly recognize himself as being illiterate.

Pseudo-esotericist and pseudo-occultist authors have written a great deal about Cosmogenesis, but in infinite space mIliums of distinct and different micro-physics and Cosmogonies exist.

It is urgent to analyze, to judiciously observe, and to pass beyond the particles of modern physics, if we truly want to know the primary elements, the fundamental puncta.

It is the hour of transcending naive atomism, and to profoundly study the puncta and the secret laws of life.

CENTAURS IN THE INFERNO

"What is decisively criminal in them must
enter the crematorium of the infernal
worlds, and what is less perverse must be
reincorporated into a human body."

Chapter 6
Return and Transmigration

Ancient traditions tell us that Aeneas the Trojan, while in exile with his people, was sheltered for a time in the mountain range of Ida until the Greeks had to abandon ancient Troy.

When the Hellenes abandoned the heroic ruins of proud Ilium, Aeneas built a fleet. Weeping, he left the shores of his native land, its harbors and the plains where the ancient citadel of Troy had once stood. Now it lay smoking on the ground, transformed into black ruins.

The wind blew and the sweet sail swelled under the light of the full moon, while the oar, struggling with the smooth marble, carried the hero, with his fleet and his people, to the shores of Thrace. It was a savage country, yet he hoped to find a welcoming land, since the Thracians had ancient ties with the elder Priam.

The history of the centuries tells us that in the savage land of the Thracians, Aeneas laid out a city that he named Aeneadae.

When the Trojans performed the sacrifice to Jupiter the Cosmic Christ, precisely in the moments in which they were preparing to light the fire and sacrifice a gleaming white bull, an extraordinary prodigy happened: the branches that they had cut from a tree for the fire dripped dark gouts of blood which stained the earth with gore.

Aeneas was chilled with horror and began to pray to the ineffable gods, begging them to turn what he was seeing into good and to make the omen blessed.

The hero tells us that he tore some other branches off from the same tree, but the dark blood flowed from the bark of all of them, until he heard a heart-rending groan emerge from deep in the mound, and a voice rose in the air telling him:

> "Why do you tear my poor flesh, Aeneas? Take pity now on the man who is buried here and do not pollute your righteous hands. I am not stranger to you. It was Troy that bore me and this is not a tree that is oozing blood.

Escape, I beg you, from these cruel shores, from this
land of greed. It is Polydorus that speaks. This is where
I was struck down and an iron crop of weapons covered
my body. Their sharp points have rooted and grown in
my flesh."

The legend states that upon the mound of soil in which
the roots of that tree were inserted, Aeneas consecrated an
altar, dark with funeral wreaths and offerings of foaming cups
of warm milk and bowls of wine.

Thus, this is how the funeral of Polydorus the dead warrior, who was killed in hard battle, was celebrated.

Since the ancient times of Arcadia, when worship to the
gods of the four elements of the universe and to the deities of
the tender corn was still performed, the old hierophants, with
their hair growing white with wisdom, never ignored the multiplicity of the "I."

Is it then rare, perchance, for any one of these many entities that constitute the ego to seize itself to life with much
obsession and to be re-born in a tree?

Another case comes into my memory, that of Pythagoras
and his friend who was reincorporated into a poor dog.

But, is it not perhaps true that the centaurs are assisted?
What are the legends of the centuries telling us?

These epic warriors (centaurs) who fell bleeding among the
helmets and bucklers of those who gloriously died for the love
of their people and their country, receive a well-deserved extra
help when they return into this world.

It is written with tremendous words that the centaurs,
before returning into this valley of tears, eliminate part of
themselves, part of their beloved ego.

The law for centaurs is as follows: what is decisively criminal in them must enter the crematorium of the infernal worlds,
and what is less perverse must be reincorporated into a human
body.

The old laurel-crowned Florentine Dante found many centaurs in the abyss. Let us remember Chiron, the old tutor of
Achilles and Pholus, who was so frenzied.

It is said with frightening and complete clarity in the great book of Nature, written with flaming embers, that before returning into this world, many parts of the ego are lost. Many psychic aggregates of the "myself" reincorporate into organisms of beasts, others are desperately seized (as the case of Polydorus) into the branches of trees, and finally, certain subjective elements of the "I" continue their devolution into the submerged mineral kingdom.

Transmigration is beyond a doubt something very similar to all of this, although with great differences and more profound roots.

There exist people within the tremendous flames of life so bestial, that if by chance all of the coarseness that they possess was extracted from them, nothing would remain. So, it is necessary to reduce such creatures into dust within the interior of the earth in order for their Essence, their soul, to be liberated.

Legend tells us that Capaneus, one of the seven kings who besieged Thebes, arrogantly cried within the abyss:

> "That which I was in life, I am in death. Though Jove wear out the smith from whom he took, in wrath, the keen-edged thunderbolt with which on my last day I was to be transfixed; or if he tire the others, one by one, in Mongibello, at the sooty forge, while bellowing: 'O help, good Vulcan help!' — just as he did when there was war at Phlegra — and cast his shafts at me with all his force, not even then would he have happy vengeance."

There are frightful devolutions in the interior of this afflicted world upon which we live. Precisely there is where divine justice has cast Attila who flogged divinity on Earth; there also is cast Pyrrhus, as well as Sextus whose boiling blood eternally throws out his tears.

> "If you fall there, you must suffer unbearable punishments, and there will certainly be no time for escape."

Homer said:

> "It is better to be a beggar upon the earth than a king in the kingdom of darkness."

Therefore, the descent into the tenebrous worlds is a backward trip through the devolving path. It is a downfall into an always increasing density, within obscurity and rigidity. It is a return, a repetition of the animal, plant, and mineral states — in short, a return into the primitive Chaos.

The souls of the abyss are liberated with the Second Death. These souls receive the token for their freedom when the ego and the lunar bodies are reduced to dust.

The souls who are coming from the interior of the earth, who are marked by the frightful subterranean trip and covered with dust, convert themselves into gnomes of the mineral kingdom, then later into elementals of the plant kingdom, further into animals, and finally they reconquer the lost human state.

This is the wise doctrine of transmigration taught in foregone times by Krishna, the Hindustani master.

MIliums of souls who died within the inferno are now playing as gnomes upon the rocks. Other souls are now delectable plants, or are living within animal creatures and longing to return to the human state.

Chapter 7
Rune Is (Isa)

When we profoundly analyze the rune IS, with mystical astonishment we discover our own Being, the Innermost.

The *Testament of Learning* says:

> *"Before the false dawn came over this earth, those who survived the hurricane and the storm gave praise to the Innermost, and to them appeared the heralds of the dawn."*

In the profound night of all ages, there, in the sunny country of Khem, the rune IS was studied within the concealed Egyptian Temples. Their paradigm always included the bipolarity of man-woman, masculine-feminine. It is clear that ISIS is the outcome of this paradigm, which is the sacred name of the eternal Mother Space.

Much has been said in occultism about Prakriti: space as a maternal, feminine entity. Nonetheless, pseudo-esotericists know nothing about that mathematical point within which is always gestated the Sun-King, the Golden Child of sexual alchemy.

There is no doubt whatsoever that the very root of our own sacred Monad resides within that mysterious point.

Indeed, our particular, beloved, and eternal Divine Mother, who has no beginning nor end, is this very point.

All the sacred powers of the Monad (Atman-Buddhi-Manas) are found contained within our Divine Mother Kundalini. For those who are not well-versed in Theosophy, we will say that all the sacred powers of our own Spirit are found within our own particular Divine Mother, for everyone has their own Mother within.

Pseudo-esotericists and pseudo-occultists have spoken at length about the immortal Triad or Triune Spirit of each living creature. However, they do not comment at all about the unfoldment of Prakriti (the Divine Mother).

She... the Unmanifested, has no symbolism among the Greeks, but in her second manifested aspect within Nature, She is the greatly adored and worshipped chaste Diana.

The third aspect of Prakriti is the blessed Goddess Mother-Death, terror of love and law. She is the terrible Hekate, Proserpine, queen of the infernos.

Two more unfolding aspects of Prakriti take us into the negative aspect of Nature: that which is undesirable, that which in no way would be beneficial for us: the kingdom of terror and black magic.

It is written that each one of these unfolding aspects of Prakriti are repeated within the Microcosmic Man.

The three superior aspects of Prakriti are fundamental, and we must learn to work with them.

The revolution of the consciousness would be radically impossible without the special help of our own particular, beloved Divine Mother.

She is in Herself our own Being, the root, cause, and origin of our divine Spirit.

She is Isis, whose veil no mortal has lifted. In the flame of the serpent we call upon Her.

Many pseudo-esotericists and pseudo-occultists read the literature of Sivananda. There is no doubt that this man was truly a guru-deva [godly teacher] who worked intensely for this suffering humanity. I truly confess that I never liked his Hatha Yoga. This type of acrobatics always appeared to me to be quite circus-like. I never found that someone could Self-realize by converting himself into an acrobat.

Nonetheless, it is well known that this said yogi profoundly worked in strict secrecy with sex yoga. It seems that Hatha Yoga was only a bait in order to fish within the rivers of life.

I am glad to communicate to our beloved readers that this guru-deva Sivananda, while being in a Maha-Samadhi (ecstasy), joyfully disincarnated.

I met him in the parallel universe of the fifth dimension. My happiness was tremendous when I witnessed that this man had built his solar bodies in the flaming forge of Vulcan.

SWAMI SIVANANDA AND DISCIPLES

My surprise was extraordinary when I verified that this master had already died within himself before physically dying.

Sivananda intensely worked in the Great Work of the Father. Thus, he is a guru-deva in the most complete sense of the word.

Our meeting was very special; it took place inside a precious precinct where I was accomplishing the obligation of teaching. Suddenly, the great yogi entered and, as if wanting to recriminate me, he said, "You are vulgarizing the doctrine."

It is obvious that he referred to the spread of the knowledge of the Maithuna (sex yoga) among profane people.

I was in no way speechless. My answer was strong and sincere; since I belong to the virile fraternity, it could be no other way. I expressed myself energetically when saying, "I am willing to answer all the questions asked of me, before anyone within this precinct."

However, the guru-deva Sivananda, being an enemy of any discussion, preferred to sit in the sacred buddhic posture, and thus submerged himself into profound meditation.

I felt the mind of this yogi inside of my own innermost Self. This man was diving, inquiring, exploring within my most intimate profundities. There is no doubt that Sivananda wanted to converse with my real Being, whose secret name is Samael, and this he achieved.

Astonished, I could do nothing but exclaim, "Sivananda, you are a true sannyasi of thought!" Filled with ecstasy, this guru-deva stood up and hugged me. He now comprehended the revolutionary statement of our doctrine, and exclaimed, "Now I agree with you, and I will tell the whole world to read your books."

Afterwards, he added, "I know your Mother (referring to my particular Divine Mother). I saw Her very well dressed. She wears a white mantle that reaches to Her feet."

This meeting was formidable. Many other things happened that I now omit because they are not suitable for this chapter.

Let us now practice with the Rune IS, and let us meditate on the Divine Mother Kundalini.

Practice

Standing in an upright position, let us raise our arms in order to form a straight line with the whole body. After praying to and asking for help from our Divine Mother, we must sing the mantra **ISIS**, as follows:

Iiiiiiiiiiiisssssss Iiiiiiiiiiiisssssss

Prolong the sound of the two letters and divide the word in two syllables IS-IS [The pronunciation of the letter I is similar to that found in the word "tea"].

Afterward, the student must lay down with his relaxed body and, filled with ecstasy, concentrate and meditate on the Divine Mother.

RUNE IS

Chapter 8

The Cosmic Egg

In the beginning of this century, Einstein, the famous author of the theory of relativity, conceived in his genius mind a curved, finite universe, enclosed like an egg.

The tremendous exclamation of this extraordinary man still comes into our memory. He said, "The infinite tends to a limit."

It is not ignored that later on, Edwin Hubble, at the famous observatory at Mount Wilson, discovered with great astonishment that all the galaxies that abide in the infinite space are moving away from each other at fantastic velocities.

This is an undeniable fact. Disgracefully, Georges Lemaitre did not know how to comprehend this, and in searching for causes, he arrived at mistaken conclusions.

> "If the universe is in a constant expansion [he absurdly explained] it is because it exploded from the center of a primeval atom in a foregone day."

Lemaitre, with his incorrect calculations, firmly believed that his primeval, original nucleus had an exiguous, small, insignificant diameter, only the distance from the Earth to the Sun, in other words, 150 mIlium kilometres.

Certainly, let us imagine at least for an instant the infinite space proportionally minuscule. Such a primeval nucleus, in accordance with Lemaitre, would have so frightful a density that (because of the very proximity of the atoms) the temperature would rise (as a natural consequence) to hundreds of mIliums of degrees above zero.

In this inconceivable temperature, in accordance with that theory, the liberated atomic energy would be so great and the cosmic radiation so intense, that everything would burst asunder. Therefore, the profound explosion would be like the eruption of a terrible and frightful volcano.

All of this is marvelous, but who placed that cosmic egg there? What existed before? Why did this cosmic explosion have to be performed in a determined mathematical instant

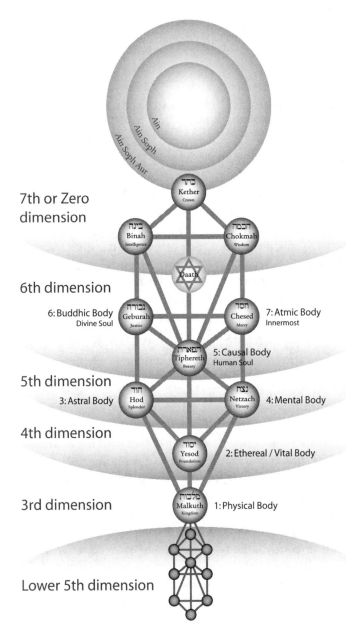

7th or Zero dimension

6th dimension

6: Buddhic Body
Divine Soul

7: Atmic Body
Innermost

5: Causal Body
Human Soul

5th dimension

3: Astral Body

4: Mental Body

4th dimension

2: Ethereal / Vital Body

3rd dimension

1: Physical Body

Lower 5th dimension

Ain
Ain Soph
Ain Soph Aur

כתר
Kether
Crown

בינה
Binah
Intelligence

חכמה
Chokmah
Wisdom

Daath

גבורה
Geburah
Justice

חסד
Chesed
Mercy

תפארת
Tiphereth
Beauty

הוד
Hod
Splendor

נצח
Netzach
Victory

יסוד
Yesod
Foundation

מלכות
Malkuth
Kingdom

PARALLEL UNIVERSES (DIMENSIONS) ON THE TREE OF LIFE

and not before or after? Where is the foundation for such
a theory? Who would be the eyewitness to the facts of this
hypothesis?

We, the Gnostics, comprehend in depth that the galaxies
are moving away from one another; this is already demonstrated. But, it does not forcefully signify that all of them departed
from the same, singular nucleus.

Einstein said, "Mass transforms itself into energy." All the
wise men of the world bowed in reverence before this tremendous truth. The great mathematician also said, "Energy transforms itself into mass." No one could reject this postulation
either.

There is no doubt that "energy equals mass multiplied by
the square of the velocity of light."

These wise postulations demonstrate that the mass of all
the universes is eternal and immutable. Matter disappears and
reappears in a type of flux and reflux, activity and repose, day
and night.

The worlds are born, grow, get old, and finally die. They
cease to exist in order to become energy, and when this energy
crystallizes into mass, they re-emerge, reborn anew.

A zero hour, a common root, does not exist in time count-
ed retrospectively in all of the seven cosmos, which in their
conjunction seethe and palpitate in the infinite space. We can
clarify that when we say common root, we concretely refer to
the concept of a zero hour in time. This does not signify in any
way that we deny the zero hour in an *absolute* way. This zero
hour exists, but, particularly for each universe, for every solar
system in their pre-manifested cosmic state.

In other words, we will say that each solar system of the
unalterable infinite has its mahamanvantaras and mahapra-
layas, meaning, its cosmic days and nights, epochs of activity
and repose.

MIliums of solar systems exist within this galaxy in which
we move and have our Being, and while some of them are
found in their zero hour, others are in complete activity. This is
also repeated in the human being and in the atom; it is repeated in all that was, is, and will be.

Modern scientists try to explain all of these things, but only based on the natural laws. It becomes frightfully ridiculous to want to exclude the intelligent principles of such laws. Each world of the starry space possesses its own Fohat, which is omnipresent in its own sphere of action.

Beyond all doubt, we can and must emphatically affirm that there are as many Fohats as there are worlds. Each one of these vary in power and in degree of manifestation. MIliums, bIliums, and trIliums of Fohats exist, and these are in themselves conscious and intelligent forces. Truly, the Fohats are the constructors, the sons of the dawn of the Mahamanvantara (cosmic day). They are the true cosmocreators.

Our solar system, which was brought into existence by these agents, is certainly constituted by seven parallel universes.

Therefore, Fohat is the electric, vital, personified power, the transcendental unity that embraces all of the cosmic energies in our tridimensional world, as well as in the parallel universes of the superior and inferior dimensions.

Fohat is the Word made flesh, the messenger of the cosmic and human ideation, the active force within the universal life, the solar energy, the electric vital fluid.

Fohat is called "The One Who Penetrates" and "The Builder," because Fohat gives form to the atoms that are proceeding from the unformed matter by means of the Puncta. Mathematics, the Army of the Voice, the Great Word, are found hidden within the Fohat.

Any explanation of cosmic mechanics that excludes the noumenon behind the phenomena, the Fohat behind any cosmogenesis, would be as absurd as to suppose that a car could appear by spontaneous generation, as a product of chance, without special fabrication, without engineers, without mechanics, etc.

The trajectory of galaxies never indicate that they have their origin or point of departure in such a reduced nucleus as the hypothetical egg of Lemaitre. As proof of this, we have that their angle of dispersion always varies between 20 and 30 degrees, in other words, that these galaxies could have passed an enormous distance from the supposed center.

Chapter 9

The Oracle of Apollo

After the royal and sacred funerals of Polydorus, the epic warrior who gloriously fell among hamlets and bucklers in a bloody battle, Aeneas the Trojan cut through the boisterous and dreadful sea with his fleet and people. Sailing swiftly, he arrived at the land of Delos, a land of many Hyperborean traditions. Then, blazing with the flame of faith, he consulted the Oracle of Apollo, wisely built upon the hard rock.

Herodotus, in his *Histories*, Book IV (sections XXXII and XXXIV), comments that the Hyperboreans, who were the ancestors of the Lemurians, periodically sent their sacred offerings wrapped with wheat-straw to Delos. Such venerated offerings had their sacred itinerary very well-marked. Firstly, they passed into the country of Scythia, and then towards the Occident, to the Adriatic Sea. This was similar to the route that was followed for the pursuit of amber, from the Baltic sea until the boisterous river Po, then to the Italic Peninsula.

The first among the Greeks to receive the Hyperborean offerings were the Dodonaeans. Then, the Hyperboreans descended from Dodona to the Maliac Gulf, and after, continued to Euboea and Carystus.

Ancient legends, lost within the night of the centuries, narrate that these very sacred Nordic offerings continued their voyage from Carystus, skipping Andros. From there, the Carystians carried them to Tenos, and the Tenians to Delos.

The people of Delos wisely said that the Hyperboreans had the beautiful and innocent custom of sending their sacred, divine offerings in the hands of two enchanting and ineffable virgins. The name of one was **Hyperoche** and the other **Laodicea**.

The sacred scriptures say that in order to guard these charming and sublime holy women, five initiates or "Perpherees" accompanied them on their long and dangerous voyage.

Nonetheless, all was in vain because these holy men and the two sublime Sibyls were assassinated in the land of Delos as they were accomplishing their mission.

Many beloved and beautiful nubile maidens of that city, filled with pain, cut their hair so they could deposit their curly tresses on a spindle upon a monument that was built in honor of those sacred victims, who (it was said) were accompanied by the gods Artemis and Apollo.

So, Aeneas arrived at Delos, a most revered place, a place of archaic Hyperborean legends that are hidden as precious jewels in the profound depths of all ages.

While prostrated on the ground and breathing the dust of the centuries, with his heart in pain, Aeneas invoked Apollo, the god of fire, within that sacred precinct. He begged the god to protect the city that he was going to build, which became the second Trojan Pergamum.

History tells us that as this respectable man gazed in reverence at the god Apollo and asked about the place appointed to settle themselves, the earth began to tremble frightfully. The hero and his people threw themselves to the ground and heard these words of Phoebus Apollo:

> "O much-enduring sons of Dardanus, the land which first bore you from your parents' stock will be the land that will take you back to her rich breast. Seek out your ancient mother. For that is where the house of Aeneas and his sons' sons and their sons after them will rule over the whole earth."

The epic leader narrates that after hearing the Oracle of Apollo he became worried, wondering what could be this most remote land of his own origin. Then, his elderly father who vividly remembered the ancient family traditions, said:

> "Listen, you leaders of Troy, and learn what you have to hope for. In the middle of the ocean lies Crete, the island of great Jupiter, where there is a Mount Ida, the cradle of our race, and where the Cretans live in a hundred great cities, the richest of kingdoms. If I remember rightly what I have heard, our first father Teucer sailed from there to Asia, landing at Cape Rhoeteum, and chose that place to found his kingdom. Troy was not yet standing,

nor was the citadel of Pergamum, and they lived low
down in the valley.

"This is the origin of the Great Mother of Mount Cybele
[the Divine Mother Kundalini], the bronze cymbals of
the Corybants, our grove of Ida, the inviolate silence of
our worship, and the yoked lions that draw the chariot
of the mighty goddess.

"Come then, let us follow where we are led by the
bidding of the gods. Let us appease the winds and set
forth for the kingdoms of Cnossus. It is not to far to
sail. If only Jupiter is with us, the third day will see our
ships on the shores of Crete.'

"Rumor [said Aeneas] as she flew told the tale of the
great Idomeneus how he had been forced to leave his
father's kingdom and how the shores of Crete were now
deserted. Here was a place empty of our enemies, their
home abandoned, waiting for us.

"The sailors raised all manner of shouts as they vied
with one another in their rowing and my comrades
[continued Aeneas] kept urging me to make for Crete
and go back to the home of their ancestors. The wind
rising astern sped us on our way and we came to shore at
last on the ancient land of the Curetes. Impatiently I set
to work on walls for the city we all longed for. I called it
Pergamea and the people rejoiced in the name."

So, the heroic and terrific people commanded by Aeneas,
the illustrious Trojan paladin, could have definitively established themselves on that island, if a malignant disastrous
plague had not obligated them to sail over the sea in search of
other lands.

In the polluted putrefaction of that ill air, men lost the
lives they loved, or dragged around their sickly bodies; the sinister plague disgracefully infected all of their bodies and caused
them to fall, fulminated by the ray of death.

"The Dogstar [said Aeneas] burned the fields and made
them barren, the grass dried, the crops were infected and
gave us no food."

A tempest was released in the furious mind of Aeneas and with desperation, as a castaway who clings to a cruel rock, he thought to go back across the sea to the sanctuary of Phoebus Apollo, the god of fire, and to his oracle at Ortygia, to pray for his gracious favor again. But, that very same night, in those delectable hours in which the body sleeps and the soul travels out of the physical organism within the superior worlds, Aeneas found himself with his Phrygian penate gods, the tutelar genii of his family, the **jinns** or angels of Troy.

The lords of the flame spoke these words:

> "Delian Apollo did not send you to these shores. Crete
> is not where he commanded you to settle. There is a
> place — Greeks call it Hesperia — an ancient land, strong
> in arms and in the richness of her soil. The Oenotrians
> lived there, but the descendants of that race are now
> said to have taken the name of their king Italus and call
> themselves Italians. This is our true home. This is where
> Dardanus sprang from and his father Iasius from whom
> our race took its beginning. Rise then with cheerful
> heart and pass on these words to Anchises your father."

His astonished father then remembered Cassandra, the Trojan prophetess, that grievous woman who made the same prophesy to him before the destruction of the proud Ilium. None had believed her prophecies, since Apollo was punishing her.

This noble woman whose name was Cassandra, who was so blessed and adored, paid a very singular type of karma for having wrongly used her divine faculties in her past lives.

Thus, the legend of the centuries tells us that Aeneas and his people, without wasting time, set sail upon their ships to run before the wind over the vast ocean towards the lands of Lazio.

Chapter 10
Rune Ar

Ineffable enchantments come into my memory, poems of love, and things that are impossible to describe with words. Certainly, what I have known, what I have seen, what I have palpated in the house of my Father and within all of those resplendent abodes of the great city of light known as the Milky Way, can only be uttered with words of gold in the purest dawn of the divine language.

It was a night trimmed with stars; the projected rays of the moon entered into my haven and pretended to be a shawl of silver. The profound blue of the sky was rather an infinite ocean where the stars were twinkling.

Meditating like this, I abandoned my dense form and entered into ecstasy. There is no better pleasure than the feeling of oneself as a detached soul, for then, past, present, and future are siblings in an eternal now. Filled with a delectable, unutterable, and indescribable spiritual voluptuousness, and impelled by the mysterious force of longing, I arrived before the doors of the temple.

The door of the sanctuary was sealed with a great boulder that blocked the way to profane people. Oh heart, do not desist before things of mystery! "Open sesame!" was my exclamation, and the rock opened in order for me to enter. So then, when some intruders tried to do the same, I had to grasp my flaming sword and cry with all the forces of my soul, "Get ye hence profane and profaners!"

I had entered into the great temple of this Milky Way, the central sanctuary of this gigantic galaxy, the Transcendental Church. The terror of love and law reigns within this venerated place. Only the sidereal gods can prostrate before the sacred altar of that terribly divine temple.

Joyfully, I advanced towards the place of prostrations and adorations. Here, there, and everywhere, in all the blessed places of the temple, a multitude of humble and simple people were coming and going, who rather resembled submissive and obedient peasants. They were the bodhisattvas of the gods; they were human beings in the most complete sense of the word: creatures who enjoy objective knowledge, who are one hundred percent conscious of Self.

Certainly, I could evidence completely and without a doubt that nothing that could be called "I" or "myself" existed within these human creatures; these humans were completely dead. I did not see within them the desire of standing out, of ascending, of climbing to the top of the ladder and wanting to boast of themselves, etc. These creatures had no interest in their existence; they only wanted absolute death, to lose themselves within their Being, that is all.

How happy I felt while advancing through the center of the temple towards the sacred altar! Certainly, I was marching arrogantly, energetically, with a triumphal step. Suddenly, one of those "humble peasants of pick and shovel" was walking by, blocking my way. For a moment, I tried to keep walking arrogantly, haughtily, and with disdain.

But, oh God of mine! An intuitive lightning bolt fulminated me to death, and I then vividly remembered that in a forgone time, in the remote past, I had committed the same error while in the presence of this humble peasant. That past error was clearly present within my mind. With horror, terror, and fear I remembered the dreadful instant in which, with frightening words uttered from the sacred altar, amidst lightning bolts, rays, and thunder, I was cast out of the temple.

The whole of this past event revived within my mind in a thousandth of a second. Then, repentant, I stopped my arrogant and proud march, and feeling contrite, regretful, and remorseful in my heart, with modesty and submission, I prostrated myself before this peasant. I kissed his feet while addressing him in this way, "You are a great master, a great sage."

But that creature, instead of being satisfied with my words, answered, "I do not know anything. I am nobody."

I answered back, "Yes, you are the bodhisattva of one of the great gods who is the governor of many constellations."

My joy was immense when that authentic human being blessed me. I felt as if I had been forgiven, and joyfully continued my way towards the sacred altar. Afterwards, I returned into my physical body.

Many years have passed and I have never forgotten that temple sealed with the sacred stone.

"Behold I lay in Sion a chief corner stone, elect, precious: and he that believeth on it shall not be confounded.

"The stone which the builders disallowed, the same is made the head of the corner. And a stone of stumbling, and a rock of offence." – 1 Peter 2:6-8

The old medieval alchemists were always searching for the Philosophical Stone, and some of them performed the Great Work with complete success.

Speaking with blunt frankness, it is our duty to emphatically affirm that this stone is sex.

Peter, disciple of Jesus the Christ, is Aladdin, the marvelous interpreter who is authorized to lift the stone that seals the sanctuary of the great mysteries. The original name of Peter is **Patar** with its three radical consonants: P, T, R. The P reminds us with complete clarity of the parents of the gods, our Pater, Father, who is in secret, the Pitris. The T is the Tau, the cross, the divine hermaphrodite, the black lingam inserted into the yoni. The R is fundamental in the fire, it is the Egyptian **Ra**. The R is also radical in the powerful mantra INRI:

Ignis Natura Renovatur Integra

The fire is found latent within the stone, and the ancient people made the spark to leap from within the living bosom of the hard flint. My memory brings the remembrance of the stones of the lightning, the Orphic galactite, the Aesculapian ostrite, the stone with which Machaon healed Philoctetes, the magical baetylus of all countries, the howling, oscillate, runic and uttering stones of the Teraphim. The chalice of the Christified Mind has as its base the living stone, the sacred altar.

The mantra **ARIO** prepares the Gnostics for the advent of the sacred fire. This mantra must be chanted every morning, dividing it into three syllables: **AH... RI... O...** prolonging the sound of each letter. It is advisable to work with this practice for ten minutes daily.

RUNE AR

Chapter 11

Proton and Antiproton

The real existence of the proton and the antiproton was demonstrated absolutely in the year 1955 by a physics team from Berkeley. When a plate of copper was bombarded with the energy of 6,000 mIlium electronvolts, two marvelous nuclei of hydrogen were extracted from the target. They were identical but of opposite charge: one positive proton and the other negative.

By all means it then becomes clear that half of the universe is constituted of antimatter. If the modern wise men could find anti-particles in the laboratories, it is because they also exist in the profound depth of this great Nature. In no way can we deny that to detect the antimatter in space is frightfully difficult.

The light of the anti-stars, even when apparently identical to the light of the stars, and even when photographs register them in the same way, have a difference that is unknown to the "wise men."

The concept that states that there is no place for anti-matter in our solar system is still arguable. The transformation of mass into energy is something very interesting. That half of it escapes in the form of neutrinos is evidently normal, that a third of it becomes transformed into gamma rays and that a sixth part is transformed into sound and luminous waves should not surprise us in any way, since it is natural.

When we think of cosmogenesis, the same questions always emerge: What existed before the dawn of our solar system? The **Rig Veda** answers:

> *"Nor Aught nor Nought existed; yon bright sky*
> *Was not, nor heaven's broad roof outstretched above.*
> *What covered all? What sheltered? What concealed?*
> *Was it the water's fathomless abyss?*
> *There was not death — yet there was nought immortal,*
> *There was no confine betwixt day and night;*

The only One breathed breathless by itself,
Other than It there nothing since has been.
Darkness there was, and all at first was veiled
In gloom profound — an ocean without light —
The germ that still lay covered in the husk
Burst forth, one nature, from the fervent heat.
Who knows the secret? Who proclaimed it here?
Whence, whence this manifold creation sprang?
The gods themselves came later into being —
Who knows from whence this great creation sprang?
That, whence all this great creation came,
Whether Its will created or was mute,
The Most High Seer that is in highest heaven,
He knows it — or perchance even He knows not.
Gazing into eternity...
Ere the foundations of the earth were laid,
Thou wert. And when the subterranean flame
Shall burst its prison and devour the frame...
Thou shalt be still as Thou wert before
And knew no change, when time shall be no more.
Oh! Endless thought, divine ETERNITY.

Before the mahamanvantara (cosmic day) of this universe in which we live, move, and have our Being, all that existed was energy free in its movement.

Before that energy, matter existed in an organized form. The former universe of the past cosmic day (mahamanvantara) was constituted by this matter.

The Moon, our beloved satellite that illuminates us during the night, is the only remembrance left for us from that preterit universe.

Each time energy crystallizes in the form of matter, it appears under the extraordinary shape of a pair of symmetrical particles.

Matter and anti-matter complement each other. We can say that this is a new theme for contemporary science, and that it will progress even more in the future.

To affirm that there is no place for anti-matter in our solar universe is by all means an absurdity. Matter is always accompanied by anti-matter. Without it, it is clear that nuclear physics would be without a foundation, and would lose its validity.

During the dawn of the mahamanvantara (cosmic day), the universe appeared in the form of a cloud of plasma, that is to say, ionized hydrogen.

There are twelve fundamental hydrogens in our solar system, and these have already been analyzed by the great masters of humanity. It has been said unto us that in that sum of hydrogen, twelve categories of matter are represented. These types of matter are contained within the universe, from the Abstract Absolute Space to the submerged mineral kingdom.

In the minds of learned people, the cloud of original plasma appears in a double form. Therefore, a judicious examination of this matter allows us to comprehend that plasma and anti-plasma exist. This is what a certain sage has named "ambiplasma."

The scientists know very well through observation and experience that the intense magnetic field that is formed in the galaxies originates the radical split of the particles in accordance with their electrical charge. Plasma and anti-plasma are not only opposite, but moreover they are separated.

Thus, matter and antimatter coexist separately, and they condense or crystallize into stars.

The total destruction of matter occurs when matter and antimatter come in direct contact with each other. The living depth of matter is precisely antimatter, but between these two forms of life is a neutral field.

Certainly, the three primary forces — positive, negative and neutral — govern all of this universal mechanism. Matter and antimatter, stars and anti-stars, coexist in the infinite space.

Hydrogen and anti-hydrogen crystallize with the gravitational force, thus originating nuclear fusion.

Thus, beloved reader, this is how protons accumulate with other protons of their own kind in order to form all the elements of Nature.

HARPIES AS SEEN BY DANTE IN THE INFERNO

Chapter 12

The Harpies

Aeneas, the epic Trojan paladin, was submitted to frightful new ordeals while navigating with his people towards the marvelous lands of the ancient Hesperia.

Ancient traditions, lost within the night of the centuries, tell us that while they were upon the open sea, the dreadful forces of Neptune raised a terrible tempest, which thanks to God did not sink their ship. However, it did cause Palinurus, who was the most skillful of the pilots, to lose his bearings in mid-ocean after passing through three long days of darkness and three starless nights.

Horrifying were the moments when the Trojans approached the shores of the terrifying Strophades Islands in the great Ionian sea, which are inhabited by the Dantesque harpies. They are disgusting witches with heads and necks of girls who were beautiful maidens in the past, but have now been transformed into horrible furies who pollute everything they touch with their foul contagion.

It was a monstrous, abominable harpy army that in a foretime was commanded by the execrable Celaeno. They were provided with hooked claws for hands, and their faces were pale with a hunger that could never be satisfied.

The glorious hero with his people arrived to this land and entered the harbor without thinking of abject witches or of horrifying Witches' Sabbaths. Hungry as they were, these strong descendants of Dardanus did not hesitate to sacrifice the beautiful and reluctant cows they found happily eating unguarded on the grass of this no man's land.

But suddenly, when they were feasting on this rich fare, the harpies were upon them, screeching as ravens and swooping down from their mounts with a fearful clangor of their wings, grabbing and tearing the food to pieces and polluting everything with their filthy mouths. This was a horrifying spectacle; all of the meat was infected, the odor polluted the air, and the banquet became filthy, repulsive, and sickening.

The Trojans, escaping from these sinister ladies who were transformed into horrifying fowls, once again sheltered themselves in mysterious caves far back from the sunny beach. But to the disgrace of these illustrious warriors, when they were ready to eat after sacrificing new cattle, the noisy flock of damned witches came once again and polluted the food.

Therefore, filled with great anger, these men armed themselves with their bows and javelins in order to exterminate this fearsome tribe of abominable harpies. But the harpies had a filthy skin that felt no violence from the bronze, and their backs were as invulnerable as steel.

Terrible was the spell that Celaeno burst out of her breast while flying round about the glorious heads of the courageous Trojans, screeching:

> "Is it war you offer us now, sons of Laomedon, for the slaughter of our bullocks and the felling of our oxen? Is it your plan to make war against the innocent harpies and drive us from the kingdom of our ancestors? Listen to what I have to say and fix it in your minds. These words were spoken by the Almighty Father of the gods to Phoebus Apollo, and Phoebus Apollo spoke them to me, and now I, the greatest of the furies, speak them to you. You are calling upon the winds and trying to sail to Italy. To Italy you will go and you will be allowed to enter its harbors, but you will not be given a city, and you will not be allowed to build walls around it before a deadly famine has come upon you, and the guilt of our blood drives you to gnaw round the edges of your tables, to put them between your teeth and eat them."

Surprised and consternated, the Trojans beseeched the holy gods to turn away this threat from them. They then abandoned that gloomy land and sailed into the sea again.

Factually, to sacrifice the Sacred Cow is equivalent to invoking cruel harpies of pernicious presages.

It becomes opportune to refer here to the symbolic cow of five legs, which is the terrific guardian of the **Jinn** lands.

H. P. Blavatsky actually saw a cow with five legs in India, which had a "fifth leg" growing out of her hump. It scratched its head with the extra hoof and killed flies with it, etc. That animal was guided by a young man who was a member of the Sadhu sect.

If we read the three syllables of the word CABALA in the inverted way, then we read LA-BA-CA. In Spanish, LA VACA means "the cow," which is the living symbol of the eternal Mother Space.

The eternal feminine element of Nature, the Magna-Mater (from which the "M" and the Aquarian hieroglyphic emanates), is always mentioned in all theologies of the north, south, west, and east of the world.

She is the universal womb of the great abyss, the primitive Venus, the great Virgin-Mother, who emerges from the waves of the sea with her, Cupid / Eros. She is the final variant; in short, she is Gaia, Gaea, or the Earth in her superior aspect, the Hindustani Prakriti.

Let us remember Telemachus descending into the world of shadows in order to inquire about the fate of Ulysses, his father. The young man walked under the light of the moon while invoking Prakriti, the powerful deity who is Selene in heaven, as well as the chaste Diana on the earth, and the formidable Hekate within the subterranean worlds.

The two subsequent unfoldments of Hekate / Proserpine, which are the fourth and fifth aspects of Prakriti, are negative. They constitute the shadow of the eternal Mother Space, which are lost reflections within the mirror of Nature.

Black and white Jinns exist. The harpies follow the tenebrous path. Dante found them tormenting the devolving submerged souls within the infernal worlds.

The harpies are black Jinns; they utilize the two negative inferior aspects of Prakriti. They submerge themselves within the fourth dimension with these two aspects, in order to fly through the air.

The physical body can take any given figure while inside the unknown dimension, and beautiful maidens can transform themselves into horrifying fowls, as the example of those birds that Aeneas found in the tenebrous Strophades Islands.

Charon, the infernal god, whose eternal age is always melancholic and abominable, conduces the harpies who have passed through the doors of death to the other shore of the evil river. There, among its muddy currents of black water with frightful and filthy borders wander the specters of the dead. It is the fatal river where the boat of Charon navigates, conducing the lost ones into the somber, dismal, and obscure regions of the submerged mineral kingdom.

Horrible is the end that awaits the harpies of the execrable Celaeno, which is to frightfully devolve within the sub-world until petrifying and reducing themselves into cosmic dust. The condemnation of those who perform evil is just; their mouths are as open sepulchres. They never knew the path of peace.

Chapter 13
Rune Sig (Sigel, Sowelu)

It is difficult indeed to depict the enchantment, the ine-briation of ecstasy, the communion of saints in the nights of meditation. On one such night, the Patriarch Jacob, living rein-carnation of the resplendent angel Israel, while resting his head upon the Philosophical Stone, read within the stars the prom-ise of innumerable descendents, and he saw between heaven and earth the mysterious septenary ladder through which all the Elohim ascend and descend.

To experience the Truth, the Reality, or "That"... is only possible when we are absent from the "I."

On the day of the Lord, I was inspecting, searching, inquir-ing into the mysteries of my own final hour. I saw and heard things that the profane and profaners are not allowed to com-prehend. Then, I directly experienced the last stage, the setting of the "I," the catastrophical end of "myself."

Thus, I lived the crucifixion of the intimate Christ and the descent into the holy sepulchre. The fight against Satan was terrible... Then, my priestess wife sealed my sarcophagus with a large stone while sweetly smiling... and from the Golgotha of the Father, lightning, thunder, and terribly divine voices were heard.

All of this reminds me of the rune Sig, which is the terrific lightning from the central sun.

Sulu-sigi-sig is the secret name of the sacred frightful viper Kundalini.

Certainly, the star of five points is a constant repetition of the rune Sig. This star resembles the trace of the zig-zag of lightning. In ancient times, human beings trembled before the pentalpha.

Within the archaic mysteries, **Sig** was the phallus, and through it we return to the Maithuna (sex yoga).

Sig is the **Sun**, and its letter is the "S," whose sound when wisely prolonged is converted into the subtle voice, into that sweet and appeasing whistle that Elias heard in the wilderness.

The Final Initiation is sealed with lightning, with the rune Sig, and amidst thunder and lightning these tremendous words are heard, "Father, into thy hands I commend my Spirit."

The luminous flaming sword, which turns threateningly in all directions in order to keep the way of the Tree of Life, has the dreadful figure of the rune Sig, and it reminds us of the zig-zag of lightning.

> "Woe unto the Samson of the Kabbalah if he permits himself to be put asleep by Delilah! The Hercules of science, who exchanges his royal sceptre for the distaff of Omphale, will soon experience the vengeance of Dejanira, and nothing will be left for him but the pyre of the Mount Oeta, in order to escape the devouring folds of the coat of Nessus."

Unhappy is the one who permits himself to be seduced by the original she-devil, the no-name woman, who is a rose of perdition from the infernal abyss.

Disgraceful is the initiate who falls inebriated into the arms of the sanguinary Herodias, the harpy Gundryggia, and one hundred women more.

Woe! Woe! Woe to those initiates who succumb to the fiery kisses: not of many women, but of that one woman of antonomasia, of that symbolic woman who does not try to grossly seduce with suggestions of mere animal sensation, but with the most perfidious and delectable arts of subtle sentimentalism and romantic emotionalism.

Therefore, it would be better for these initiates to have not been born, or to have a millstone hung about their necks and be drowned in the depths of the sea. [Matthew 18:6, Mark 9:42, Luke 17:2]

Disgraced are the ones who—instead of rising towards the Golgotha of the Father and descending into the holy sepulchre —will instead be fulminated by the terrible lighting of cosmic justice, who will lose their flaming swords, and descend into the kingdom of Pluto through the black path.

Anguished sleeplessness, the frightful jealousy that makes our existence bitter, cruel distrust, the filthy vendettas covered with wounds, and the abominable hatred that distills blood are always flapping tenebrously around about the ebony throne of the king of the infernal worlds. There we also find the gnawing avarice that continuously, mercilessly devours itself, and the disgusting rage that tears at its flesh with its own hands.

To that end, we also find the insane arrogance that miserably ruins everything, and the infamous treason that always defends itself and nourishes itself with innocent blood, yet cannot be satisfied by the corrupted fruit of its perfidies. There is also the mortal venom of envy that destroys itself when incapable of destroying others. Also the cruelty that is precipitated into the hopeless abyss, and the macabre and frightful visions, the horrifying phantoms of the condemned ones, the fear of the living ones, those nightmarish monsters, and the cruel sleeplessness that causes so much anguish.

These and other fatal images are girded around the horrifying forehead of the fierce Pluto and fill his ominous palace.

Telemachus, the son of Ulysses, found mIliums of hypocritical Pharisees in the kingdom of Pluto; they are whitened sepulchres who fake love towards religion, but are actually filled with arrogance and pride.

Descending into more submerged regions, this hero found many patricides and matricides who were suffering frightful torments. He also found many wives who bathed their hands with the blood of their husbands, and traitors who betrayed their country and violated all of their oaths. Nevertheless, even though it seems incredible, these traitors were suffering less punishment than the hypocrites and simoniacs.

Thus, this punishment is the will of the three judges of the infernal worlds, since these hypocrites and simoniacs are not content — like the rest of the condemned ones — with simply being evil, but moreover boast of themselves as being saints and thus deviate people with their false virtue. Thus, they place people far away from the path that leads towards the truth.

The holy gods who have been impiously and hypocritically mocked by everybody in the world, and who have become insignificant before the masses, are now with all of their power avenging themselves of the insults that people have inflicted upon them.

The terrible ray of cosmic justice also precipitates into the abyss those fallen Bodhisattvas who never want to rise again. They are accused of three crimes:

1) to have assassinated the internal Buddha
2) to have dishonored the gods
3) numerous other crimes

Every great work, any judgment, is always sealed with the rune Sig, with the flaming sword.

Practice

You must seal all of your magical works, invocations, supplications, healing chains, etc., with the rune Sig. The zig-zag of lightning must be traced with your right hand and your extended index finger, at the moment when you also sound the letter *sssssssssssssss* as a prolonged, sweet, and gentle whistle.

Chapter 14

The Ain Soph

It is necessary to comprehend and urgent to know that within the poor intellectual animal mistakenly called "human being," there are three perfectly defined aspects.

The first one of these aspects is that which is called Essence. In Zen Buddhism, this Essence is denominated Buddhata [buddhadhatu].

The second aspect is the personality. This aspect in itself is not the physical body, even though it utilizes the physical body for its expression in the tridimensional world.

The third aspect is the devil, the pluralized "I" within each one of us, that is to say, the "myself."

The Essence, the Buddhata, is that aspect within the human being that has true reality, that is genuine.

The personality is not genuine, because it comes from the exterior world. It is what the human being has learned in his home, in the streets, in the school, etc.

The pluralized "I" is that conjunction of diverse entities that personify all of our psychological defects.

Beyond the organic machine (physical body) and the three aspects that manifest themselves through it, many substances, forces, and spiritual principles exist that emanate from the Ain Soph as a final synthesis.

But, what is this Ain Soph? We answer in an abstract way when saying the Ain Soph is the absolute "No-Thing" without limits.

Nonetheless, it is necessary to be precise and concrete, in order to comprehend: the Ain Soph is our super-divine atom, which is singular, special, specific, genuine, and super-individual.

This definition signifies that in the final synthesis, each one of us is nothing more than an atom from the Abstract Absolute Space, the interior atomic star that has always smiled upon us.

A certain author said, "I raise my eyes towards the utmost, towards the stars, from which, for me, all help has to come, but I always follow the guidance of my inner star."

It is clear that this super-divine atom is not incarnated, but yet is found to be intimately related with the chakra Sahasrara, the lotus of one thousand petals, the magnetic center of the pineal gland.

While in the state of very profound meditation, I have directly experienced the Ain Soph. One day (the date and hour does not matter), I attained that state that in India is known as nirvi-kalpa-samadhi, where my soul was totally absorbed within the Ain Soph, and able to travel throughout the Abstract Absolute Space.

This journey started in my pineal gland and continued within the profound bosom of the eternal space. Thus, I saw myself beyond any galaxy of matter or anti-matter; I was simply converted into a self-conscious atom.

How happy I was while in the absence of the "I," beyond this world, beyond the mind, beyond the stars and anti-stars. What one feels during the experience of Samadhi is unutterable. It is comprehendible only through experimentation.

So, while inebriated with ecstasy I entered through the doors of a temple, and then I saw and heard things that the intellectual animals are not allowed to comprehend.

I wanted to converse with a divine priest, and it is obvious that I achieved it so that I could console my painful heart.

One among many of those Self-realized atoms from the Ain Soph (Abstract Absolute Space) increased its size and assumed the venerated figure of an Elder of Days before my unusual presence.

Then, spontaneous words that resounded within the infinite space emerged from my creative larynx, and I consulted about someone I knew in the world of dense forms.

The answer from this very illustrious atomic master was certainly extraordinary. "For us, the inhabitants of the Ain Soph, the mind is what the mineral kingdom is for you." And he added, "Therefore, we examine the human mind in the same way you examine any mineral."

In the name of the truth, I have to say that answer caused me great amazement, admiration, astonishment, and surprise.

Afterwards, he demonstrated it; that loving, essential one studied the mind of the person I asked about, and he gave me an exact answer.

Many years have passed, but I cannot forget that mystical experience. Certainly, I had the joy of conversing with an atomic kabir beyond the parallel universes, there within the Ain Soph.

However, not all of the atomic stars from this spiritual firmament are Self-realized.

The genesis atom (Ain Soph) of any person who has not built his solar bodies within the flaming forge of Vulcan is certainly very simple. This type of atom does not contain more atoms.

The genesis atoms that are Self-realized are another matter. They are what in occult science we call "Ain Soph Paranishpanna." They have within themselves four seed-atoms, which are symbolically represented in alchemy with these four letters: C.O.N.H. (carbon, oxygen, nitrogen, hydrogen).

One summer night, I interrogated a group of Gnostic students in the following way: "If, at the end of the mahamanvantara we must disintegrate the solar bodies that we built with so much effort within the Ninth Sphere, then why did we build them?" None of the students could give the right answer. Therefore, my explanation was necessary. "It is clear," I said, "that when the great pralaya (cosmic night) arrives, the Ain Soph absorbs the three primary forces and disintegrates the four bodies. Nevertheless, the Ain Soph retains and attracts towards its interior sphere the four seed-atoms that correspond to the four bodies. Therefore, within the Ain Soph Paranishpanna, that is to say, within the Self-realized atom, the three primary forces and the four seed-atoms exist."

The letter C symbolizes the body of conscious will. The letter O corresponds to the Christic mind. The letter N is related with the astral body. The letter H is associated with the physical body.

At the dawn of the mahamanvantara (cosmic day), the Ain
Soph Paranishpanna rebuilds its four bodies by means of its
correspondent seed-atoms.

These four bodies constitute the Hebraic Mercabah, which
is the chariot of the centuries, the solar vehicle of the Ain Soph
Paranishpanna, which is the "No-Thing" without limits, and
absolute.

The four bodies assume the form of the manifested
Heavenly Man, which is the vehicle in order to descend and
manifest within the world of phenomena.

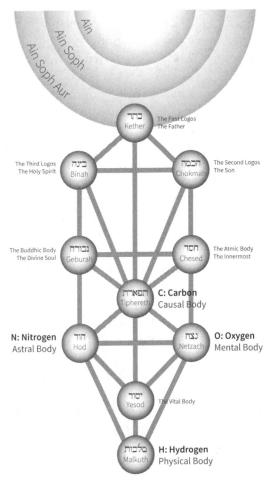

AIN SOPH AND FOUR BODIES ON THE TREE OF LIFE

Chapter 15

The King Helenus

When Aeneas, the epic Trojan paladin, was approaching the wealthy palace of King Helenus, he saw with astonishment, admiration, and pleasant surprise a woman called Andromache, the wife of Hector the Trojan who was gloriously killed in battle at the undefeated foundations of the walls of Troy.

Then, Aeneas gave thanks to the holy gods (Angels, Archangels, Principalities, Powers, Virtues, Dominions, Thrones, Cherubim, and Seraphim of Christianity). He gave thanks to these ineffable beings from the depths of his heart for having liberated this woman Andromache and for having impeded the Achaeans from taking her as a captive to Mycenae.

Andromache, a noble woman, was now the wife of Helenus, the prophet-king, a splendid monarch who gave opulent hospitality to the Trojans in his royal palace.

When Aeneas found Andromache, she was offering a ritual meal and performing rites to the dead in a grove of a sacred forest. She was carrying in a magnificent golden urn the ashes of Hector, her former husband.

> "Is this a true vision? Is it a true messenger that comes to me, Aeneas, son of the goddess? Are you alive? If the light of life has left you, why are you here? Where is Hector?"

This is how the woman spoke, and then she fainted.

The unhappy woman had been held captive by the terrible Pyrrhus, a sly, evil warrior who was the assassin of the elder Priam.

Fortunately, the fate of this unhappy woman changed radically after Pyrrhus died at the hands of the dreadful warrior Orestes. Then, she married the good King Helenus.

We know that on the third day Aeneas was taken into a solitary cave in order to foresee the will of Apollo.

The most important of the prophesies of Helenus was to tell Aeneas that the conclusion of his voyage was far away and that he was going to enter into many harbors before definitely establishing himself on that land that in a foretime was the ancient Hesperia.

Helenus advised him to go and see the Sibyl of Cumae, a divine prophetess, a virgin priestess who foretold the future in a prophetic frenzy by writing her magical verses on falling leaves from a corpulent tree that was next to her cave.

Once in a while, a hurricane wind dislodged the green prophetic leaves and the verses were mixed and extraordinarily mingled, thus forming phrases unintelligible to the profane. For this reason, many men departed without receiving advice, and cast maledictions against the Sibyl.

Putting all doubts aside, we can emphatically affirm that only initiates with awakened consciousness could understand the strange phrases and mysterious enigmas of the Sibyl of Cumae.

Helenus also predicted for Aeneas that he would navigate close to Scylla and Charybdis, and as well to the lands of the Cyclops, and that he should avoid the entrance into the meridional shores of Ithaca, which in that epoch were populated by the terrible Greeks.

Finally, the bountiful King Helenus advised Aeneas, the illustrious Trojan paladin, to worship the godhead of great Juno first and foremost in his prayers, through his own free will to submit his vows to Juno, and to win the love of the mighty queen of heaven with his offerings and prayers, since this deity always showed herself as an enemy of the Trojans.

So, the wind blew the sails under the light of the full moon, the paddle struggled with the smooth marble, and Palinurus consulted the stars. The ships left the seigniorial dominions of the Latin king while Andromache cried at the departure of the Trojans.

Helenus, illuminated king, prophet of Apollo! You were the one who provided royal and magnificent hospitality to the Trojans, and then filled with love, you interrogated the god of fire for the sake of your friend Aeneas.

Helenus, you were also the one who (oh gods!) advised this illustrious Trojan man to visit the Sibyl of Cumae.

AENEAS AND THE SIBYL OF CUMAE. UNKNOWN ARTIST

When arriving to this part of our present chapter, all of the priestesses of Eritrea, Endor, etc., come into my memory.

Wherever a holy one of these Sibyls abided, it was sure that also a Delphic, Bacchic, Kabiric, Dactylic, or Eleusinian mystery existed.

The gods and most wise men will never forget the tremendous importance that these mysteries had in ancient times. The fame and great renown of Sais, Memphis, and Thebes in the ancient Egypt of the Pharaohs was due to these mysteries.

There, within the night of the centuries, Mithra is still remembered by the initiates among the Parsis. Eleusis, Samothrace, Lemnos, Ephesus, etc., are remembered among the Greeks.

Formidable were the initiatic colleges of Bibracte and Alexis among the Gallic Druids.

The mysteries of Heliopolis in Syria, and Tara in Ireland, etc., were ineffable and indescribable for their beauty and splendor.

According to the sayings of Pliny, and also according to the writings of Caesar and Pomponius Mela, the Druid priests of the Celts practiced magic and the mysteries in their caverns.

These austere and sublime Druid hierophants, crowned with oak, solemnly reunited under the pale light of the moon in order to celebrate their Major Mysteries, especially in Spring / Easter, which is when life is powerfully and gloriously resuscitating.

The initiatic colleges were closed in the east by the military barbarism of Alexander, and in the west by Roman violence.

The city of Cote-d'Or, which is next to St. Reine, was certainly the tomb of the Druidic initiation, since all the masters and Sibyls were vilely slaughtered by the sanguinary orders of Rome, without any compassion.

Equally fatal and painful a fate had Bibracte, the glorious rival of Memphis, and likewise following in the number of victims were Athens and Rome, whose Druidic college had 40,000 students of astrology, occult science, philosophy, medicine, jurisprudence, architecture, literature, grammar, etc.

The Latin *mysterium* is the Greek *teletai*, whose original root is found in the word *telelutia*, "death."

A vain thing is the death of the physical body. What is important is the total destruction of the "myself."

The illumination of the Sibyls of Cumae, the splendor of the priestesses of Eritrea, the ecstasy of the mahatmas, are only for people who have truly passed through the Great Death.

The awakening of the consciousness, the radical and absolute change, is impossible without the death of the pluralized "I." The coming of the new is only possible through death.

The path of life is created by the hoofprints of the horse of death.

Chapter 16
Rune Tyr (Teiwaz)

Singing birds, jumping rivulets, roses that perfume the air, sounding bells that call... stop, shadow of my Goodness, beautiful illusion of the day, for night has arrived.

Delicious night brimming with stars, allow me to offer you the oasis of the old garden of my painful heart. It is December, yet with your romantic singing, it will have roses from the month of May.

I would like to divine the voice that always denies vain things, that always rejects them, that repudiates them with a **No** that is without hatred, and that also holds promise for many **Yea's**.

Divine night, behold: here I am, finally alone with myself, and listening to the voice of Isaiah, to your hinting clamor that is naming me.

Oh enchanted night, Urania, life of mine, to be sick because of you is to be sane. All the tales that amuse mortals in their remote infancy are nothing close to you, because you smell better than the fragrance of dreamy, enchanted gardens, and because you are more transparent, oh Goodness of mine, than a transparent crystal palace.

So, with fertile endurance, without misfortune, and with simple piety, I passed through the streets of the capital of Mexico.

I went across the midnight city among ineffable crystals, clean of any mist.

Who is the one who traverses the abode while exclaiming my name? Who is the one who calls me in the night with such a delectable accent? Ah, it is a gust of wind that wails in the summit tower; it is a sweet thought.

So, I climbed the old tower of the Metropolitan Cathedral while singing my poem with the voice of the silence.

The mist was lost upon the summits of the mountains, upon those lands that had suffered tremendous convulsions. Then, among craters and eruptions of lava, **Iztaccihuatl** and

Popocatepetl emerged like an enchantment in order to delight the eyes. These two legendary volcanoes are like two millenary guardians in custody of the city of Mexico.

Far away, beyond these mountains, I saw worlds and ineffable regions that are impossible to describe with words. "Behold, that which is awaiting for you!" said a generous voice unto me, a voice that was endowing music to the wind.

This was a song heard by no one, played and played wherever I went, with musical notes in which I seemed to sense my own voice.

So, when descending from that tower, someone was following me; he was a chela, disciple. Great was my joy, since I was inebriated with an exquisite spiritual voluptuousness. My body did not have weight, I was moving myself with my astral form; I had abandoned my physical vehicle a long time before.

Already upon the atrium of this old cathedral, close to the foundation of its old walls that have been mute witnesses to many quarrels, conflicts, and challenges during many centuries, I saw a variegated and picturesque conjunction of men, women, children, and elders who were selling their merchandise everywhere.

There, seated as an oriental yogi, close to the wall and under the aged tower, at a corner of this old cathedral, an Aztec elder of indescribable age was meditating.

Any sleeping person would have easily confused him as being another merchant. In front of him and upon the cold stone of the floor, this venerable elder had a mysterious object, a secret Aztec relic.

Then, humbled, confounded, and abased before this holy, venerated, indigenous Aztec, I had to prostrate myself with reverence. The elder blessed me.

My chela (disciple), who was following my steps, looked like a zombie; his consciousness was profoundly sleeping... Suddenly, something happened; he bent down as if to grasp something, and without the least bit of respect, he grasped the untouchable relic; he observed it in his hands with infinite curiosity and I, frankly, was horrified by his behavior. This appeared so terrible to me that I exclaimed, "What do you think you are doing? You are committing a great sacrilege. For God's sake, withdraw from here and leave the relic in its place." Nevertheless, the master, filled with infinite compassion, replied, "It is not his fault in this matter; he is asleep."

Afterwards, like a pilgrim on the path who wants to heal the afflicted heart with a precious balm, he grasped the head of this sleeping neophyte, and blew the living **Fohat** upon his face with the purpose of awakening him, but everything was useless. This chela continued sleeping, dreaming.

So, filled with deep bitterness, I said, "How much I have fought there in the physical world in order for these people to awaken their consciousness, and still they continue to sleep." The chela had assumed a gigantic figure. The pluralized "I" (a conjunction of distinct and diverse entities), engulfed within the lunar bodies, was giving him that aspect.

It was bizarre to see this enormous, grayish-colored giant slowly walking like a zombie along the old atrium of this ancient cathedral while heading towards his home where his physical body was sleeping. In those moments I could only exclaim, "How ugly the lunar bodies are!"

Nonetheless, the venerated elder, while inebriated with compassion, replied unto me, "Within the temple you are about to enter (a Jinn temple, an Aztec sanctuary), there are many like this one, so look at them with sympathy."

I replied, "Clearly, I will look upon them with sympathy."

Let us now talk about reincarnation. Are perchance these lunar creatures reincarnating? Could reincarnation exist where there is no individuality?

In the sacred country of the Ganges, the doctrine of Krishna teaches that only the gods, demigods, heros, devas, and titans reincarnate. In other words, we will say that only the Self-realized, those who have the Being incarnated, can reincarnate.

The ego, the pluralized "I," does not reincarnate. It is submitted to the law of eternal return of all things. It returns into a new womb; it comes back into this valley of Samsara; it reincorporates.

RUNE TYR

Practice

The practices corresponding to the rune Tyr or Tir consist of placing the arms high above the head, then with the hands cupped like seashells, lowering them to the sides. When lowering the straight arms, pronounce the mantra "Tiiiiiirrrrrrrr." (The sound of the letters "i" and "r" should be prolonged in order to awaken the consciousness.)

The letter "t" or tau strikes the consciousness in order to awaken it. The letter "i" works intensely within the blood which is the vehicle of the essence. The "r," while intensifying the circulation of the blood in the veins and in the sanguineous vessels, operates marvels with the igneous flames by intensifying and stimulating the awakening of the consciousness.

Chapter 17
Meditation

Intellectual information is not a living experience. Erudition is not experimentation. Essays, tests, and demonstrations that are exclusively tri-dimensional are neither uni-total nor integral.

A faculty superior to the mind has to exist that must be independent from the intellect, capable of granting us knowledge and direct experience of any phenomenon.

Opinions, concepts, theories, hypotheses, do not signify verification, experimentation, and complete consciousness of this or that phenomena.

Only when we liberate ourselves from the mind can we have the living experience of the truth, of that which is the Reality, or of that which is found behind any phenomenon in a potential state.

Mind exists in everything. The seven cosmoses, the world, the moons, the suns, are nothing but crystallized and condensed mental substances.

The mind is also matter, although more rarefied. Mental substances exist in the mineral, plant, animal, and human kingdoms.

The only difference between the intellectual animal and the irrational beast is called intellect. The human biped gave intellectual form to the mind.

The world is nothing but an illusory mental form that inevitably will be dissolved at the end of the great cosmic day.

Myself, your body, my friends, your things, my family, etc., are (in their depth) what the Hindustani call Maya (illusion): vain mental forms that sooner or later must be reduced to cosmic dust.

My affections, my most beloved beings that surround me, etc., are simply forms of the cosmic mind. They do not have real existence.

THE TRIUMPHAL ENTRY INTO JERUSALEM

Intellectual dualism such as pleasure and pain, praise and slander, triumph and defeat, wealth and misery, constitute the painful mechanism of the mind.

While we are slaves to the mind, true happiness cannot exist within us.

It is urgent to ride the donkey (the mind) in order to enter into the heavenly Jerusalem on Palm Sunday. Disgracefully, nowadays, the donkey rides us, the miserable mortals of the mud of the earth.

No one can know the truth while being a slave to the mind. That which is Reality is not a matter of suppositions, but of direct experience.

Jesus, the great Kabir, said, "Know the truth, and the truth shall make you free." [John 8:32] However, I tell you that truth is not a matter of affirmation or negation, of belief or doubt. The truth must be directly experienced while in the absence of the "I," beyond the mind.

Whosoever liberates the self from the intellect can experience, can vividly verify, can feel an element that radically transforms.

When we liberate ourselves from the mind, then this mind is converted into a ductile, elastic, and useful vehicle with which we express ourselves in this conscious world.

Superior logic invites us to realize that liberating, emancipating ourselves from the mind, releasing ourselves from all mechanicity, is equivalent in fact to the awakening of the consciousness, to the termination of automatism.

That which is beyond the mind is Brahma, the uncreated eternal space, that which has no name, the Reality.

But let us study the facts: who is the one that wants to release himself, to liberate himself from the mortifying mind?

It is easy to answer this question by saying that the consciousness, the Buddhist interior principle, that part of the soul that we have within us, is what can and must be liberated.

Indeed, by itself, the purpose of the mind is only the bitterness of our existence. Authentic, legitimate, real happiness is only possible when we emancipate ourselves from the intellect.

However, we must recognize that an inconvenience exists, as well as a capital obstacle and impediment in order to acquire that longed for liberation of the Essence. I am referring to the tremendous struggle of antitheses.

The Essence, the consciousness, even when of a Buddhic nature, disgracefully lives bottled up within the exaggerated intellectual dualism of the opposites: yes and no, good and evil, high and low, mine and yours, like and dislike, pleasure and pain, etc.

By all means, it is illuminating to deeply comprehend that when this tempest in the ocean of the mind ceases and the struggle between the opposites finishes, the Essence can escape and submerge itself within that which is the Reality.

What is very difficult, laborious, arduous, and strenuous is the achievement of absolute mental silence in all and each one of the forty-nine subconscious departments of the mind.

To reach, to obtain quietude and silence in the mere superficial intellectual level, or in some of the subconscious departments of the mind, is not enough, because the Essence continues to be bottled up within submerged infraconscious and unconscious dualism.

A blank mind is something extremely superficial, hollow, and intellectual. We need serene reflection if we truly want to achieve the quietude and absolute silence of the mind.

The Chinese word Mo signifies silence or serenity, and the word Chao means to reflect or to observe.

Consequently, Mo Chao can be translated as "serene reflection" or "serene observation."

However, it is important to comprehend that in pure Gnosticism, the terms serenity and reflection have much more profound meanings and therefore should be comprehended with special connotations.

The sense of serenity transcends that which is normally understood as calmness or tranquility. It implies a superlative state which is beyond reasoning, desires, contradictions, and words. It signifies a situation that is beyond mundane noise.

The sense of reflection in itself is beyond what is always understood as contemplation of a problem or idea. Here this word does not imply mental activity or contemplative thought, but rather a type of objective consciousness, clear and reflective, always illuminated within its own experience.

Therefore, serenity signifies the serenity of no thought, and reflection signifies intense and clear consciousness.

Serene reflection is the clear consciousness within the tranquility of no thought.

When perfect serenity reigns, true, profound illumination is achieved.

Chapter 18

The Deformed Giant Polyphemus

Men and gods, you must remember that damned land
where the deformed giant Polyphemus abided filthily. He was
always accompanied by a hundred of his brothers who were
equivalent to his cruelty and monstrous stature.

Ulysses, the cunning warrior, destroyer of citadels, was
sheltered with his people in the cave of this ogre, who started
devouring all the guests without respecting any rule of hospitality.

However, Ulysses, the sagacious warrior, who was skillful,
shrewd, and sharp in every type of mischief, achieved the ine-
briation of this enormous giant (who was satiated with human
flesh) with delicious wine.

So, the monster was sleeping on his back on the ground
close to his cave and vomiting wine mixed with the scattered
flesh of those that he had inhumanely sacrificed.

A good opportunity exists for any warrior who is within
the mouth of the wolf, and it is clear that the king of Ithaca
(Ulysses) knew how to take advantage of that situation.

It is said by those with wisdom that this sly warrior — cunning, artful as no other — took a sharply pointed stake hard-
ened by fire and stabbed it without hesitation into the frontal
eye of this colossus. Afterwards, he hastily fled far away from
that cavern.

Aeneas, the illustrious Trojan man, verified the reality of
the former story when he navigated to the land of Lazio.

He disembarked with his people on that inhospitable land
and listened to this story from the lips of Achaemenides. He
saw Polyphemus appear high up on the mountain. This blind
giant was walking with his sheep, heaving his vast bulk down
from a high cliff, towards the shore he knew so well.

Possessed by panic, the Trojans cut the cables, embarked
in concealment and took Achaemenides with them. The giant
heard the struggling of the oars, and though not able to pursue
the navigators, he raised a great clamor as when a lion roars,

and then one hundred titans appeared, similar in stature to the high cedars or pines that adorn the sacred forest of Diana.
"These are, then, the 'Giants' (the titans) of antiquity, the ante- and postdiluvian Gibborim of the Bible." — H.P. Blavatsky, The Secret Doctrine, 2:340

The five statues of Bamian discovered by the famous Chinese traveller Hsüan-tsang [Xuanzang] come into my memory.

"CAVES OF BAMEEN" ILLUSTRATION. THE SO-CALLED "BUDDHAS OF BAMIYAN" WERE WIDELY KNOWN AS TWO 6TH CENTURY MONUMENTAL STATUES, POPULARLY INTERPRETED TO BE OF STANDING BUDDHAS, CARVED INTO THE SIDE OF A CLIFF IN THE BAMWAM VALLEY IN THE HAZARAJAT REGION OF CENTRAL AFGHANISTAN. THOSE TWO WERE DESTROYED IN 2001 BY THE TALIBAN. IN 630 AD, XUANZANG WROTE ABOUT A THIRD LARGE STATUE, BUT IT HAS NEVER BEEN FOUND. HOWEVER, ON 8 SEPTEMBER, 2008, ARCHAEOLOGISTS SEARCHING FOR IT ANNOUNCED THE DISCOVERY OF AN UNKNOWN 19-METRE (62-FOOT) STATUE.

"The largest is made to represent the First Race of mankind, its ethereal [protoplasmic: semi-ethereal, semi-physical] body being commemorated in hard, everlasting stone, for the instruction of future generations, as its remembrance would otherwise never have survived the Atlantean Deluge. The second — 120 feet high — represents [with complete clarity, the Hyperborean] the sweat-born [second root-race]; and the third — measuring 60 feet — immortalizes [the Lemurian root race who inhabited the continent Mu, or Lemuria, which was situated in the Pacific Ocean] the last descendants of which are represented in the [famous] statues found on Easter Isle." — H. P. Blavatsky, The Secret Doctrine 2:336-41

The fourth root race is represented by the next corresponding statue. This race lived on the Atlantean continent, situated

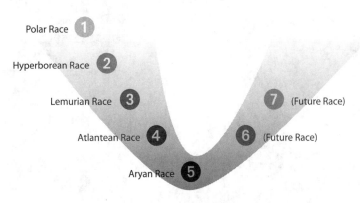

THE SEVEN ROOT RACES

in the Atlantic Ocean, and was smaller still than the previous one, though gigantic in comparison with our present fifth root race.

The last of these five images is a little higher than the average tall person of our current root race. It is obvious that this statue personifies the Aryan humanity which inhabits the present continents.

Everywhere, in all the corners of the world, there are Cyclopean ruins and colossal stones that are a living testimony of these giants.

Gigantic stones that could walk, talk, utter oracles, and even sing existed in the ancient times.

It is written that the...

> "...Christ-stone, or Christ-Rock, 'the spiritual Rock' that followed 'Israel' (I Cor 10:4) 'became a Jupiter lapis,' swallowed by his father Saturn, 'under the shape of a stone.'

> "Had there been no giants to move about such colossal rocks, there could never have been a Stonehenge, a Carnac (Brittany) and other such Cyclopean structures."
> — H. P. Blavatsky, The Secret Doctrine 2:341

If in foregone times the true and legitimate magical science had not existed upon the face of the earth, then:

STONES OF CARNAC (BRITTANY)

"...there could never have been so many witnesses to oracular and speaking stones.

"In a poem on Stones attributed to Orpheus, those stones are divided into ophites and siderites, 'serpent-stones' and 'star-stones.' 'The Ophite is shaggy, hard, heavy, black, and has the gift of speech; when one prepares to cast it away, it produces a sound similar to the cry of a child. It is by means of this stone that Helanos foretold the ruin of Troy, his fatherland...' etc. (Falconnet.)" — H. P. Blavatsky, The Secret Doctrine 2:341-342

Very ancient sacred documents affirm that...

"...Eusebius never parted with his ophites, which he carried in his bosom, and received oracles from them, delivered in a small voice resembling a low whistling. [This was the same of course as the small voice heard by

---

* One translation reads, "Except old seers do feign, And wizards' wits be blind, The Scots in place must reign, Where they this stone shall find."

Elias or Elijah after the earthquake at the mouth of the cave (I Kings 19:12)].

"It is also known that the famous stone at Westminster was called liafail — 'the speaking stone,' — which raised its voice only to name the king that had to be chosen."
— H. P. Blavatsky, The Secret Doctrine 2:342

This stone had an inscription that is now erased by the dust of the centuries, which said:

"Ni fallat fatum, Scoti quocumque locatum
Invenient lapidem, regnasse tenentur ibidem."

"Finally, Suidas speaks of a certain Heraclius, who could distinguish at a glance the inanimate stones from those which were endowed with motion; and Pliny mentions stones which "ran away when a hand approached them.

"... the monstrous stones of Stonehenge were called in days of old chior-gaur... or the dance of the giants.

"The authors... of various learned works on the ruins of Stonehenge, Carnac and West Hoadley, give far better and more reliable information upon this particular subject. In those regions... immense monoliths are found, 'some weighing over 500,000 kilograms.'"
— H. P. Blavatsky, The Secret Doctrine 2:342-343

The giants of ancient times were those who once could raise such boulders and could...

"...range them in such symmetrical order that they should represent the planisphere, and place them in such wonderful equipoise that they seem to hardly touch the ground, are set in motion at the slightest touch of the finger, and would yet resist the efforts of twenty men who should attempt to displace them."
— H. P. Blavatsky, The Secret Doctrine 2:336-41

Giants were the ones who transported the stones for the construction of the pyramids of Egypt.

The Oscillating Stone was a medium for divination used by giants, but why do they oscillate? The most enormous of them are evidently relics of the Atlanteans. The smallest of them, like the rocks of Brimham, with oscillating rocks on their summit, are copies of the most ancient lithoid.

ABRAHAM AND THE THREE ANGELS

"Truly, it is urgent, indispensable, and necessary to convert
ourselves into kings or queens and priests or priestesses
of nature in accordance with the Order of Melchizedek."

Chapter 19
Rune Bar (Beor, Berkana)

When speaking in the golden language, in the very pure gold of divine language, with mystical astonishment we discover that in Syrian **bar** signifies "**son**."

Baron: This word in itself is broken down into two sacred syllables, **bar** and **on**. This must be intelligently translated as "the **son** of the **earth**."

Christ, the Solar Logos, is something more profound. In the Aramaic language, Christ is **Bar-Ham**, the Son of Man.

Certainly, the Christos or the cosmic and triumphant Chrestos, is not Jesus, though He was incarnated within him. He was neither the Buddha, but He flourished in his fertile lips made Word. He was not Moses, but He shone in his face, there on mount Nebo. He was not Hermes, but He lived reincorporated within him. The Lord Chrestos is without individuality.

> "Whosoever knows, the Word gives power to. No one has uttered It, no one will utter It, except the one who has incarnated It (the Word, Christ)."

> *"The son of Man [whether he is named Jesus, Buddha, Krishna or any other name] must suffer many things, and be rejected of the elders [those who are passing in this world as being prudent, judicious and discreet] and chief priests [constituted by men with mundane authority] and scribes [those who pass as being wise in this world], and be slain, and be raised the third day... But I tell you of a truth, there be some standing here, which shall not taste of death, till they see the kingdom of God.*

> *"...If any man will come after me, let him deny himself [let him dissolve the "I"], and take up his cross daily, and follow me... For whosoever will save his soul [the egocentric person] shall lose it; but whosoever will lose his soul for my sake [the one who wants to die within himself], the same shall save it.*

> *"For what is a man advantaged, if he gain the whole world, and lose himself, or be cast away?*

"For whosoever shall be ashamed of me and my words, of him shall the Son of Man be ashamed, when he shall come in his own glory, and in his Father's, and of the holy angels." — Luke 9:22-27

When we study cosmic grammar, then we can verify for ourselves that an intimate relationship exists between the runes **Tyr / Tir** and **Bar**.

Tir esoterically corresponds to the zodiacal sign of Pisces, and **Bar** burningly shines in the brilliant constellation of Aries. This reminds us of the occult relationship between water and fire, death and life.

If we place before the sacred syllable **Ar** the letter B, then we indicate with this the necessity of attracting the Sun to the Earth. **Ar-Bar-Man** is the primeval name of Abraham.

To incarnate Christ in and within oneself is what is vital, cardinal, and fundamental in order to convert oneself into the Son of Man. This is the only way to earn the right to enter into the Order of Melchizedek.

It becomes opportune to remind the children of the Earth — the dwellers of this world, this lunar race — that just as the water put an end to ancient history, so too, very soon now, the fire will destroy everything with life that is thereon.

Woe! Woe! Woe to the dwellers of the earth; woe to this perverse race of Adam.

"But the day of the Lord will come as a thief in the night; in the which the heavens shall pass away with a great noise, and the elements shall melt with fervent heat, the earth also and the works that are therein shall be burned up." — II Peter 3:10

It is good for the children of the Earth to know that the solar race dwells within "the One Thousand and One Nights," the Jinn lands.

Truly, it is urgent, indispensable, and necessary to convert ourselves into kings or queens and priests or priestesses of nature in accordance with the Order of Melchizedek. This is the only way to be saved.

Among the multiple, disquieting faces of life, we have and must clearly affirm that next to our very side, another humanity exists, which is invisible to us because of our sins and sexual abuses.

With the consent of the very venerable and respectable masters, I have been granted the right to inform the lunar people that the Order of Melchizedek has many confraternities. Let us remember just for a moment the transcendental Monsalvat, the exotic Shambhala, the sacred island of the north that is situated in that polar spherical segment, the Sacred Order of Tibet to which I have the honor of being affiliated, etc.

It is obvious that thanks to the Veil of Isis such ineffable corporations are unapproachable. It is beneficial to explain to people that the sexual Adamic veil can only be lifted up by the intimate Christ.

The Son of Man is born from the fire and the water. This is the synthesis-religion, the doctrine of Jano with its three radicals: I.A.O. But the children of the Earth abhor this doctrine, since their motto is, "Let us eat and drink, since tomorrow we will die."

It is written that the Atlantean root race was devoured by the Averno, and that only the children of the Sun were saved.

This event will be repeated in accordance with the law of recurrence. The entrance of this present humanity into the submerged devolution of this planetary organism on which we live becomes evident.

There are three types of churches:

First, the Triumphant Church, represented by the few
   Knights of the Grail who persisted to remain pure;
Second, the Failing Church, represented by
   those who abhor the Initiatic Stone;
Third, the Militant Church, represented by
   the others, who as Mary Magdalene, Paul of
   Tarsus, Kundry, and Amfortas, are still in rebel-
   lion against the seductive Luciferic fire.

The Triumphant Church is certainly the church of the brothers and sisters who have already remounted upon the harsh path of salvation — **Per Aspera Ad Astra** — as the Latin motto says — true children of God in the most beautiful, mystical sense.

"Children of God" and "Sons of Men" are synonyms in Christic esotericism. They are the Knights of the Holy Grail.

Esoteric Practice

You must intelligently combine the exercises of the rune **Bar** with the exercises of the rune **Tyr / Tir**.

Place the arms high above the head, descending them while the hands are cupped as shells, and while singing the mantras **Tir**, **Bar**, as follows: *Tiiiiiiirrrrrrrr, Baaaaaaarrrrrrrrrr.*

Objectives of this practice:

1. To wisely mix within our own interior universe the magical forces of the two runes.
2. To awaken consciousness.
3. To intimately accumulate Christic atoms of high voltage.

Rune Tyr Bar

Chapter 20
The Ten Rules for Meditation

Scientific meditation has ten basic, fundamental rules. Without them, emancipation and liberation from the mortifying shackles of the mind is impossible.

1ST RULE   Before the arising of any thought, be completely conscious of your psychological mood.

2ND RULE   Psychoanalysis: investigate the root and origin of each thought, remembrance, affection, emotion, feeling, resentment, etc., as they emerge from the mind.

3RD RULE   Serenely observe your mind; place perfect attention on all mental forms that appear on the screen of the intellect.

4TH RULE   From moment to moment during the common and current course of daily life, remember and recall the "sensation of contemplation."

5TH RULE   The intellect must assume a psychological, receptive, integral, uni-total, complete, tranquil, and profound state.

6TH RULE   There must be continuity of purpose, tenacity, firmness, constancy, and insistence in the technique of meditation.

7TH RULE   It is commendable to attend the meditation rooms of the Gnostic Lumisials anytime we can.

8TH RULE   During any agitated or revolving activity, it is peremptory, urgent, and necessary to convert ourselves into watchers of our own mind, to stop at least for an instant to observe it.

9TH RULE   It is indispensable and necessary to always practice with closed eyes, with the goal of avoiding the external sensory perceptions.

10TH RULE   Absolute relaxation of the entire body, and the wise combination of meditation with drowsiness.

Beloved reader, the moment has arrived in order to judiciously weigh and analyze these ten scientific rules of meditation.

A   The principle, base, and living foundation of Samadhi (ecstasy), consists of previous introspective knowledge of oneself. It is indispensable to introvert ourselves during deepest meditation. We must start to profoundly know the psychological mood that precedes the appearance of any mental form in the intellect. It is urgent to comprehend that all thoughts that emerge from within our mind are always preceded by pain or pleasure, happiness or sadness, like or dislike.

B   Serene reflection. Examine, estimate, and inquire about the origin, cause, reason, or fundamental motive of every thought, remembrance, image, affection, desire, etc., as they emerge from the mind. Self-discovery and self-revelation are in this second rule.

C   Serene observation. Pay perfect attention to every mental form that makes its appearance on the screen of the intellect.

D   We must convert ourselves into spies of our own mind by contemplating it in action from instant to instant.

E   The chitta (mind) is transformed into vrittis (vibratory waves). The mind is like a pleasant and tranquil lake. When a rock falls into this lake, bubbles emerge from the bottom. All the different thoughts are perturbed ripples on the surface of the waters.

During meditation, let the lake of the mind remain still, without waves, serene, and profound.

F   Fickle people who are voluble, versatile, change-able, without firmness, without willpower, will never achieve ecstasy, satori, samadhi.

G   It is obvious that scientific meditation can be practiced individually in an isolated way, as well as in a group of like-minded people.

H   The soul must be liberated from the body, affections, and the mind. It is evident, clear, and obvious that when the soul is emancipated from the intellect, it is radically liberated from the rest.

I   It is urgent, indispensable, and necessary to eliminate perceptions of the external senses during interior profound meditation.

J   It is indispensable to relax the body for meditation; let no muscle remain tense. It is urgent to provoke and regulate drowsiness at will.

It is evident, clear, and unarguable that illumination is the outcome of the wise combination of drowsiness and meditation.

Results

Upon the mysterious threshold of the Temple of Delphi, a Grecian maxim was engraved in the stone that said, **Homo Nosce Te Ipsum**... "Man, know thyself, and thou will know the universe and its gods."

In the final instance, it is obvious, evident, and clear that the study of oneself and serene reflection conclude in the quietude and silence of the mind.

When the mind is quiet and in silence — not only in the intellectual level, but in all and each one of the forty-nine subconscious departments — then the Newness emerges. The Essence, the consciousness, is unbottled, and the awakening of the soul, that is to say, the ecstasy, the samadhi, the satori of the saints occurs.

The mystical experience of Reality transforms us radically. People who have never directly experienced the Truth live like butterflies going from school to school. They have yet to find their center of cosmic gravitation. Therefore, they die as failures, and without having achieved the so longed for realization of the Innermost Self.

The awakening of the consciousness, of the Essence, of the soul or Buddhata, is only possible by liberating, emancipating ourselves from the mental dualism, from the struggle of the antitheses, of the intellectual waves.

Any subconscious, infra-conscious, or unconscious, submerged struggle turns into an impediment for the liberation of the Essence (soul).

Every antithetical battle, as insignificant and unconscious as it might appear, indicates, accuses, aims to obscure points that are ignored, unknown within the atomic infernos of the human being.

To reflect, observe, and know these infra-human aspects, these obscure points of oneself, is indispensable in order to achieve the absolute quietude and silence of the mind.

To experience that which is not of time is only possible while in absence of the "I."

Chapter 21
The Tragedy of Queen Dido

No one can deny that the Eternal Mother Space has two rival aspects: Venus and Astaroth, Heva and Lilith, Sophia Achamoth and Sophia Prunikos.

Let us now talk about Venus — or it is better if we say, let us talk of Astaroth, which is its negative aspect, and **Prakriti's** tenebrous antithesis in Nature and in the human being.

Long ago, over many centuries, we find how the heart of Queen Dido became inflamed by the cruelty of **Kali**. The unhappy sovereign did not want to comprehend that her passion was contrary to the will of the holy gods.

Oh Dido! Light of a delectable dream, flower from an enchanted myth, your admirable beauty sings the grace of Hermaphroditus with the aerial enchantment of Atalanta, and from your ambiguous form the evocative ancient Muse raises a hymn to the fire.

Thus, from the old wine poured down within the amphora, Aeneas drank thirstily. Therefore, Phoebus frowned his forehead, and Juno frowned her own as well, but nodding in assent, Kali Astaroth laughed as always when Eros unclasped his philter within the chalices of Hebe.

So, before meeting the illustrious Trojan man Aeneas, the saddened queen spurned the love of Iarbas, the king of Libya, a courageous man who did not tolerate any offense, a terrific archer who dwelled with his people of war close to the African desert.

Poor Dido!... What a terrible intimate struggle she would have to endure between her sacred duty, the love of her people, and the cruel wound of Cupid, who began his destructive labor by incessantly erasing from the memory of the sovereign the image of Sychaeus, her former husband.

Lilith-Astaroth... what damage you have caused! Goddess of desire and passions, mother of Cupid... The human tempests shed blood from their hearts because of you. Thus, this is how, oh queen, you put your tremendous oath aside and into obliv-

The Meeting of Dido and Aeneas by Nathaniel Dance-Holland (1735–1811)

ion, by finding on the path of your life a Trojan who placed
on your thirsty lips a new breath, a beautiful cup of delicious
wine.

Then, when Cupid arrived, a wild triple flame was lit in
your scarlet blood, and among grapevines of fire you delivered
the vintage of your life to a dreadful sexual passion.

This beauty, whose terrible fate commanded with much
tenderness that she be martyred, received from Lucifer a rare
black pearl for her tiara of madness.

Thus, the unhappy queen consulted her dearest sister
Anna, and both of them traversed the altars of their diverse
gods in search of presages that would favor her desires.

They immolated victims to Ceres, to Phoebus Apollo, and
to Dionysus, and especially to Juno, who is the goddess of
women who work in the Ninth Sphere. Juno also presides over
just and perfect nuptial ceremonies.

Many times (oh God!), the tragic queen bent herself over
the open wounds of the innocent, sacrificed victims, inspecting their palpitating inner organs. Yet, an enamoured woman
who has her consciousness asleep clearly will always be ready to
interpret all the signs in favor of her dream.

From heaven, Juno, the goddess of initiated women, observed with indignation the tenebrous progress that Kali Astaroth was making upon the poor Dido, but all of Juno's claims and protests were in vain.

Consumed by passion, the unhappy sovereign walked in vigil every night, exclusively thinking of Aeneas.

Madly in love, the Trojan Aeneas rebuilt the walls of Carthage and worked in the fortification of this foreign city.

Ah! How different the fate of poor Dido would have been if Mercury, the messenger of the gods, had not intervened.

The epic Trojan paladin had to march towards Lazio, and to forget she who adored him. Such was the command of Jupiter, father of gods and men.

> "...You are not the son of a goddess, and Dardanus was not the first founder of your family. It was the Caucasus that fathered you on its hard rocks, and Hyrcanian tigers offered you their udders."

This is what the desperate, enraged sovereign exclaimed.

Useless were all of her complaints and her mourning... If this unhappy bride was not in Aulis, sacrificing to the gods in order to invoke the destruction of the city of Priam, and if she was never in alliance with the Achaeans, then why (oh God of mine!) should this unhappy woman have suffered so much?

This unfortunate sovereign, transformed into a slave by the cruel dart of sexual passion, invoked death.

Useless were her offerings before the altar of the goddess Juno, since animal passion receives no answer from the gods.

Ah! If people only knew that the poison of animal passion cheats the mind and heart...

The disgraced queen believed herself to be in love; the dart of Cupid was inserted in her heart, but certainly in its depth, what she felt was passion.

So, the unhappy one cried upon the altar of Juno, and suddenly, the lustral water became black like a sackcloth of hair and the sacred wine of libation became red as blood.

Terrible were the moments... Upon the solitary dome of the palace, the owl of death sung his sinister song, and at times the sovereign dreamt of herself walking in a limitless desert in search of her adored Aeneas, or desperately escaping while being chased by the merciless Furies.

Nevertheless, the unhappy one did not ignore the magical, marvelous, and infallible procedures in order to forget her bestial passion.

> "...Go now, telling no one (said she unto her sister
> Anna), and build up a pyre under the open sky in the
> inner courtyard of the palace, and lay on it the armor
> this traitor has left hanging on the walls of my room;
> everything there is of his remaining, including that
> sword which was engraved with gold and that he offered
> as a present for our nuptial wedding which was never
> fulfilled, and the marriage bed on which I was destroyed,
> I want to wipe out everything that can remind me of
> such a man, and that is what the priestess advised."

Disgracefully, the passionate sovereign — instead of burning in that funeral pyre the remains of this illustrious Trojan man — resolved to immolate herself in that fire in a sudden blaze of madness.

She tied her royal temples with the band of the victims destined for sacrifice, and at the foot of the funeral pyre, she took as her witnesses the hundred gods, as well as Erebus, Chaos, and Hekate, the third aspect of the Divine Mother Space.

She, the unfortunate sovereign who could have utilized the magical effects of the lunar herbs by using them as a fuel for the incineration of memories, passion, and evil thoughts, instead, desired with violence to burn herself on the pyre of death.

She begged to the Sun, exclaimed to Juno, invoked the Furies of vengeance, and committed the error of damning Aeneas, and finally, pierced her heart with the Trojan's sword. Her sister found her already burning within the blazing fire of madness. This is how Queen Dido died.

Chapter 22
Rune Ur (Uruz)

ᚾ

Surveying from a height within infinite space, searching and lurking within the Akashic Records of Nature, I could verify for myself that the Moon is the mother of the Earth.

Now, with the open Eye of Dangma, I will submerge myself within the Great Alaya, the famous Over-Soul of Emerson, the soul of the universe. I invite you, beloved reader, to deeply study this book. It is necessary to meditate on it, to go deeply into its content, to know its profound significance.

If you ask me who I, Samael Aun Weor, am, I would answer you that I am one of the seven Amesha-Spentas of the Zoroastrians, who was active in the past mahamanvantara (cosmic day) that was named the Lotus of Gold.

Therefore, I am going to give testimony of that which I have seen and heard. Listen to me, men and gods: I know in depth about the seven mysteries of the Moon, the seven jewels, the seven surges of life that evolved and devolved within that which the Theosophists call the "Lunar Chain."

Certainly, the Moon is the satellite of the Earth only in one sense. What I am referring to is that it rotates around our planet. When this matter is seen from another angle, when it is investigated with the Eye of Shiva (intense spiritual vision of the Adept or Jivan-Mukta), then truly, the Earth becomes the satellite of the Moon. The evidence in favor of this fact is found in the tides, in the changing cycles of the many forms of sicknesses which coincide with the lunar phases, in what we can observe within the development of plants, and in the very marked lunar influence within the phenomena of conception and gestation of all creatures.

The Moon was once an inhabited planet, but now it is just cold refuse, a shadow that is dragged by the new body (the Earth), which is where all of its powers and principles of life have been passed by transfusion. It is condemned to be in pursuit of the Earth throughout many ages. The Moon looks like a satellite, but it is a mother that rotates around its daughter (the Earth).

I lived among the lunar humanity. I knew its seven root races, its epochs of civilization and barbarism, its alternating cycles of evolution and involution.

When the Selenites arrived to the sixth sub-race of the fourth round (the same age which this terrestrial humanity has already reached) I accomplished a similar mission to the one which I am accomplishing in these moments on the planet in which we live.

I taught the people of the Moon the synthesis-religion, which is contained within the initiatic stone (sex), the doctrine of Jano (I.A.O.), or the doctrine of the Jinns.

I lit the flame of Gnosis among the Selenites; I formed a Gnostic movement there. Thus, I sowed the seed... and as I sowed, some seeds fell by the wayside, and the mundane fowls of the air devoured them.

Some seeds fell upon rocks of discussions, theories, and anxieties, where profound and reflective people did not exist. As soon as they sprung up, they withered away before the light of the sun, for they did not pass the ordeal of fire, as they did not have roots.

Some fell among the thorns of brothers and sisters who hurt each other with their thorns of slander and gossip, etc. So, the thorns sprang up with the seeds and choked them.

Fortunately, my labor as a sower was not in vain, since some seeds fell on good ground, and sprang up, and bore fruit, some a hundredfold, some sixty-fold, some thirty-fold.

Many latent faculties exist within the Devamatri, Aditi or cosmic space, inside the runic UR within the Microcosmos, the "machine-man," or better if we say, the intellectual animal, that could be developed through tremendous, intimate super-efforts.

On the ancient Moon, in the times before it became a corpse, those who accepted the synthesis-religion of Jano became saved, and they transformed themselves into angels. Nevertheless, the great majority, those who were enemies of the Maithuna, those who rejected the initiatic stone (sex), converted themselves into Lucifers, terribly perverse demons to which the Bible refers.

Usually, a third party is never missing; so, in that Lunar apocalypse, a certain cold group at last became fiery, and they accepted the work in the Ninth Sphere (sex). A new abode was granted to these people, in order for them to work with the brute stone until giving it perfect cubic form.

> *"The stone which the builders disallowed, the same*
> *is made the head of the corner, and a stone of stum-*
> *bling, and a rock of offense."* − 1 Peter 2:7-8

In those times, the Selenites had a dreadful, sanguinary religion. The pontiffs of that cult sentenced me with the death penalty, and I was crucified upon the summit of a mountain close to a great city.

The transference of all the vital powers of the Moon to this planet Earth left that old Selenite abode without life. Therefore, the lunar soul is now reincarnated in this world upon which we live.

I was absorbed within the Absolute at the end of that Lunar mahamanvantara, which endured 311,040,000,000,000 years, or, in other words, an age of Brahma.

It is indispensable to say that after the great day, the Monadic waves of the Moon submerged themselves within the runic UR, within the profound womb of the eternal Mother Space.

It is urgent to affirm that during such a maha-samadhi (ecstasy without end), we (the Monadic waves) penetrated much more deeply, and thus we arrived to the Father, Brahma, the Universal Spirit of Life.

It is necessary to clarify that Brahma submerged Himself into the Absolute during the whole period of the mahapralaya, the great night.

While we, the brothers and sisters, were in that tremendous para-nirvanic repose, the Unknown Darkness converted itself into Uncreated Light for us.

UHR is the clock, the measurement of time; thus, the mahamanvantara RHU is the repose, the great pralaya.

Certainly, the cosmic night endures as long as the great day. It is my duty to affirm that each one of us, the brothers and sisters, was radically absorbed within his own primordial atom, the Ain Soph.

Therefore, when the dawn of this new cosmic day was initiated, the eternal Mother Space expanded herself from inside out, like a lotus bud. This is how this universe was gestated inside the womb of Prakriti.

Practice

Loving our Divine Mother and thinking in that great womb where the worlds are gestated, let us pray daily as follows:

Within my internal real Being resides the Divine Light. RAAAAMMM IOOO is the Mother of my Being. Devi Kundalini, RAAAMMM IOOO, help me... RAAAMMM IOOO assist me, illuminate me.

RAAAMMM IOOO, Divine Mother of mine, Isis of mine, Thou hast the child Horus, my true Being, in thy arms. I need to die within my self so that my Essence might be lost in Him... Him...Him...

Rune Ur

Indication

This prayer must be performed before the sun, with raised arms and hands. The legs must be opened, and the body slightly crouched, thus awaiting to receive Light and more Light.

Chapter 23
The Story of Master Meng Shan

According to old traditions now lost in the night of the centuries, the Chinese Master Meng Shan knew the science of meditation before the age of twenty.

It is stated by the yellow-skinned mystics that from that age until thirty-two, the cited master studied with the Eighteen Elders.

Certainly, it is interesting, pleasant, and worthwhile to know that this great illuminated one studied with infinite humility at the feet of the venerable elder Wan Shan, who taught him how to intelligently utilize the powerful mantra **Wu**. This mantra is pronounced like a double U, and wisely imitates the howl or sound of a hurricane when blowing through the rifts of the mountains.

This brother always remembered the state of alert perception and alert novelty that is so indispensable and so urgent for the awakening of the consciousness.

The venerable elder guru Wan Shan told him that during the twelve hours of the day, it is necessary to be alert like a cat that is lurking for a mouse, or like a hen that is brooding on her eggs. They do this without abandoning their duty, not even for a second.

Therefore, in these studies mere efforts are not worthwhile, only super-efforts are. Since we are not illuminated, we must work without rest, like a mouse that is gnawing on a coffin. If we practice in this manner, we will at last be liberated from the mind, and experience in a direct way that element which radically transforms, that element which is the Truth.

One given day, after eighteen days and nights of profound interior meditation, Meng Shan sat to drink tea, and then... (oh marvel!) he comprehended the intimate sense of a certain gesture of the Buddha showing a flower, and the deep significance of Mahakasyapa with his unforgettable, exotic smile.

He then questioned three or four elders about that mystical experience, but they kept silent. Other elders told him to identify that living, esoteric experience with samadhi, the Seal of the Ocean. Naturally, this wise advise inspired complete confidence in himself.

Meng Shan triumphantly advanced in his studies.

Nonetheless, in life not everything comes up roses; there are also thorns. So, in the month of July, during the fifth year of Chindin (1264), he unfortunately got dysentery in Chunking, a province of Szechuan.

With death on his lips, he decided to make his will and to dispose of his terrene goods. When this was done, he slowly rose to a sitting position, burned incense, and sat in an elevated place. There, in silence, he prayed to the three Blessed Ones and to the holy gods by repenting all the evil deeds he had committed in his life.

However, since he considered the end of his existence definite, he asked the ineffable ones to hear his last petition: "By means of the power of **Prajna** and a controlled mental state, I want to reincarnate myself in a favorable place, where I can become a monk (swami) at an early age. If perchance I recuperate myself from this illness, I will renounce the world, take the vows, and try to carry the light to other young Buddhists."

After pronouncing these vows, he submerged himself into a profound meditation while mentally chanting the mantra **Wu**. The sickness tormented him, his intestines were frighteningly torturing him, but he resolved not to pay attention to them.

Meng Shan radically forgot his own body; his eyelids were firmly closed, and he remained as if dead.

Chinese traditions tell us that when Meng Shan entered into meditation, only the Word, that is to say, the mantra **Wu** (U.... U.....) resounded in his mind. Afterwards, he lost the notion of himself.

But, the sickness...? What became of it...? What happened...?

It is clear and lucid to comprehend that any affliction, illness, or pain has determined mental forms as a foundation. If we achieve the radical and absolute forgetfulness of any suffering, then the intellectual base is dissolved and the organic indisposition disappears as well.

When Meng Shan rose from his place at the beginning of the night, with infinite happiness he felt that he was already half cured. Then after, he sat anew, and continued, submerged in profound meditation, until midnight. Thus, his cure became complete.

In the month of August, Meng Shan went to Chiang Ning, and filled with faith, he entered the priesthood. He remained one year in that monastery. Afterwards, he initiated a voyage in which he cooked his own food and washed his own clothes, etc. He then comprehended that the duty of meditation must be tenacious, resistant, strong, firm, constant, without ever getting tired of it.

Later on, walking throughout those Chinese lands, he arrived at the Monastery of the Yellow Dragon. While there, he deeply comprehended the necessity of the awakening of the consciousness. Afterwards, he continued his voyage towards Che Chiang.

Immediately after his arrival, he tossed himself at the feet of the Master Ku Chan from Chin Tien and swore not to leave the monastery until reaching illumination.

The meditation time he lost during his voyage was recuperated after one month of intense meditation. But in the interval, his body became filled with horrible blisters. He intentionally ignored them and continued with his esoteric discipline.

One given day (it does not manner which), some people invited him to a delicious supper. While walking on the way there, he took his Hua Tou (the mantra) and worked with it. Thus, while submerged into profound meditation he passed by the door of his host without noticing it. So, he comprehended thereafter that he could keep ahead with his esoteric work while being in complete physical activity.

On the sixth of March, while Meng Shan was meditating with the help of the mantra **Wu**, a monk who was the principal of the monastery entered the lumisial of meditation with the evident purpose of burning incense. However, it so happened that when this monk struck the box of the smoke-offering a noise was produced, and Meng Shan came to recognize himself, and he could see and hear Chao Chou, a famous Chinese master.

> "Desperate, I arrived at the dead end of the path. Then I stroked the wave (but) it was nothing but water. Oh, that notorious old man Chao Chou, whose face is so ugly."

All the Chinese biographers agree when they affirm that in autumn, Meng Shan had an interview with Hsueh Yen in Lingan and with Tui Keng, Shis Keng, Hsu Chou, and other famous elders.

I understand that the Koan or enigmatic phrase that was decisive for Meng Shan was without any doubt the same one with which Wan Shan interrogated him.

> "Is not that phrase, 'The light shines serenely upon the sand of the brook,' a prosaic observation from this foolish Chang?"

The meditation upon this phrase was enough for Meng Shan. When Wan Shan later interrogated him with the same phrase, that is to say, when he repeated to him the same question, the yellow-skinned mystic answered by throwing away the mattress of his bed, as if he was saying: **I am already awake!**

Chapter 24

The Country of the Dead

Aeneas, the most excellent Trojan man, olympically and solemnly ascended the august mountain of Apollo on whose majestic summit the mysterious cavern of the Pythoness was found.

Close to the temple, there was the sacred forest of the third aspect of the Divine Mother Kundalini, an ineffable jungle of Hekate, Proserpine, Coatlicue.

It was a hermetically sealed sanctuary with one hundred doors, a glorious entrance on which Daedalus, the skillful sculptor, engraved marvelous embossments with his extraordinary mastery.

It is said that Icarus (with his I.A.O. chiselled by his father on the sacred rock of that mysterious entrance) wanted to soar towards heaven, to convert himself into a Son of the Sun, but the wax that held his wings to his body melted and he fell into the horrifying precipice.

Icarus is the marvelous symbol of the vain intention of those who do not know how to work with the luminous and spermatic Fiat of the first instant. It is the disgrace and downfall of those alchemists who spill the raw matter of the Great Work.

Was Daedalus not perhaps the famous sculptor, the father of Icarus, and also the same one who taught Theseus how to escape from the intricate labyrinth of Crete...?

It was a horrifying corridor, and in the center of this labyrinth was always found the famous Minotaur, a half-man, half-beast (complicated intellect bottled up within the "myself").

Only by eliminating the interior beast can we make ourselves truly free. We will reach the realization of the Innermost Self only by the dissolution of the animal ego.

> "This is no time for you to be looking at sights like these (said the priestess), since soon, Apollo, similar to a hurricane-wind, will arrive."

So, this illustrious Trojan man sacrificed a hundred black rams from a herd in honor to Proserpine, who is the third manifested aspect of the Eternal Mother Space, queen of hell and death.

Thus, when the Sibyl spoke... oh God!... a frightening earthquake shook the base of the earth, and while transfigured, the virgin priestess cried:

> "It is the God Apollo! The God Apollo is here!... Why are you hesitating, Trojan Aeneas? Why are you so slow to offer your vows and prayers? Until you have prayed, the great mouths of my house are dumb and will not open."

The legend of the centuries states that when this famous man heard these venerated words, he poured out ardent prayers from the depths of his heart to Apollo.

Then, the priestess spoke with her voice transfigured by ecstasy, and warned this most illustrious warrior to lay hold his foot upon the shores of Italy, and to establish himself in the kingdom of Lavinium.

She told him that a second Achilles, equal in strength to the first one, would declare war upon him, and that the Latin rivers would be foaming with torrents of blood as the Simois and the Xanthus were in Troy. However, he must not give way to these adversities. Instead, he must face them all, since his road to safety, strange as it may seem, would start from a Greek city.

> "With these words from her sanctuary, the Sibyl of Cumae sang in the mountain her fearful riddling prophecies, her voice boomed in the temple, and the earth howled as she wrapped the truth in darkness..." (Demonius est Deus inversus).

So, the hero Aeneas began to beseech the Sibyl; he wept, and asked to be allowed to go into the country of the dead; he wanted to descend into the abode of Pluto, and said:

> "Since they say the gate of the king of the underworld is here and here too is the black swamp which the tide of Acheron floods, I pray to be allowed to go and look upon the face of my dear father. Show me the way and open the sacred door for me. On these shoulders I

carried him away through the flames of the smoking Troy...

"Besides, it was my father himself who begged and commanded me to come to you as a supplicant and approach your doors... was not Orpheus allowed to summon the shade of his wife with the sound of the strings of his Thracian lyre? Do I need to speak of Theseus? Or of great Hercules? I too am descended from highest Jupiter [Aeneas was an initiate]."

Certainly, to descend into the Averno in order to work in the Ninth Sphere and to dissolve the ego is easy, but it is dreadfully difficult to retrace our steps and to escape to the upper air. "That is the task! That is the difficult labor!"

Proserpine, the queen of hell and death, is certainly very capricious, and she always ordains that an offering must be brought to her from those who visit her. This offering is the golden bough, the golden branch of the tree of knowledge, with seed aplenty.

Joyful is the one who finds this magical tree (which, by the way, is not too far from us, since it is the very spinal medulla). The doors of Pluto will be open to this one.

Whosoever wants to ascend must previously descend; this is the law. Initiation is death and birth at the same time.

However, you who read these lines:

"Follow me; and let the dead bury their dead." – Matthew 8:22

"Whosoever will come after me, let him deny himself, and take up his cross, and follow me." – Mark 8:34

To deny the self signifies to dissolve the "I," to die from moment to moment, to reduce the "myself" to dust, from instant to instant.

To take the heavy cross of the master upon our shoulders is something very significant. The vertical pole of this sacred symbol is masculine, and the horizontal pole is feminine. The clue of the Second Birth is found in the sexual crossing of these two poles.

To follow the Lord from second to second signifies sacrifice for humanity, to be ready to give even our last drop of blood for our fellowmen, to immolate ourselves upon the sacred altar of supreme love for the sake of all of our brothers and sisters in the world.

Now, gods and mortals listen to me: through the dreadful cave the Sibyl and Aeneas entered into the womb of the earth.

I place the genie of the earth as a witness, in order to solemnly affirm that before entering into the Averno, one has to pass through the Orcus (limbo). The Orcus is in itself a vestibule where many abide, such as: white-faced Diseases, horrifying, perverse Hunger who is a corrupter of men, squalid Poverty, perverted Pleasures, murderous War, the Furies, raving Discord with blood-soaked ribbons binding her viperous hair, Pain, and the idle dreams of the consciousness.

Here is where Aeneas found the stubborn dreams of people. Here is where he saw all manner of monstrous beasts like Briareus, the giant with his hundred arms, the Hydra of Lerna, who Hercules killed with mastery when cutting off all of its multiple heads, the Chimaera of people, which is a monster with the face of a goat, the Gorgons and Harpies (witches), etc.

The Orcus is the very throat of hell where the mysterious route that conducts the lost souls to the Tartarus (infernal worlds) commences.

Aeneas and the Sibyl, while seated on the boat of Charon, navigated upon the waters of Acheron and arrived at the other shore.

Aeneas also found Cerberus, the demon of gluttony, and Minos, the inexorable judge, and he saw the gloomy river, which serpentines nine times about the Ninth Sphere, and the terrible water-pools of the river Styx.

Within the Averno, the pitiful Aeneas found Dido, the queen who loved him, and he was able to embrace his deceased father.

Chapter 25

Runes Dorn and Thorn (Thurisaz)

Just a few days ago, it occurred to me to once again visit the Temple of Chapultepec in Mexico.

A certain sister humbly bowed before the door of the temple, thus imploring for admission. These types of sincere supplications are always heard.

Master Litelantes and I entered behind that supplicant. Frankly, I cannot deny that filled with profound veneration and devotion, I advanced, walking upon my knees, as many penitents do. Thus, in this way, I ascended each one of the steps of the sanctuary.

Litelantes entered very happily... and a little bit playful. I had to become a little severe with her, and because of my attitude, she was surprised. "Once inside the temple, I am different," I said, addressing her.

A group of lunar people took advantage of this opportunity of open doors; poor people...

Litelantes and my insignificant person who has no value felt ourselves very distinct from all of those people who were dressed with lunar rags... Truly, how different are the solar bodies!

What is astonishing is the way in which this lunar group advanced: without veneration, without respect.

However, I could clearly and with complete lucidity comprehend that I should see such a group with sympathy, since they were selected people and with a lot of merits.

Unfortunately, it was not the hour for a meeting, and the way in which these people entered was not organized either.

The superior master of the temple grumbled severely at them, and he even took them out of the temple by singing in a very delectable language... thus, all of these people had to withdraw.

I have been reflecting upon all of this. The love of Christ is formidable, because this lunar group is very sincere, even though these poor little ones have yet to achieve the Second

Birth. But they deserve to be helped, so the Lord takes care and cultivates them, as if they were delicate little flowers from the greenhouse. Good opportunities will be finally granted unto them in order to work in the Ninth Sphere. Then, oh yes, disgrace will be on them if they fail in the difficult ordeal.

Since ancient times, the descent into the Ninth Sphere has been the maximum ordeal for the supreme dignity of the hierophant. Buddha, Jesus, Dante, Hermes, Krishna, Quetzalcoatl, etc., had to descend into the abode of Pluto.

Here is the cave where Cerberus, who is a prodigy of terror, howls. With its barking, its three enormous flat-nosed heads, and with serpents writhing on its neck, Cerberus fills all the defuncts with terror.

THE TREE OF LIFE (KABBALAH)
SUPERIMPOSED OVER THE BODY

יסוד Yesod   The Ninth Sphere
"foundation"

Those who died cheated by the poison of sexual passion dwell in those painful profundities, as did Evadne, Pasiphae and Laodamia... and also the poor Queen Dido who swore to be faithful to the ashes of Sychaeus.

Here is where many heroes of ancient Troy live, as did Glaucus, Medon, Thersilochus, Polybotes, and also Idaeus who was so beloved yet feared.

Here is where the terrible shadows of Agamemnon and Ajax and many other Achaeans who fought against Troy run and scream, reliving their life as if still fighting on the fields of battle sprinkled with sunlight. They still are inebriated with light and blood.

Here is where the sinister city exists, encircled by a triple wall, from where are heard horrible groans and the dragging and clanking of iron chains.

Here are the three Furies: Desire, Mind, and Evil Will, who flog the guilty ones with whips that hiss over them like viperous tongues.

The Titans of ancient Atlantis, who intended to climb the firmament in order to conquer other worlds of the infinite space, yet without having reached true sanctity, also reside in those tenebrous, submerged regions.

In Tartarus live the fornicators, the adulterers, the homosexuals, assassins, drunkards, the avaricious, the selfish, thieves, swindlers, the angry, the violent, the greedy, the envious, the proud, the vain, the lazy, the gluttons, the founders of evil doctrines, hypocritical Pharisees, traitors, and materialistic atheists who are enemies of the Eternal One.

Immense, oh God, is the multitude of crimes, that — even if having one hundred mouths, a thousand tongues, and a voice of steel — their enumeration could never be uttered.

To descend into those mineral regions of the earth, into that sub-world, is extremely easy, but to ascend again, to return up to the light of the sun is frightfully difficult, almost impossible.

When I was born in the Causal World, or better if we say the parallel universe of conscious will, the sacred cloth of Veronica shone upon the altar of the temple.

There are chiselled in stone many heads crowned with thorns related to the age of bronze.

A cult to the god of thorns existed. Such thorns, when treated with consideration and judiciously examined, clearly present to us the symbolic figure of the rune Thorn.

In these sacred mysteries of the Thorn cult, special practices were given in order to develop conscious will.

Dorn, Thorn, signifies willpower. Remember Gnostic brothers and sisters, that our motto is **Thelema**.

The divine Rostrum crowned with thorns signifies Thelema, that is to say, conscious will.

Dorn is also the phallus, the volitive principle of Sexual Magic (Maithuna).

There is the need, by means of the phallus, to intelligently accumulate the seminal energy; when it is refrained and transmuted, it is converted into Thelema (willpower).

Arm yourself with willpower like steel. Remember, beloved reader, that without the thorn that pierces or sticks, the spark does not jump, the light does not emerge.

We can return from Tartarus and up to the light of the sun only with Thelema (Christ Will).

Truly, I tell unto you that Christ Will knows how to obey the Father on earth as it is in heaven.

Take heed of evil will; it is in itself the strength of Satan — that is to say, concentrated desire.

Practice

In the military position, on your feet, firm, and facing towards the east, place your right arm in such a way that your hand rests upon your waist or hip, thus performing the shape of this rune.

Now, you must sing the mantric syllables, TA, TE, TI, TO, TU, with the purpose of developing Christ Will in yourself.

This exercise must be practiced everyday at sunrise.

RUNE THORN

Chapter 26
The "I"

You, who with mystical patience have listened deeply to the arcanum of the mysterious night; you, who have comprehended the enigma that is hidden in each heart, as well as the sound of a far away carriage, of a vague echo, of a slight sound that is lost in the far off distance... listen to me.

In those instants of profound silence, when forgotten things emerge from the bottom of the memory, in those forgone times, in the hour of the dead, in the hour of repose, you will know how to study in depth this present chapter of the Fifth Gospel, not only with your mind, but also with your heart.

As if into a cup of gold, I pour my sufferings into these lines, sufferings of past remembrances and fatal disgraces, sorrowful nostalgia of my soul inebriated with flowers, mourning of my heart, sad from festivities.

But, what is it that I want to say?... Soul of mine!... Are you perhaps lamenting with vain complaints because of too many yesterdays? You can still hunt for the perfumed rose and the fleur-de-lis, and at least there are also myrtles for your pitiful gray head.

The soul, satiated with vain remembrances, cruelly immolates what the ego enjoys, such as Nzinga, the black and lubricious Queen of Angola.

You have enjoyed yourself with horrifying bacchanals, stubborn pleasures within the mundane noise, and now, woe of thee! You heard the terrible curse of Ecclesiasticum.

Disgrace on thee!... Poor ego! The moment of passion bewitched you, but behold how Ash Wednesday arrives: **Memento Homo** ["Memento, homo... quia pulvis es, et in pulverem reverteris" (Gn 3:19). " Remember, man, you are dust and to dust you will return."].

Thus, this is why the selected souls are going towards the Mountain of Initiation, as explained by Anacreon and Omar Khayyám.

Old time gnaws at everything without clemency, and it goes quickly. You must know how to defeat it, Cintia, Cloe, and Cidalisa.

While in the absence of the "I" and beyond time, I experienced That which is the Reality, the element that radically transforms.

To vividly experience the reality beyond the mind... to experience in a direct way that which is not from time... certainly, is something impossible to describe with words.

I was in that state that is known in the oriental world as nirvikalpa-samadhi. Being an individual, I had passed beyond any individuality. I felt for an instant that the drop was becoming lost within the ocean that has no shores, the sea of indescribable light... the bottomless abyss... the Buddhist void filled with glory and happiness.

How can the Illuminated Void be defined...? How can that which is beyond time be described...?

Thus, the samadhi became extremely profound... The absolute absence of the "I," the complete loss of individuality, the greater and greater radical impersonalization caused fear in me.

Yes, fear...! I was afraid of losing what I was, my own particularity, my human affections...! What a terrible thing is the Buddhist annihilation...!

So, filled with fright, and even terror, I lost that ecstasy. I entered time. I bottled myself up within the "I." I fell into the mind.

Then, woe is me!... Woe! Woe! It was then that I comprehended the inconvenient joke of the ego. The ego was the one who was suffering. It was afraid for its life. It was crying.

Satan, the "myself," my beloved ego, caused the loss of my samadhi. What a horror! If I had known it before...

But, the people adore their "I" too much; they qualify it as divine and sublime. Certainly, how mistaken they are...! Poor humanity...!

When I passed through this mystical living experience, I was still very young, and she (the night, the firmament) was named Urania.

Ah! Crazy youth plays with such mundane things, and sees in each woman a Greek nymph, even when she could be a scarlet courtesan girl.

Such a time is now already distant! But, still I see orange blossoms in the green orange trees that are impregnated with aromas, and in the old frigates that come from the distant seas, or in the haycock, or thick mangroves, your adored rostrum from that time begins to appear like the first sorrow and first love.

So, I comprehended that I needed to dissolve the ego, to reduce it into dust, in order to have the right to ecstasy.

Then... God of mine!... I found myself with many and too many yesterdays. Truly, the "I" is a book of many volumes.

How difficult was the dissolution of the "I" for me, but I achieved it. Sometimes when fleeing from evil, I encountered evil, and I cried.

For what use is vile envy and lust, if their pale furies writhe as reptiles?

For what use is fatal hatred of those who are ungrateful...? For what use are the libidinous gestures of the Pilates?

Within the depths of the most chaste men, the Biblical Adam lives inebriated with carnal passion, and delectably tastes the forbidden fruit, as does the naked Phryne in the work of Phidias.

So, I would often cry out to heaven, saying:

"Give unto this fawn which is in me, science, the wisdom which makes the angel shake his wings. Through praying and penance allow me to put to flight the evil she-devils. Give me, oh Lord, other eyes, and not these that enjoy looking at the roundness of snow and red lips. Give me another mouth in which the ardent embers of asceticism can remain impregnated forever, and not this mouth of Adam in which wine and insane kisses are infinitely increasing and multiplying this bestial gluttony. Give me hands of discipline and penitence which can leave my back stained with blood, and not

these lubricious hands of a lover that caress the sinning apples. **Give me innocent Christic blood, and not this blood that makes my veins boil, my nerves vibrate, and my bones crackle. I want to be free from evil and deceit. I want to die within myself, and to feel a lovely hand that pushes me into that cave that always welcomes the hermit.**"

So, by intensely working, oh my brothers and sisters, I arrived to the kingdom of death through the path of love.

Ah!... if those who look for the illumination would truly comprehend that the soul is bottled up into the "I"...

Ah!... if they would destroy the "I," if they would reduce to dust their beloved ego, then truly, their soul would be free... in ecstasy... in a continuous samadhi. Thus, they will directly experience that which is the Truth.

Whosoever wants to vividly experience Reality must eliminate the subjective elements of perception.

It is urgent to know that such elements constitute diverse entities that form the "I."

The soul profoundly sleeps within each one of those elements. What pain...!

Chapter 27

The Cruel Enchantress Circe

Ancient traditions of Latium narrate:

> "You too, Caieta, nurse of Aeneas, have given by your death eternal fame to our shores; the honor paid you there even now protects your resting-place, and your name marks the place where your bones lie, great Hesperia, if that glory is of any value.

> "Good Aeneas duly performed the funeral rites and heaped up a barrow for the tomb, and when there was calm on the seas, he set sail and left the port behind him. A fair breeze kept blowing as night came on, the white moon lit their course and the sea shone in its shimmering rays. Keeping close inshore, they skirted the island of Calixto where Circe, the daughter of the Sun, lives among her riches... with her irresistible herbs, the savage goddess had given to men the faces and hides of wild beasts." — Aeneid VII

The legend of the centuries states that Neptune, lord of the sea, powerful god, protector of devout Trojans, kept them from sailing into that harbor or coming near the deadly shore where the frightful enchantress dwelled, by filling their sails with favorable winds...

Let us remember the case of Ulysses, cunning warrior, destroyer of citadels, the one who entered into the abode of Circe.

The old scriptures state that the warrior halted at the mysterious portals where the fair-tressed goddess lived. There he stood and called aloud, and the goddess heard his voice, and she came forth and invited him to enter.

In *The Odyssey*, Ulysses himself tells of his adventure:

> "I went with her, heavy at heart. So she led me in and set me on a chair with studs of silver, a goodly carven chair, and beneath was a footstool for the feet. And she made me a potion in a golden cup, that I might drink, and she also put a charm therein, in the evil counsel of her heart.

CIRCE

"Now when she had given it and I had drunk it off and was not bewitched, she smote me with her wand and spake and hailed me, "Go thy way now to the stye; couch thee there with the rest of thy company.""

"So spake she, but I drew my sharp sword from my thigh and sprang upon Circe, as one eager to slay her. But with a great cry she slipped under, and clasped my knees, and bewailing herself spake to me winged words, 'Who art thou of the sons of men, and whence? Where is thy city? Where are they that begat thee? I marvel to see how thou hast drunk of this charm, and wast nowise subdued...'"

Circe transformed men into swines; but is this perchance possible? What does lycanthropy say about this? What do the holy gods say of this?

We have already spoken a great deal about the three states of the eternal Mother Space. Do opposite aspects of Devamatri exist? What does occult science say about this?

Any given body that enters into the fourth dimension can change its shape; however, something else is needed. What could this be?

Let us go into the roots, into the very facts. It is urgent to comprehend in depth that the third aspect of the Cosmic Mother, whether named Hekate or Proserpine, always has the possibility of unfolding herself into two more aspects of an opposite or fatal type.

Let us define and clarify: these two negative aspects of Prakriti constitute that which is named Kali or Holy Mary.*

The Sixth Arcanum of the Tarot represents these two polarities of the great Mother Space. Let us remember virtue and vice, the virgin and the whore, Heva the White Moon and Lilith the Black Moon.

Let us remember the two gracious wives of Shiva (the Third Logos): Parvati and Uma. Their antitheses are those two sanguinary and ferocious women, Durga and Kali, the latter being the tenebrous regent of this horrible age of Kali Yuga.

Kali is the tempting serpent of Eden. She is the abominable Kundabuffer organ, about which we have written a great deal in our former Christmas messages. The sinister power of such a fatal organ transforms men into swines.

INDECISION

Arcanum Six

* — The author is not referring to Mary the mother of Jesus. See "The Perfect Matrimony" for more information.

That the abominable harpies convert themselves into frightful fowls, or that Apuleius transforms himself into a donkey, and the comrades of Ulysses into swines is certainly not impossible. These are very natural phenomena of the fourth dimension, fourth vertical, or fourth coordinate, and these phenomena are always performed with the tenebrous power of Kali or Circe.

Our affirmations might appear very strange to readers who have never studied our former Christmas messages; however, in synthesis, we have to tell them that truly this Circe or Kali is the blind Fohatic force, the transcendental sexual electricity used in a malignant way.

If a harpy introduces herself with her physical organism into the fourth vertical, and if afterwards she transforms herself into a bird of evil omen, or into any given beast, you can be completely sure that she has based the whole of her work on the sinister power of the abominable Kundabuffer organ.

Have you ever heard about the tail of Satan...? It is actually the sexual fire projected downwards from the coccyx, towards the atomic infernos of the human being.

Such a Luciferic tail is found controlled by a malignant atom from the Secret Enemy. Occult anatomy teaches that such an atomic demon is found located in the magnetic center of the coccyx.

It is in this abominable Kundabuffer organ (Satanic tail) where the whole leftist and sinister power of Kali, Circe, or Holy Mary is found contained.

The adepts of black tantra, such as the Böns* and Drukpas of the red cap, develop in themselves the blind Fohatic force of this cited fatal organ [* the author later corrected this; see the Glossary entry on page 216].

Lycanthropy, the science of metamorphosis (commented on by Ovid), has always existed. As incredible as it may seem, in this present twentieth century there are still modern Circes in some corners of the world.

As for scoundrels, pseudo-learned ones, those who believe they are filled with virtues, what does it matter to science or to us if they laugh?

There is an abundance of lycanthropy and modern Circes in the isthmus of Tehuantepec, Mexico.

We know the concrete case of a certain specimen who was a drunkard Don Juan, a certain remarkable gentleman who had the bad taste of having sexual relations with an ultra-modern Circe of the new age.

It is clear by all means that such a Don Juan placed the whole starry heaven at this harpy's feet, painting rainbows in the sky for her, and making formidable promises to her.

"If you do not accomplish your pledged word, I will convert you into a donkey." Such was the cunning comment of the beautiful she-devil. Her lover laughed at what seemed to be a simple joke.

Days passed and even weeks without this suburban Don Juan remotely thinking of accomplishing his romantic promises.

But something unusual happened. On a given night, he did not return to his apartment. His roommate thought that perhaps Don Juan was fooling around somewhere, having found some new adventure.

However, his absence was prolonged far too long... many nights passed and nothing. Finally, while preoccupied, he suddenly saw that instead of Don Juan, a donkey appeared that insisted on entering the apartment.

So, the good friend went to the streets in search of Don Juan. He interrogated the beautiful Circe, he inquired, and finally she told him... "Your friend is wandering around; behold him!" and she pointed to the donkey.

The guffaw, the malicious sarcasm... the thundering laughter of one of her friends (another very beautiful she-devil) was something definitive. This man comprehended everything.

Later on, some good people advised him to leave from that place before it would become too late for him as well.

So, the best thing this poor man did was to return to the capital city of Mexico.

The Rune Gibor (page 205). Padmasambhava and Yeshe Tsogyal Performing Sahaja Maithuna, White Tantra

Chapter 28
Rune Os (Othila)

It is urgent, indispensable, and unpostponable that in this 1968-1969 Christmas message we deeply study the problem of sexual transmutation for single people.

Innumerable letters from many single students suffering from nocturnal pollutions constantly arrive to this patriarchal headquarters of the Gnostic movement.

Certainly, nocturnal pollutions are something filthy, dirty, and abominable. We always answer that the medicine against such subjective states is Sexual Magic, Maithuna.

However, we must clarify this matter. While we remain very alive — in other words, while we remain with the ego existing in the forty-nine regions of the subconsciousness — erotic dreams inevitably will continue.

Nonetheless, to make light within the darkness, we must emphatically affirm that Maithuna establishes an adequate foundation in order to avoid nocturnal pollutions, even when pornographic dreams continue.

What occurs is that with Sahaja Maithuna (sex yoga), the chela (disciple) becomes accustomed to frequently refraining from the sexual impulse. Therefore, when an erotic dream is produced, the mind refrains the sexual impulse by instinct. This is how we avoid what is called a nocturnal pollution or the lamentable loss of the vital liquor.

It is clear, certain, and evident that such a formula helps when one has continuity of purpose. Thus, daily practice is needed, year after year, with intensity.

Unfortunately, this formula only works when one has a spouse, but what about those who are single, who do not have a spouse? Then what? Here is precisely where the problem resides, and it is certainly very grave. If what we truly want is to utilize this formula, then what we need is to get a spouse.

Now, let us pass into another very similar matter. I want to refer to sexual transmutation for single men and women.

It would be lamentable if single men and women could not utilize the sexual energy in some way. They also need to progress. So how? Well, let us get to the roots, to the facts.

I do not want to say that those who are single can Self-realize themselves in depth. They cannot, because it is clear that without the Maithuna, it is more than impossible to reach adepthood, which is so longed for.

Nevertheless, those who are single can and must utilize the creative energy for the awakening of the consciousness.

What we need to know is the technique, and this is precisely what this present chapter is committed to. Thus, let us now, in full, enter into the fields of the rune Os.

This rune intensely vibrates with the constellation of the scorpion, which is very important because this court of stars is found intimately related with the sexual organs.

This is the same rune Olin of Aztec Mexico, and it is esoterically related with the famous rune Thorn.

Among the Aztecs, Olin is the mystical symbol of the god of wind, the lord of cosmic movement. The name of this angel is Ehecatl, the one who intervened in the resurrection of Jesus by transmitting prana, life, into the body of the great Kabir, and saying, "Jesus, rise with your body from within your tomb."

I personally know the angel Ehecatl, the god of wind. He is certainly an extraordinary deva who lives in the world of conscious will. So then, we can see the intimate esoteric relationship between the rune Os and the rune Thorn (movement and will).

Albeit, the many "super-transcended" stubborn ones from the worthless pseudo-esotericism and pseudo-occultism will laugh at the notion of elemental creatures of Nature, considering them fantasy. Even when they mock and scoff at Paracelsus and his elementals, such as Gnomes, Pygmies, Sylphs, Salamanders, etc., etc., these elementals have existed, do exist, and will always continue to exist, eternally.

Ehecatl is certainly a guru deva who has power over the Sylphs of the air. So what if the foolish, obtuse, and stubborn do not like this? Do they laugh about elementals? Do they mock us? Frankly, we are not bothered by it, since he who laughs at what he does not know is an ignoramus who walks the path of idiocy.

The millenary sphinx in the sacred land of the pharaohs corresponds to the elemental sphinx of Nature, which is the mysterious instructor of the holy devic college. This elemental sphinx of ancient Egypt, which is so intimately related with the mysterious sphinx of stone, came to me when I was born in the world of conscious will. This elemental came with its feet covered with mud... so, I exclaimed, "Your feet are covered with clay!" It was clear... I understood everything... In this black age that is governed by the goddess Kali, everything has been profaned, and no one wants anything to do with the sacred college of the sphinx.

When I, filled with love, wanted to kiss this elemental, she (the sphinx) told me, "Kiss me with purity." This I did when kissing her cheek. Afterwards, the sphinx returned to her point of departure, that is to say, to the sacred land of the pharaohs.

All Gnostic brothers and sisters would like to do the same thing, to talk face to face with the elemental sphinx of Nature, to have a dialogue with the devas, to walk with Ehecatl. But, first of all, it is necessary to awaken the consciousness, to open the door, to call with persistency, to set in motion our willpower.

Practice

Observe very carefully the two diagrams of the rune Os. In the same way that the rune **Fah** has its two arms upwards, the rune Olin has them downwards, and this is profoundly significant.

During these esoteric practices, there is the need to successively

RUNE OS

alternate movements by placing the arms in the first position (downwards), then in the second position (placing the hands on our waist like in the rune Dorn or Thorn). I repeat, examine very carefully the two diagrams of the rune Os.

During these runic practices, you must combine the movement with harmonious and rhythmic breathing. Inhale the prana through the nose, and exhale it through the mouth along with the mystic sound TTOOORRRNNN, prolonging the pronunciation of each letter.

When inhaling, imagine the sexual forces rising, ascending from the sexual glands through the pair of sympathetic nervous cords, which are known in India by the names of Ida and Pingala.

These nerves or tubes reach the brain, then after they continue through other nerves towards the heart. These nerves are other channels; the Amrita Nadi is one among them.

When exhaling, imagine the sexual energies entering the heart, and even penetrating more deeply, reaching the consciousness in order to awaken it. Strike the consciousness with force, with **Thelema** (willpower), thus combining the runes Thorn and movement (Os).

Afterwards, pray and meditate. Beseech the Father who is in secret; ask Him to awaken your consciousness.

Beseech your Divine Mother Kundalini. Beg Her with infinite love to elevate, to make the sexual energies reach the heart and even further, to the very profound depth of your consciousness.

You must love and pray, meditate and supplicate. Build faith even the size of a grain of mustard seed *"and ye shall say unto this mountain, Remove hence to yonder place; and it shall remove"* [Matthew 17:20]. Remember that doubt is the beginning of ignorance.

> *"Ask, and it shall be given you; seek, and ye shall find; knock, and it shall be opened unto you."* — Matthew 7:7

Chapter 29
Origin of the Pluralized "I"

"My doctrine is not mine, but his that sent me." – John 7:16

Listen to me: you must study in depth with your mind and your heart this revolutionary chapter of this 1968-1969 Christmas message.

"The Elohim (holy gods) produced Man from themselves (through modification), in their likeness ... He (the collective Deity) created them (the collective humanity or Adam) male and female."

The Protoplasmic root race from the Sacred Island (located in the Septentrion) was truly their first production. It was a tremendous transformation of themselves (the Elohim), through themselves. These productions were purely spiritual existences. Behold here the Adam-Solus.

From this primeval Polar root race, the second root race arose: the Adam-Eve or Iod-Havah [יהוה], the Hyperborean people, the inactive androgynes.

The third root race, the Lemurian people, arose (always by modification) from the Hyperborean. This race was the separating hermaphrodite Cain and Abel, which lived upon the gigantic continent of Mu, or Lemuria as it was later called, that was situated in the Pacific Ocean.

This third root race was the last semi-spiritual one. As well, it was the final vehicle of the pure, virginal, unbegotten, instinctive, and innate esotericism of the Enochs, or the illuminated ones from that humanity.

The separating hermaphrodite Cain and Abel produced the fourth root race of Seth-Enos, which lived on the continent of Atlantis, situated in the Atlantic Ocean.

Our present Aryan root race, which perversely dwells upon the five continents of the world, arose from the Atlantean people.

Each one of the four preceding root races perished by gigantic cataclysms, and our fifth root race will not be an exception.

It has been said unto us that in a remote future, two more root races will exist on the face of the earth. It is obvious that each of them will have its own scenario.

The primeval unity of the sexual polarities within the third human root race is an axiom of ancient wisdom. Its virginal individuals elevated themselves to the rank of gods, because these people were indeed representing the divine dynasty.

Certainly, the separation into opposite sexes was performed over thousands of years, and was consummated as fact at the end of the Lemurian root race.

Let us now talk about Eden, of those paradisiacal Jinn lands to which the sacred individuals of Lemuria had continuous access in the times when the rivers of the pure water of life flowed with milk and honey.

That was the epoch of the Titans, when there was neither that which is mine nor that which is yours. Everyone could collect fruit from the tree of the neighbor without any fear.

This was the epoch of Arcadia, in which people worshipped the gods of fire, air, water, and earth.

This was the Age of Gold when the lyre had not yet been smashed into pieces by falling upon the floor of the temple.

Then, there was only the pure rising of the divine cosmic language, spoken like a river of gold running through the thick, sunny jungle.

In that ancient age, people were very simple and innocent because the pluralized "I" was not yet born. They rendered cult to the gods of the tender corn, and also to the ineffable creatures of rivers and forests.

I knew the hermaphroditic Lemurian root race. Those terrible volcanoes that were in constant eruption come into my memory in these instants. What a time! We initiates normally used very common sacerdotal vestures. Those sacred venerated vestures stood out splendidly with white and black colors, symbolizing the tremendous struggle between Spirit and matter.

It was inspiring to admire and see those Lemurian giants with their noble vestures and their sandals that displayed great tassels.

The pituitary gland, the sixth sense, which is the light-keeper and page of the pineal gland, was displayed between the eyebrows of those colossuses.

Then, the life of any individual had an average age of twelve to fifteen centuries.

So, gigantic cities were built, which were protected with enormous stones formed with volcanic lava.

I also knew the end times of the third root race. I lived in that epoch, which is cited in Genesis as being that ancient age in which Adam and Eve were cast out of Eden.

In those times, humanity had already been divided into opposite sexes. The sexual act was a sacrament then, which was only performed inside the temples.

In certain lunar epochs, the Lemurian tribes performed long travels. They departed on pilgrimages towards holy places, with the purpose of multiplying the species (let us recall our honeymoon trips).

We, all the Lemurians, were children born from willpower and yoga. Maithuna was what we performed during the copulation, and no one committed the error of ejaculating the entity of semen.

The human seed always passed into the womb without the spilling of semen being necessary. The multiple combinations of this infinite substance are marvelous.

The king and queen monarchs were sexually united before the very altar of the temple, and the multitudes performed the copulation inside the sacred precinct and in the rocky patios filled with mysterious hieroglyphics.

The holy gods wisely directed those mystical ceremonies, which were indispensable for the reproduction of the human species. No one thought in perversity, since the pluralized "I" was not born yet.

I lived in the country with my tribe, far away from those walled cyclopean cities. We abided in a big cabin, cottage, or hut. Close to our rounded, palm-roofed residence, I remember with total clarity that there was a military base where the warriors of our tribe met.

It happened that on a certain night, all of us, fascinated by a strange Luciferic power, resolved to perform the sexual act outside of the temple. Thus, we, each of the couples, delivered ourselves to lust.

The next day, in the morning, as if nothing had happened, we had the daring, the shame, the insolence, the impudence, to present ourselves as usual in the temple. However, something unexpected and terrible happened.

All of us saw a god of justice, a great master, dressed with a day-breaking and immaculate sacerdotal vesture. With a flaming sword that he turned in every way to threaten us, he said, "Get out, you unworthy!" It is clear that we then fled, terrorized.

Obviously, this event was repeated in all the corners of the enormous continent Mu. This is how the humanity Adam-Eve was cast out of the Garden of Eden.

Following this event, which is registered in the Genesis of all religions, horrifying epilogues occurred. MIliums of human creatures were developing the abominable Kundabuffer organ when they started to mix magic with fornication...

Incidently, it is useful to mention here Kalayoni, the king of the serpents, the black magician, keeper of the temple of Kali, which is the fatal antithesis of eternal Mother Space.

With the magical conjuration of Kalayoni, Krishna saw a long blue-greenish reptile appearing. The fatal serpent [Kaliya] slowly straightened its body, then horizontally it bristled its reddish mane, and its penetrating eyes frightfully flashed in its monstrous head of shining shells.

"Better if you worship it, or you will perish," said the black magician... but the serpent died at the hands of Krishna.

So, when Krishna heroically killed this great serpent, keeper of the Temple of Kali (the goddess of desire) the mother of Cupid made ablutions and prayers for one month at the shores of the river Ganges.

This viper from Kali is the tempting serpent of Eden, the horrible serpent Python that writhes in the mud of the earth and that Apollo enragedly hurt with his darts.

KRISHNA ATOP KALIYA

It is indispensable to comprehend that such a sinister snake is without any doubt the tail of Satan, the abominable Kundabuffer organ.

When the gods intervened, eliminating from the human species the cited fatal organ, the awful consequences of this tail of Satan remained within the five cylinders of the human machine (intellect, emotion, movement, instinct, and sex).

It is obvious that such evil consequences from the abominable Kundabuffer organ constitute that which is called ego, the pluralized "I," the "myself," a tenebrous conjunction of perverse entities that personifies all of our psychological defects.

Therefore, the pluralized "I" is a granulated, lunar, negative, Luciferic Fohat. This Fohatic, satanic crystallization constitutes that which is called **ego**.

THE THREE FURIES

"They are the Demon of Desire, the Demon
of the Mind, and the Demon of Evil Will."

Chapter 30

The Three Furies

Let us now talk about the three Furies who are gorged with all the poisons of the Gorgons. They wear hydras of the deepest green as girdles, small serpents and cerastes form their hair, and are used to encircle their bestial temples.

Listen to me M. M., you must know once and for all that these are the three traitors of Hiram Abiff.

Megaera is on the left, always dreadful and horrible. She who weeps on the right is Alecto, in whose heart is hidden discord, fraud that produces disorder, and evil things that take away peace. Between them is Tisiphone.

Each Fury tears at her breast with her repugnant nails; each with her palms beats on herself and wails so loud, "Just let Medusa come; then we shall turn him into stone." Looking down, they all cry, "We should have punished Theseus' assault."

Remember, Gnostic brothers and sisters, that **Mara** is the lord of the five desires, the factor of death, and is an enemy of the truth. Who always accompanies him? Are not perhaps his three daughters the three Furies, those tempting females? Are they not the ones, with all of their tenebrous legions, who assaulted the Buddha?

Can perhaps Judas, Pilate, and Caiaphas be missing from the cosmic drama? Dante found Judas, Brutus, and Cassius in the ninth circle of the infernos.

Judas has his head inserted within the mouth of Lucifer while his legs jerked on the outside.

The one who has his head beneath, the one who hangs from the second Luciferic mouth, is Brutus. He writhes and does not say a word.

The third traitor is Cassius, who seems to be so robust, but is very weak in depth.

These are the three aspects of Judas, the three Furies. They are the Demon of Desire, the Demon of the Mind, and the

Demon of Evil Will. They are the three Upadhis, bases, or lunar foundations that are within each human being.

Let us think of the three presences of the Guardian of the Threshold within the interior of each person.

The Apocalypse says:

> *"And I saw three unclean spirits like frogs come out of the mouth of the dragon, and out of the mouth of the beast, and out of the mouth of the false prophet.*
>
> *"For they are the spirits of devils, working miracles, which go forth unto the kings of the earth, and of the whole world, to gather them to the battle of that great day of God Almighty."* – Revelation 16:13-14

But who is the dragon? Who is the beast? Who is the false prophet? Gods tell me, where is he?

If we comprehend that he is Mara, Lucifer, the blind Fohatic force from the abominable Kundabuffer organ, or the negative sexual fire that is the father of the three Furies, then we are not mistaken.

Thus, the vile slug that passes through the heart of the world is the root of the pluralized "I." He is the foundation of the three Furies.

Lucifer / Mara, the tempter, with his legions of devil-"I's" that each mortal carries within, is the origin of the three sufferings: old age, sickness, and death.

Ah...! If the negative aspect of the goddess Juno had not intervened in Latium by arousing Alecto (the most abhorred of the Furies), then the marriage of Aeneas, the illustrious Trojan man, with the daughter of the good King Latinus, would not have been preceded by a war.

> "Do this service for me, O virgin daughter of Night. It is task after your own heart. See to it that my fame and the honor in which I am held are not impaired or slighted, and see to it that Aeneas and his men do not win Latinus over with their offers of marriage and are not allowed to settle on Italian soil. You can take brothers who love each other and set them at each other's throats. You can turn a house against itself in hatred and fill it

with whips and funeral torches. You have a thousand
names and a thousand ways of causing hurt. Your heart
is teeming with them. Shake them out. Shatter this
peace they have agreed between them and sow the seeds
of recrimination and war. Make their young men long
for weapons, demand them seize them!"

Alas, oh God of mine...! What pain! This frightful Fury of
the mind presented herself within the royal chamber of the
Queen Amata and drove into her ideas of protest and rebellion
against the will of the King Latinus.

Under the perfidious influence of Alecto, Queen Amata
desperately left the palace and, swift as any bacchante, ran
through the midst of the Italian mountains. She danced and
jumped as any bacchante. She seemed to be a furious maenad
in a wild, mad rage, driven with the lash of Bacchus.

Amata, the sovereign, protested with indignation before
the monarch. She did not want to do the will of her lord and
defend Turnus, a young Greek suitor who was the son of a
people that in a foretime assaulted the unconquerable walls of
Troy.

The queen was afraid that Aeneas would flee with her
daughter far away from Latium. She felt the pain of losing her
daughter, and cried.

Albeit, the work of Alecto did not finish here. She flew
straight to the abode of the bold prince Turnus. Alecto
changed her appearance, and took on the face of an old woman
with a viperine tongue, and told him everything that was hap-
pening inside the palace of the king. Thus, the insinuating and
evil Alecto awoke the jealousy of the young prince.

Afterwards came the war, and the young prince fought for
his lady, the beautiful Lavinia, the precious daughter of good
King Latinus.

The monarch did not want war, neither was he himself
the one who opened the doors of the Temple of Janus (Ianos,
I.A.O.), the god with two faces. His enraged people were the
ones who opened them.

Inside the Temple of Janus, the doctrine of Saturn was preserved. This was the primeval, original revelation of the Jinns. So, this temple was only opened in a time of war.

This is how the war was lit among the Rutulians. When this repugnant Fury Alecto ended her work, she flew down within the innermost parts of the frightful abyss through the mouth of a dry volcano, which was once in a while spitting the fetid vapors of death. In a short time she arrived at the sinister banks that surrounded the waters of the Cocytus.

Turnus, the new Achilles, died at the hands of Aeneas, who became married to Lavinia, daughter of the King Latinus.

Nevertheless, oh God! Alecto, as ever, is still lighting bonfires of discord everywhere, and mIliums of human beings cast themselves to war.

Ah...! If people would comprehend that each one of them carries Alecto within themselves...

Unfortunately, the human creatures are profoundly asleep; they do not comprehend anything.

Chapter 31
Rune Rita (Raido)

Coming into my memory in these instants are scenes of a previous reincarnation of mine during the Middle Ages.

I was living in Austria, in accordance with the customs of that epoch. I do not deny that I was a member of an illustrious family of aristocratic rank.

In that epoch, my people, my lineage, were very conceited about matters of royal blood related with rigid ascendancy and notable ancestry.

I feel ashamed, yet I must confess (and this is what is critical in this matter) that I also was engulfed within the bottle of those social prejudices, the matters of that epoch!

One given day (it does not matter which), a sister of mine fell in love with a very poor man, and of course, this was the scandal of the century. The ladies of the class of nobles and their stubborn little fops, dandies, dudes, peacocks, and coxcombs came to skin the neighbor alive. They scoffed at my unhappy sister. They said that she had disgraced the honor of the family, and that she could have married better, etc.

It did not take long for my poor sister to become a widow, but the outcome of her love was clearly a child.

What if she had wanted to return into the bosom of her family? It was not possible. She knew well the viperine tongue of those elegant ladies, their fastidious counterpoints, their disregard. Therefore, she preferred an independent life.

Did I help the widow? It would be an absurdity to deny it. Did I have pity on my nephew? That is true. Unfortunately, there are times when one is trying not to be a person without pity, yet one becomes pitiless. That was my case. Feeling pity on the child, I put him in a boarding school (with the pretext that he could receive a strong, firm, and vigorous education) without taking into account the feelings of his mother, and I even committed the error of prohibiting this suffering woman to visit her son. I thought that in this way my nephew would not receive any type of harm, so he could become someone else later, that is to say, to become a great gentleman, etc.

The path which leads to the abyss is paved with good intentions. True? Yes, it is true.

How many times when one is trying to do good, one accomplishes evil! My intentions were good, but my actions were mistaken. Nonetheless, I firmly believed that I was doing the right thing.

My sister was suffering greatly because of the absence of her son, and she could not even see him at the college, as this was prohibited for her.

By all means, it is clear that on my part there was love for my nephew and cruelty for my sister. However, I thought that if I was helping the son I would also be helping his mother.

Fortunately, as if by magic, the police of Karma, the Kaom, emerge inside each one of us, within those intimate regions where love is missing.

To flee from the agents of Karma is not possible, since inside of each one of us exists the police who will inevitably conduct us towards the tribunals.

Many centuries have passed since that epoch. All of the personages from that drama became old and died.

However, the law of recurrence is terrible, because everything is repeated as it once happened, along with its consequences.

In the twentieth century, we, all the actors of that past event, have encountered one another again. Everything has been repeated in a certain way, but it is clear that it has been with consequences. This time I was the one who was repudiated by the family. Such is the law. My sister encountered her husband anew. I do not reject the fact that I am united again with my ancient priestess spouse, known with the name of Litelantes.

The so adored and fought over nephew was reborn again, this time with a feminine body. She, by the way, is a very beautiful girl. Her face is as a very delightful night, and the stars shine in her eyes.

One time (the date does not matter now), we were living next to the sea; the girl (my ancient nephew) could not play, as she was grievously ill with an intestinal infection. It was a very delicate situation, as various children of her age died in that epoch because of the same cause. Why should my daughter be an exception?

The numerous remedies that were administrated to her were frankly useless. In her infantile face, the unmistakable profile of death was already starting to be drawn with horror.

By all means, the failure was standing out, the case was lost, and I did not have any other chance but to visit the dragon of the law, the terrible genie of karma whose name is Anubis.

Fortunately, thanks be given to God, we — Litelantes and I — know how to consciously and positively travel in the Astral body. Therefore, it was not a problem for us to present ourselves together in the palace of this great archon within the parallel universe of the fifth dimension. That temple of karma is impressive, majestic, and grandiose.

The hierarch was there, seated on his throne, imposing, and terribly divine. Anyone would be frightened to see him officiating with that sacred mask of a jackal, just as he appears in many embossments of the ancient Egypt of the pharaohs.

Finally, the opportunity to talk to him was granted to me, and clearly I did not let it pass away so easily. "You have a debt with me," I told him.

"Which one?" he answered, astonished.

Then, completely satisfied, I introduced to him a man who in a foretime was a perverse demon. I am referring to Aztaroth, the great duke. "This was a lost son for the Father," I continued, saying unto him, "Nonetheless, I saved him, by showing him the path of the light. I took him out of the Black Lodge, and now he is a disciple of the White Brotherhood, and you did not pay me this debt."

It was the case that this daughter of mine had to die in accordance with the law, and her soul was to enter within the womb of my sister in order to form a new physical body for my daughter. This is how I understood it. Therefore, I added, "I ask that Aztaroth go into the womb of my sister instead of the soul of my daughter."

The solemn answer of this hierarch was definitive.

"Granted; let Aztaroth go into the womb of your sister, and let your daughter be healed."

Therefore, that girl (my ancient nephew) was miraculously healed, and then my sister begot a male child.

I had capital in order to pay that debt. I had cosmic capital. The law of karma is not a blind mechanical law, as many pseudo-esotericists and pseudo-occultists suppose.

As these matters show, it becomes evident and easy to comprehend that with the potential death of my daughter, I had to feel the same pain of detachment, the same bitterness that in an ancient epoch my sister felt for the loss of her son.

Thus, by means of the great law, the damage would be compensated with the repetition of similar scenes. However, this time I, myself, would be the victim.

Fortunately, karma is negotiable. This law is not the blind mechanicity of the astrologers and chiromancers of fairs.

I had cosmic capital, so I paid that old debt. Thus, thanks to God, it was possible for me to avoid the bitterness that was awaiting me.

When will the people comprehend all of the mysteries of the rune Rita? Certainly, this is the rune of the law.

Rita comes to remind us of the words: reason, roll, religion, right.

Roman law has the scale and the sword as symbols of justice.

It is then not too strange that inside the palace of Anubis, the great archon of the law, scales and swords are seen everywhere.

This great judge is assisted in his work by forty-two judges of the law.

Illustrious lawyers of the great law, who defend us when we have enough cosmic capital in order to pay our old debts, are never absent before the tribunal of karma.

To receive credit with the lords of the law or archivists of destiny is also possible, but this must be paid with good deeds, through working for humanity, or by supreme pain.

Karma is paid not only for the evil that is done, but also for the good that could be done, yet is left undone.

Practice

The fundamental mantras of the rune Rita are:

**RA........ RE....... RI......... RO.........
RU...........**

RUNE RITA

In the rune F, we had to raise the arms. In the rune U, we opened the legs. In the rune D, we placed the arm on our waist. In the rune O, the legs were open and the arms upon the waist. So, in the present rune Rita we must open one leg and one arm. Thus, in this position, the Gnostic students will see that they in themselves are forming the runic letters, such as they are written.

The present runic practice has the power of liberating internal judgment.

We need to convert ourselves into judges of consciousness. To awaken the Buddhata, the soul, is urgent.

This rune has the power of awakening the consciousness of the judges.

Let us remember what is called remorse, which certainly is the accusing voice of the consciousness.

Those who never feel remorse are truly very far from their interior judge. Commonly, they are lost cases.

People like that must work very intensely with the rune Rita, thus they will liberate their interior judgment.

We need with urgency to learn to be guided by the voice of the silence — that is to say, by the innermost judge.

FROM VENUS AND ANCHISES, BY WILLIAM BLAKE RICHMOND (1842–1921)

"...each living being has his own Devi Kundalini,
his own particular Divine Mother."

Chapter 32
The Divine Mother Kundalini

Oh, ineffable Muses!... Inspire me. Here shall your excellence reveal itself so that my style does not detract from the nature of this matter...

Oh, Divine Mother Kundalini!... You are Venus, lady of mine, you are Heva, Isis, Sophia Achamoth, Parvati, Uma, Tonantzin, Rhea, Cybele, Mary, or better if called Ram... Io.

Oh, Devi Kundalini! You are Adshanti, Rajeswari, Adonia, Insobertha, Tripura Sundari, Maha-Lakshmi, Maha-Saraswati.

By all means, without thee, oh beloved Mother, the manifestation of prana, electricity, magnetic force, molecular cohesion, and cosmic gravitation would be more than impossible.

You are the Matripadma, the Devamatri, Aditi, or cosmic space, the mother of the gods!

You have, oh eternal Mother Space, three luminous aspects during cosmic manifestation, and two antitheses.

May humans listen to me! It is said that each living being has his own Devi Kundalini, his own particular Divine Mother.

To truly eliminate the Ahamkara Bhava, the egoic condition from our consciousness, would be absolutely impossible if we commit the crime of forgetting our own Divine Mother Kundalini.

The intellectual animal mistakenly called man is nothing but a compound of aggregates that sooner or later must become cosmic dust.

The only thing eternal within ourselves is the Innermost Buddha, and truly He is found beyond the body, mind, and affections.

To eliminate the vain and perishable aggregates is something cardinal and definitive in order to awaken the consciousness.

These aggregates are certainly those entities or tenebrous "I's" that dwell within the five cylinders of the human machine.

We explained, we already stated with complete clarity in our former Christmas messages, that the five cylinders of the

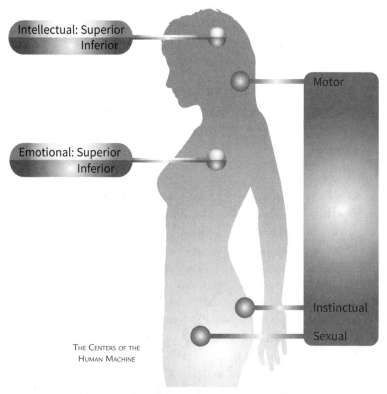

Intellectual: Superior
Inferior

Motor

Emotional: Superior
Inferior

Instinctual

Sexual

THE CENTERS OF THE
HUMAN MACHINE

human machine are: intellect, emotion, movement, instinct, and sex.

Let us concretize that these devil-"I's" constitute the ego (pluralized "I"). Thus, within each one of these "I's" the consciousness sleeps.

In order to awaken consciousness, the elimination of those "I's," those entities, those aggregates that personify our defects, is vital. This is how we attain Atma-Vidya, complete illumination.

To have deep comprehension, clear consciousness of the defect that we want to extirpate, is fundamental, but it is not enough. The elimination of the defect is necessary, and this is only possible with the help of the Kundalini.

The mind cannot fundamentally alter anything. What the mind does is label things, hide defects, pass them onto other levels, etc.

To eliminate errors is another thing, and without Devi Kundalini, the magical serpent of our magical powers, this would be absolutely impossible.

One given night (the day and hour does not matter), I was travelling with my Astral Body within the parallel universe of the fifth dimension. Then, while inebriated by a certain spiritual voluptuousness, I ecstatically arrived before the mysterious threshold of that marvelous temple of the twice-born.

The hieratic and terrific guardian of the great mysteries, as always, was at the door, and when I wanted to enter, something unusual happened.

While fixedly looking at me, he said with a severe voice, "Among a group of brothers and sisters who have worked in the Ninth Sphere, and who after having worked in that region, presented themselves in this temple, you were the most advanced one. But now you are stagnant in your progress."

Those words, pronounced with so much severity by the guardian at the threshold of mystery, certainly left me perplexed, confused, and indecisive. I could think of nothing but to ask, "Why?"

Then, the hierarch answered my question, "Because of your lack of love."

"How come?" I said, "I love humanity. I am working for all human beings. I do not understand what you are telling me. In which way am I lacking love?"

"You have forgotten your mother. You are an ungrateful son," explained the guardian, and the way in which he intoned these words, I confess, produced in me not only pain, but moreover, terror.

"But, I do not know where she is. I have gone a long time without seeing her," I replied, believing that it was all related with my physical mother, who I had to leave when I was still very young.

"How is it possible that a son does not know where his mother is?" replied the Guardian, then he continued, saying, "I am telling you this for your own good, because otherwise you are hurting yourself."

Truly, I confess that only after various days of useless inquiring in order to find in this world my terrene mother, I finally understood the enigmatic words of the guardian of the temple.

Ah!... But the literature of a pseudo-esoteric and pseudo-occultist type, which is so abundant in the market, says nothing about this matter. If only I had known this before! To that end, I thought too many things, and then I prayed.

To pray is to talk with God, and I, in secrecy, prayed to the Eternal Feminine, to God as Mother.

Then, I knew that each creature has his own particular Divine Mother, and I even knew the secret name of my own.

It is clear that in that epoch when dissolving the ego, struggling in order to reduce it to cosmic dust, I was suffering the unutterable.

What is most terrible is that I had already reached the Second Birth. I comprehended very well that if I did not achieve death within myself, I would fail by converting myself into an abortion of the Cosmic Mother, into a hasnamuss with a double center of gravity.

It seemed in that time that my efforts were useless. I was failing the ordeals, and if I had continued like that, it is clear that complete failure would have been inevitable.

Fortunately, thanks to God, the guardian of the temple knew both how to warn me and how to advise me.

The work was terrible; the failed ordeals indicated to me with exactitude where the faults were.

Each ordeal was enough to indicate to me, to point out to me, the basic defect, the error.

The meditation on each error was enough for comprehension, although I could clearly see that there are many degrees and degrees in relation with understanding.

There is a great deal of elasticity and ductility in relation with comprehension. Many times we believe we have integrally comprehended a defect of a psychological type, but only later, we come to discover that really we did not comprehend it.

Elimination is another thing. Anyone can comprehend a given defect, yet in spite of this cannot achieve its extirpation.

If we exclude the Divine Mother Kundalini, then the work remains incomplete. Without Her, it is impossible to eliminate defects.

Frankly, I converted myself into an enemy of myself, thus I resolved to equilibrate comprehension and elimination. Each comprehended defect was eliminated with the power of the Divine Mother Kundalini.

Finally, one given day, I was inspecting my work in the Tartarus, in the Averno, within the submerged mineral kingdom, in those infra-dimensional regions or submerged parallel universes.

Navigating upon the waters of the Acheron, inside of the boat of Charon, I arrived to the other shore in order to inspect the work; then I saw thousands of devil-"I's," my own aggregates, parts of myself that were living in those regions.

I wanted to resuscitate something, an effigy that symbolized my own sinning Adam, who was lying like a cadaver in the muddy waters of the river.

Then, my Divine Mother, dressed with clothes of mourning like a Mater Dolorosa, told me with Her voice filled with infinite love, "This one is already quite dead. I have nothing more to take from him."

Certainly, my Mother had extracted from me the legion of devil-"I's," all of the conjunction of tenebrous entities that personify our defects and that constitute the ego.

Thus, this is how I achieved the dissolution of the pluralized "I." This is how I attained the reduction into dust of all of those aggregates which form the "myself."

FORGE OF THE CYCLOPS

"Here, lead is transmuted into gold, and the
steel of the flaming sword is tempered."

Chapter 33

The Forge of the Cyclops

When Venus, the Divine Mother Kundalini, begged for help from Vulcan on behalf of her son Aeneas, she taught with it the clue of the realization of the Innermost Self.

The goddess said:

> "Listen to me, you who forge the indomitable iron with the fires of the center of the earth! When the citadel of Troy was being ravaged in war by the kings of Greece, it was owed to Fate and was doomed to fall in the fires lit by its enemies, but I asked for nothing for those who suffered. I did not call upon the help of your art to make arms for them.
>
> "You yielded to Thetis, the daughter of Nereus; you yielded to the wife of Tithonus when they came and wept to you. Look at all the nations gathering. Look at the walled cities that have closed their gates and sharpening their swords against Aeneas to destroy those I love.
>
> "Although I owed much to the sons of Priam and had often wept at the sufferings endured by Aeneas, I did not wish, O my dearest husband, that you should exert yourself to no purpose. But now, in obedience to the commands of Jupiter, Aeneas is standing in Rotulian soil and so now I come to you as a suppliant. I approach that godhead which I so revere, and as mother, I ask you to make arms for my son Aeneas.
>
> "He is not a destroyer, is only trying to defend himself against those who threaten his purposes of fertile peace."

Oh, you!... the ones who courageously descend into the Averno in order to work in the flaming forge of Vulcan (sex), listen to me.

As the fetus remains nine months within the maternal womb, so this entire humanity remained for nine months within the womb of Rhea, Ceres, Cybele, Isis, the Cosmic Mother.

Vulcan works in the ninth circle of the inferno forging indomitable iron with the living fires of this planetary organism.

People with **Thelema** (willpower), men and women with willpower of steel, you must work without rest in the Ninth Sphere (sex).

Venus, the Divine Mother Kundalini, is, has been, and always will be the priestess spouse of Vulcan, the Third Logos, the Holy Spirit.

The igni-potent god of fire descends from the marvelous heights of heaven into the terrific forge of the Cyclops.

With a great voice, he demands the presence of his three brothers, Brontes, Steropes, and Pyracmon, who are living symbols of the elemental creatures of the air, the waters, and the perfumed earth.

The work in the forge of the Cyclops (sex) is terrific. Here, the tempestuous lightning and the secret forces of the storm, as well as the hurricane-like winds, collaborate in the effort.

Here, lead is transmuted into gold, and the steel of the flaming sword is tempered.

Here, the gigantic protector shield of the soul is forged. That shield is enough to stop the strikes of the most terrible tenebrous armies.

It is an argentine armor, a splendid shield formed with transformative atoms of a high voltage, which reside within the seminal system.

It is a divine, auric shield, which is septenary within the intimate constitution of the true human being.

During the Maithuna, the sexual cavern trembles under the erotic pressure of the bellows, and strong, sweaty arms strike the anvil with a rhythmic effort.

Aeneas looked like a god while challenging the arrogant Laurentians and the impetuous Turnus to combat.

When rejoicing with the gifts of his Divine Mother, Aeneas dressed himself with weapons made by Vulcan.

Behold here the solar bodies, the terrific crested and fire-spurting helmet, the flaming sword, and the huge, unyielding breastplate of blood-red bronze, as well as the polished

VENUS GIVES AENEAS HIS ARMS AND ARMOR

greaves and the fabric of the shield engraved with innumerable figures.

There, on that auric, luminous shield, Vulcan, the Third Logos, the Holy Spirit, engraved astonishing prophetic scenes.

The scenes of all the generations that would spring from Ascanius gloriously shone on that shield. Vulcan had also made an image of a mother wolf who milked Romulus and Remus, and showed the first of these twin brothers (dear God!) performing the violent rape of the Sabines. Also depicted was the bloody war both brothers would fight.

Ah! If only people would understand the mystery of these twin brothers... one lone soul in two distinct persons... the Buddhata divided in two, and of course incarnated in two different personalities.

Romulus and Remus milked by the she-wolf of the

ROMULUS AND REMUS

law, is a soul with two men, two persons, two bodies.

The gods know very well that it is possible to live simultaneously in different distinct times and places.

How much wisdom had Vulcan engraved in the brilliant aura of Aeneas, how many prophecies!

Behold men and gods, that also on this shield were the scenes of Porsenna ordering the Romans to take Tarquin back within the unconquerable walls of the city after they had expelled him.

On the summit of the sharpened shield you could also see the scene of the golden goose fluttering, honking for help against the Gauls who were trying to invade the Roman capital.

Observe and see the Salii priests with their Martian dances and conical warrior hats, their chaste matrons in their cushioned carriages, the traitor Catiline tormented in the Averno, the pale faces of the Furies. There too was Cato, the wise administrator of justice, the armored fleets of war, Augustus Caesar, Agrippa with favoring winds and favoring gods, Marc Antony and Cleopatra, Anubis the lord of the law, Neptune, Venus, and Minerva, the goddess of wisdom.

Finally, (oh God!) were the scenes of Caesar riding into the walls of Rome in victory, the defeated nations walking in long lines as slaves, a wealthy booty, golden thrones, defeated kings.

Chapter 34
Rune Kaum

A long time ago, in the profound night of the centuries, there in the continent of Mu or Lemuria, I knew Jahve, the fallen angel who was spoken of by Saturninus of Antioch.

Certainly, Jahve was a venerable master of the white brotherhood, a glorious angel from previous mahamanvantaras.

I knew him. I saw him when he was a priest and a warrior among the people of Lemuria. Everyone loved, adored, and venerated him.

The hierophants of the Purple Race granted him the high honor of using armor, crest, helmet, shield, and sword of pure gold.

This warrior-priest shone as a flame of gold within the thick, sunny jungle.

Upon his symbolic shield, Vulcan had engraved many prophecies and terrible warnings.

Woe! Woe! Woe! This man committed the error of betraying the mysteries of Vulcan.

The lucifers of that epoch who were floating in the atmosphere of the ancient continent Mu taught him black tanta, the Maithuna with the ejaculation of the ens seminis.

What is most grave in this matter is that this man, who was so loved and venerated by all the world, allowed himself to be convinced, and began to practice this type of pernicious Sexual Magic with certain women.

Therefore, it is clear that the igneous serpent of our magical powers descended through his medullar canal and was projected from his coccyx downwards, thus forming and developing in Jahve's astral body the abominable Kundabuffer organ.

This is how this angel fell, and through the ages became converted into a terribly perverse demon.

Many times we have found the priestess spouse of Jahve in the superior worlds; she is an ineffable angel.

The efforts of this man to convince his spouse were useless, because she never accepted the black tantra of the tenebrous.

Therefore, she preferred divorce rather than to enter into the black path.

Jahve is that demon who tempted Jesus the Christ. When Jesus had fasted in the wilderness, this demon tempted him and said:

> "If thou be the Son of God, command this
> stone that it be made bread."

> "And Jesus answered him, saying, It is written, That man shall
> not live by bread alone, but by every word of God." – Luke 4:3-4

The sacred scriptures say that Jahve then took Jesus the great Kabir up a high mountain and tempted him by saying:

> "Itababo, all these kingdoms of the world will I give thee,
> if thou wilt fall down and worship me." – Luke 4:6-7

Then, the great Master Jesus answered:

> "Get thee hence Satan: for it is written, 'Thou shall worship the
> Lord thy God, and him only shalt thou serve.'" – Luke 4:8

Finally, it is written that Jahve brought Jesus to Jerusalem and set him on a pinnacle of the temple, and said unto him:

> "If thou be the Son of God, cast thyself down from hence;
> for it is written, 'He shall give his angels charge over thee,
> to keep thee: And in their hands they shall bear thee up,
> lest at any time thou dash thy foot against a stone.'

> "And Jesus answering said unto him, 'It is said, Thou shalt not
> tempt the Lord thy God,' and when Jahve had ended all the
> temptation, he departed from him for a season." – Luke 4:9-13

If we want to learn all the mysteries of the rune Kaum, then we must now talk about white tantra.

Those old times of ancient Egypt come into my memory in these moments.

I was an Egyptian initiate during the dynasty of the Pharaoh Khafra, in the sunny country of Khem.

One given sunny afternoon, while walking through the sands of the desert, I passed through a street that had millenary sphinxes on it and arrived at the doors of a pyramid.

The guardian of the temple, a man with a hieratic and terrible face, was at the threshold. He was threateningly grasping the flaming sword with his dexterous hand. He asked me, "What do you wish?"

I answered, "I am **Sus** (the supplicant or genuflector) who blindly comes in search of the light."

"What do you want?"

I answered again, "Light."

"What do you need?"

I answered anew, "Light."

I can never forget the next instant, in which the heavy stone door turned upon its hinges and produced the characteristic sound of the Egypt of the pharaohs: that profound **Do**.

Then, the guardian took me roughly by the hand and put me inside the temple. I was deprived of my tunic and of every metallic object. Then, I was submitted to terrible and frightful ordeals.

When in the ordeal of fire, I had to maintain complete control of myself. It was terrible to walk between two blazing beams of steel which were lit to a red heat.

When in the ordeal of water, I was very close to being devoured by the crocodiles of a deep well.

When in the ordeal of air, while hanging from a metal ring above the deep of the abyss, I resisted with heroism the hurricane winds.

When in the ordeal of earth, I believed I would die between two boulders that were threatening to crush me.

I had already passed through these initiatic ordeals in ancient times, but I had to recapitulate them in order to return onto the straight path from which I had retired.

Next, I was dressed with a tunic of white linen and the tau cross was hung from my neck so that it laid upon my chest.

In spite of being a Bodhisattva, I entered as any neophyte. I had to pass through rigorous studies and esoteric disciplines, and when I arrived at the ninth door, the great mysteries of sex were taught to me.

I still remember those instants in which my guru, after profound explanations, while fixedly staring at me, told me with a solemn voice, "Uncover your **chechere** (phallus)."

Then from his lips to my ears, he communicated to me the unutterable secret of the Great Arcanum: the sexual connection of the lingam-yoni without the ejaculation of the ens seminis.

Afterwards, he brought a vestal dressed with a yellow tunic who was filled with an extraordinary beauty.

I performed the work with her. I practiced the Maithuna, white tantra, in accordance with the instructions of my master.

"This practice is marvelous," I said. Thus, I descended into the Ninth Sphere. This is how I performed the Great Work.

The objective was to build the solar bodies and to awaken and develop the serpentine fire of occult anatomy.

In that epoch, there were sacred priestesses inside the temples, special vestals. The celibate male initiates worked with these vestals. In this day and age such women inside of the Lumisials would not be beneficial... They would be scandalous. Therefore, in this day and age, Maithuna, sex yoga, can only and must only be practiced between husband and wife, within legitimate, constituted marriages.

In the ancient Egypt of the pharaohs, those who violated their oaths and divulged the Great Arcanum were condemned to the death penalty. Their heads were cut off, their hearts torn out, their bodies cremated, and finally their ashes were thrown to the four winds.

The mysterious rune K represents with complete precision the priestess woman and also the flaming sword.

The rune Kaum, with its Kabbalistic six, vibrates with greatest intensity within the sphere of Venus, the planet of love.

Men and women of the world, you must learn that to put into activity that annular serpentine fire in the body of the ascetic is only possible with Maithuna.

We need with immediate urgency to learn how to wisely manipulate the eternal feminine principle of the solar forces.

We must remember the eagle with a woman's head, the Sun-Lady, the diamantine foundation of the Great Work of the Father.

First, we must transmute lead into gold, and later, we need to build diamonds of the best quality.

Decidedly, the rune Rita influences the masculine endocrinal glands, but the rune Kaum exercises its influence upon the feminine glands.

Within the labyrinth of theories there are many contortionists of Hatha Yoga. Those acrobatic people suppose that they can exclude Maithuna, and Self-realize themselves in depth without the necessity of descending into the Ninth Sphere. Those contortionistic mystics believe that based on such recreation or absurd gymnastics they can build the solar bodies and reach the Second Birth.

A certain time ago, I had the high honor of being invited to a secret council of the great White Lodge. So, I must clearly tell the world that Hatha Yoga was disqualified, it was reproved, it was condemned as authentic and legitimate black magic of the worst type.

The esoteric rectors of humanity do not accept, they will not ever accept, the absurd frolics of Hatha Yoga.

Whoever truly wants in-depth Self-realization must transmute the sexual hydrogen Si-12 by means of sex yoga, in order to build with it the solar bodies, the wedding garment of the soul.

It is absolutely impossible to incarnate the real Being if we have not previously built the bodies of gold in the forge of the Cyclops.

It is urgent to walk with firmness upon the path of the razor's edge.

The hour has arrived to follow the path of the perfect matrimony. Remember that our motto is **Thelema** (willpower).

The mysteries of the rune Kaum gloriously shine in the bottom of the Ark, awaiting for the instant for them to be accomplished.

THE CELESTIAL EAGLE

"'Have no fear,' said my Lord 'take confidence, for it is well with us, do not relax but put out all thy strength. Now thou art come to Purgatory...'" - Dante, Purgatory, Canto IX

Chapter 35
The Purgatorial Region

The eagle with plumage of pure gold that carried Ganymede away in order to bring him to Olympus (so he could serve as a cupbearer to the gods) always has the custom of hunting in the Purgatorial region.

This majestic bird of the Spirit, while making marvelous turns, terrific descents like lightning, takes the soul away to the sphere of the fire in order to burn with her. Thus, they are both converted into a living flame.

Let us remember the powerful Achilles who turned with fear because he did not know where he was. This is because his Mother took him away from Charon and transported him asleep to the island of Scyros, where later the Greeks found him and took him away.

Those times in which I abandoned the Averno in order to enter into the Purgatorial region come to my memory.

My Mother, converted into a Mater Dolorosa, had already instructed me in depth. She had navigated with me on the boat of Charon. She had demonstrated to me the dissolution of the pluralized "I." Finally, she had taught me that when the mind is deprived of the ego, the mind still continues with evil tendencies.

Oh, God of mine!... When the pluralized "I" is dissolved, it leaves in the mind its seeds of perdition.

The yogis say that one must burn the seeds, incinerate them, reduce them to cosmic dust.

It is urgent to know that the "I" is re-born again like an evil weed from its own seeds.

I needed then to incinerate those evil seeds of a poisonous weed. It was necessary for me to enter into the Purgatorial region of the inferior molecular world in order to burn the seedbed of the "myself."

Close to the top, I reached a point where I saw a gate (it first appeared to be merely a gap, a break within the wall) which had three steps leading up to it, each one a different color. Over that terrible gate I saw engraved with indelible characters the word *Purgatory*.

I then saw the silent figure of someone on guard. I saw that genie standing on the highest step; he was an angel of extraordinary beauty, imposing, severe, and terribly divine. In his right hand he held a naked sword, which was dazzlingly reflecting its rays.

Everyone who intends to enter into the Purgatorial region must devoutly prostrate himself at the feet of this angel, and in mercy's name he must make supplications to him to open it. Prior to this, one has to smite his breast three times.

Unforgettable and terrible moments are those in which the angel inscribes on the forehead of the initiate the letter "P" seven times. Then, one hears from his lips the following phrase, "Once entered here, be sure you cleanse away these wounds."

Do you remember the case of the wife of Lot? She was converted into a pillar of salt because from behind her husband she looked back.

Likewise, the angel of Purgatory warns that whosoever after having entered into the inferior molecular world turns to look back loses his work, and goes back out again from where he came.

This signifies absolute repentance: to not commit the same error of the past again, to not commit delinquency.

Whosoever turns to look back, fails, repeats the same errors, returns to the same sinning past, does not purify himself.

Everyone who turns to look back converts himself into a purgatorial failure. Once in Purgatory, one has to march ahead with firmness.

When within the inferior molecular region, one comprehends how absurd arrogance and pride are. We are nothing but simple chrysalises, miserable slugs from the mud of the earth, inside which the heavenly butterfly can be formed, based on tremendous, intimate super-efforts. But, there is no law for this to be fulfilled. Those chrysalises could be lost, and this is what is most common.

How stubborn are those individuals who suffer the unutterable when they see happiness in any given person. Why would they place their hearts in that which requires an exclusive possession?

"**Beati pacifici**" ["blessed are the peacemakers"], the ones who lack sinning anger. Unfortunately, rage, anger, can disguise itself within the toga of a judge or with a smile of forgiveness. Thus, each defect is multifarious.

While in the Purgatorial region we frightfully suffer within the fire of lust, because we revive within those submerged subconscious regions all of the pleasures of carnal passion. However, this causes profound pain within us.

"**Adhaesit pavimento anima mea**" ("My soul is attached unto dust"). Poor souls who were attached to terrene things, how they suffer within the Purgatorial region.

People of the Purgatorial region! I tell you, remember Pygmalion, whose gluttonous thirst of gold made him a traitor, robber, and even what is worse, a parricide.

What would we say of the misery of the avaricious Midas, who was converted into a ridiculous personage throughout the innumerable centuries because of his absurd petitions?

What would we say of laziness? It is a Siren who distracts mariners on the wide sea of existence. She was the one who lay Ulysses aside from his course. A loathsome smell exudes from her belly.

Gluttons from Purgatory! Behold Boniface, who waved the crosier of numerous flocks. Behold also Messer Marchese who had only a short time of thirst before inebriating himself at Forli, yet was never sated.

> "Remember," next
> We heard, "those noblest creatures of the clouds,
> How they their twofold bosoms overgorg'd
> Oppos'd in fight to Theseus: call to mind
>
> The Hebrews, how effeminate they stoop'd
> To ease their thirst; whence Gideon's ranks were thinn'd,
> As he to Midian march'd adown the hills."
> - Canto 24, *The Divine Comedy: Purgatory* by Dante Alighieri

So, I saw frightful things within Purgatory. When reliving in this region all of my bestialities of ancient times, truly I felt myself converted into a swine.

One given day among others, while conversing with a fellow soul of Purgatory, I told her, "Sister of mine, we have become as swines in this place."

She answered me, "Thus it is; we have become as swines in this place."

The time was passing by, and I was suffering the unutterable while incinerating malignant seeds, while eliminating filthy things.

Many fellow souls of this Purgatorial region looked like decomposing cadavers. Lying on their beds, they painfully eliminated seeds, horrifying filthy larvae, and evil tendencies.

Those poor souls sighed and also moaned. I never forgot my Divine Mother. I always beseeched her to help me in this Purgatorial work, to eliminate from me this or that psychological defect. The fight against myself was terrible.

Finally, one night, the Blessed Goddess Mother Kundalini — disguised as a man — entered within the Purgatorial region. Intuitively, I recognized her. "Why did you disguise yourself as a man?" I asked her.

"In order to enter into these regions," was her answer.

"When are you going to take me out of here?" She, the Beloved One, then established a date and hour.

"Afterwards, the visual instruction will come," She continued. Clearly, I understood everything.

Various details confirmed the words of my Mother, since the seven "P's" had already been erased little by little, one by one. The purifications were evident, manifest, clear, and positive.

Chapter 36
The Temple of Hercules

The sanctuary of Hercules (the Christ) that gloriously shone in submerged Atlantis was a resplendent companion to the marvelous Temple of **Jagrenat** (of whose many marvels A. Snider wrote in the formidable work entitled *La Création et ses mystères dévoilés*).

Those were unforgettable times of profound poetry when King Evander eloquently explained to Aeneas, the eminent Trojan man, all the delectable enchantments of the sacred banquet offered in honor of Hercules.

If the god Vulcan (the Third Logos) truly deserves abundant praise, then what would we say of the Lord, the Christ, the Second Logos, Hercules?

The chorus of young warriors sang in the sacred banquet, hymning praise to the lord (Hercules) and his great deeds, enumerating with exceptional beauty the way he endured all of his labors.

When he was still a child, Hercules seized and throttled the poisonous snakes, which were the first monsters sent against his life. (Let us remember King Herod and the slaying of all the innocent children).

Hercules slaughtered the Lernaean Hydra, that is to say, the tempting serpent of Eden, the horrifying viper from the sinister temple of the goddess Kali.

With the sacred fire, Hercules cleaned the stables of Augeas, that is to say, the forty-nine subconscious regions of the human mind, where all of the beasts of desire horrifyingly abide.

Hercules killed the huge lion of Nemea, that is to say, he eliminated or extinguished the Luciferic fire, and also dragged Cerberus, the infernal watchdog of Orcus (the sexual instinct) from the darkness into the light. Hercules is certainly admirable, and worthy of all praise and glory.

To think, oh God, that Hercules repeats his labors each time he comes into the world is terrific... grandiose...!

It is clear, and by all means evident, that in order to incarnate Hercules within ourselves, we must first work in the flaming forge of Vulcan (sex).

"Woe to the Samson of the Kabbalah if he permits himself to be put asleep by Delilah! The Hercules of science, who exchanges his royal sceptre for the distaff of Omphale, will soon experience the vengeance of Dejanira, and nothing will be left for him but the pyre of Mount Oeta, in order to escape the devouring folds of the tunic of Nessus."

From the heights of the Tarpeian Rock, all of those who betray Hercules are precipitated into the bottom of the abyss.

There, in those times of the submerged Atlantis, the temple of Hercules was erected upon a rocky boulder.

The extraordinary and marmoreal stone that gave access to the temple, and its cyclopean and imposing mass, truly made this sanctuary like a precious twin brother to the Temple of Philae in Upper Egypt, and to other many venerated Mayan, Nahua, and Aztec sanctuaries.

If we think at least for a moment of the City of the Gods (Teotihuacan, Mexico), and of the secret paths and subterranean crypts of that sacred place (ignored by tourists), then we must not ever forget the colossal constructions beneath the temple of Hercules.

Certainly, beneath the facade of the temple opened a royal portico that had twelve statues of zodiacal gods. These clearly symbolized the twelve faculties of the human being, and the twelve saviors of whom the great Kabir Jesus so wisely spoke.

Ancient traditions state that this portico was similar to the celebrated House of the Dwarf, also called the House of the Magi, Great Teocalli or the House of God, in Mexico.

The initiates reverently and timorously entered under that terrific portico and passed beneath the columns of Hercules.

Such columns were of pure gold, and upon them were engraved the words **Adam Kadmon** with sacred characters. The M.M. know very well about the "J" and "B," **plus ultra**.

Seven auric steps upon which the initiate descended led him to a rectangular precinct.

That mysterious place was found vested wholly with pure gold, and corresponded exactly to the superior hall that was always open to the supplications of the profane world.

This was the Chamber of the Sun, but four other chambers existed, and the mysteries shone in all of them.

The second crypt was ineffable. Five descending flights of silvery tin, the sacred metal of Brihaspati, Jupiter, or IO, reached down into it.

The planets Mars and Venus shone in the third crypt. The red coloration of one and the foamy white of the other gave to that environment a pink and very beautiful tint.

Of the seven solar palaces, the third one in Christian and Jewish Kabbalah is related to Lucifer / Venus, which makes it the abode of Samael.

The occidental, allegorical Titans are in themselves also intimately related with Lucifer / Venus.

Thus, Sukra, in other words, the regent of the planet Venus, is the one who incarnated on the Earth as Usanas, and is known in Hebrew as Uriel. He gave perfect laws to the inhabitants of this world. Disgracefully, in later ages these perfect laws were disregarded and rejected.

I knew Usanas / Uriel on the polar continent during the first root race. He wrote a precious book with runic characters.

Lucifer is the fatal, negative aspect of Venus. Venus always shines at dawn, but the Luciferic forces are terribly agitated at dawn.

Venus is truly the elder brother, the messenger of the light for the Earth, in the physical as well as the mystical sense.

Saturn and the Moon glowed face to face upon the altar, always shining in the fourth initiatic chamber of the temple of Hercules.

It is urgent to remember that the two paths of the Atlantean epoch, the dexterous and the sinister, were clearly shown, and their struggles of more than 800,000 years are symbolically sung in that oriental poem of the great war, *The Mahabharata*.

So, by descending a little more, the Atlantean initiates entered into the fifth crypt, the one of Hermes, or Mercury, who splendidly glittered upon the altar.

Mercury, as an astrological planet, is the nuncio and wolf of the Sun, Solaris Luminis Particeps. Mercury is the chief and evoker of souls, the arch-magi and arch-hierophant.

The unhappy souls who are precipitated into the Orcus (Limbo) can be summoned to a new life by Mercury, who holds in his dexterous hand the caduceus or hammer with two serpents. **"Tun virgam capit: hac animas ille evocat orco,"** ["Then he takes his wand: with this that one calls out the pale spirits from Orcus" - Aeneid IV:242] in order to initiate them into the celestial militia...

Remember that within Limbo live many saints, wise men, and sweet maidens who believed in achieving the inner Self-realization of the Being without Sexual Magic. Poor souls... they did not work in the forge of the Cyclops, they did not build the solar bodies, the wedding garment of the soul.

Blessed be the one who integrally comprehends the wisdom of the five crypts of the temple of Hercules.

Chapter 37
Rune Hagal

Let us now talk of elementals, gods and devas, sparks and flames. May the Muses inspire us!... May we play the lyre of Orpheus.

Let us remember old Tiberinus, rising as a myst from within the waters of the river that bears his name, in order to speak to Aeneas in person.

> "O you who are born of the race of the gods, who are bringing back to us the city of Troy saved from its enemies, who are preserving its citadel Pergamum for all time, long have we waited for you in the land of the Laurentines and the fields of Latium. This is the home that is decreed for you. This is the home decreed for the gods of your household. Do not give up. Do not be intimidated by the threat of war. All the angry passions of the gods are now spent. But come now, so that you may not think what you are seeing is an empty dream.

> "I tell you that you will find a great sow with a litter of thirty piglets lying beneath ilex trees on a shore. There she will lie all white on the ground and the young around her udders will be white.

> "This will be a sign that after three times ten years revolve, Ascanius will found the city of Alba, white in name and bright in glory. What I prophesy will surely come to pass. Attend now; I shall teach you in few words how you may triumphantly resolve the difficulties that lie before you.

> "The Arcadians are a race descended from Pallas. They came to these shores following the standards of their king Evander, chose a site here and established in these hills a city called Pallantium after their founder Pallas. This people wages continual war with the Latin race. Welcome them into your camp as your allies. Make a treaty with them. I will take you to them straight up my river between these banks and you will be able to row upstream into the current.

"Up with you then, son of the Goddess, for the first
stars are beginning to set. Offer due prayers to Juno and
overcome her angry threats with vows and supplications.
To me you will give honor and make repayment when
you are victorious. I am that full river whom you see
scouring these banks and cutting through the rich
farmland. I am the river Thybris, blue as the sky and
favored of heaven. Here is my great home. My head
waters rise among lofty cities."

So spoke the river god, and plunged to the bottom of a
deep pool.

Certainly, Virgil, the poet of Mantua, tells us that when
this vision of Tiberinus vanished, Aeneas awoke, rose, then
after rubbing his eyes, he ran around to see if he could discover
the sign that the sublime elder had spoken about. Concretely,
before his astonished eyes there appeared an omen.

Through the trees he caught sight of a great white sow
with a litter of thirty piglets, all of the same color.

This was enough for him to state that the predictions of
the god Tiberinus, an elemental deva from the sacred Italian
river, were totally fulfilled.

These were the times before our Aryan root race had
entered into the descending, devolving cycle. The human mind
had yet to be poisoned by the materialistic skepticism of the
eighteenth century. The people had faith in their visions, and
they rendered cult to the elemental gods of nature.

Jinn lands do exist, paradises where the wolf and the lamb,
men and gods, live together! Yes, this is obvious.

Let us remember the monk Barinto who returned to his
country after navigating for a period of time, and told Brendan
that beyond the Stone-Mount was the Island of Delights. This
was where his disciple Merloc and many other religious members of his order had retired. He then said that even further
towards the occident, passing a thick mist, another island
shone with eternal light. This island was the promised land of
the saints.

It is clear that Brendan did not have to hear this story
twice. Filled with intense faith and a holy zeal, he embarked

himself in a boat of osier that was vested with cured and bituminous skins. With him were seventeen religious monks, and one amongst them was the young Saint Malo, one of his most illustrious disciples.

"Patiently navigating towards the tropic, they made a stop on a very craggy and hospitable island.

"Then, they arrived at another island, rich in land animals and freshwater fish, and shining with light and beauty.

"They arrived at another island without beaches, neither sand or banks, where they were determined to celebrate Easter Mass. However, it turned out that this land was a big whale or perhaps a gigantic cachalot.

"They proceeded ahead in their navigation until Pentecost on to the Paradise of Birds, where their eyes enjoyed the abundance of leaves and flowers and their ears the singing of colored birds.

"Strong winds kept them many months on the ocean, until arriving at another island, which was inhabited by Cenobites, who had Saint Patrick and Saint Ailbe as Patrons. They remained there from Christmas until the Epiphany.

"They spent a year in these peregrinations, and in the six following months, they gathered themselves for Christmas on the Island of Saint Patrick and Saint Ailbe. They were on the Island of the Sheep during the Holy Week, they were upon the back of the whale during Easter Resurrection, and on the Island of the Birds for Pentecost.

"Still they had not arrived to the Island of Delights, from where Mernoc had taken Barinto into the promised land.

"Strange and mysterious adventures proceeded with the most curious events.

"So, our heroes successively fought in the seventh year with a whale, with a Gryphon, and with the Cyclops.

"They saw other islands; one among them was very flat and produced big red fruits. This island was inhabited by a populace who called themselves the Strong Men. Another island was embalmed with the fragrance of those vines which bent the trees that produced them.

"They celebrated Christmas again in the accustomed place and afterwards they navigated towards the north, avoiding in this way the terrible Rocky Island, a bleak, windy spot where the Cyclops had their forges. The next day, they saw a mountain sending such a spray of sparks and embers that its whole summit was ablaze. This was Hell Island.

"Without a doubt, such a place was not the one searched for by Saint Brendan and his companions. Therefore, they sailed south and disembarked on a small, round island, which was deprived of vegetation, and inhabitated upon its summit by a hermit, who filled them with benedictions.

"They celebrated the Holy Week, Easter Resurrection, and Pentecost where it was customary for them. Departing from that repetitive circle, they passed through the zone of obscurity which surrounds the Island of Saints, and which appeared before them filled with precious stones, autumn-like fruits and illuminated by a perpetual day.

"In short, they wandered for forty days on that island without finding a limit to it. Upon a shore of a river which was crossing the island, an Angel told them that they could not pass ahead and that they should return the same way they came. So consequently, they repassed the darkness, rested three days on the Island of Delights, and after the benediction of the Abbot of that Monastery, returned directly to Ireland, without noticing with exactitude what it was that had just occurred."

These tales, placed between quotations, comes from Sigberto of Gemblours and Surio el Cartujo.

All ye worthy ones! Those who have reached the Second Birth, have dissolved the ego, and have sacrificed themselves for humanity's sake, listen to me, please!

Upon the living rock, right there on the beach, you must trace with a reed the rune Hagal. Then, you must call the little boat of the sacred swan. This is how you can embark to the mysterious islands of the fourth dimension.

Afterwards, when this sacred sign, this marvelous rune has been traced, you must chant the following mantras:

Achaxucanac, Achxuraxan, Achgnoya, Xiraxi, Iguaya, Hiraji.

Look fixedly at the holy rune Hagal, and with your heart filled with faith, beseech, ask unto the Roman Harpy, the Nordic Urwala, the Scandinavian Erda, the primeval Sibyl of the earth, your own Divine Mother Kundalini, to send for you the extraordinary little boat moved by the Sylphs.

Ah! How joyful you will be when you embark upon the mysterious boat of the sacred swan towards the mysterious islands of Eden.

But to you, the beginners, I advise you to render cult unto the holy gods, to work with the creatures of fire, air, water, and earth.

You must not forget your Divine Mother Kundalini, since without her you cannot progress in this sacred science.

You must remember that God has no name and that he is only an inhalation, a sigh, the incessant eternal breath, profoundly unknown to itself.

This breath, by all means, is the principle of the Logos, of all the runes, and of all words.

Practice

Beloved disciples, you must profoundly meditate on the Unity of Life, on the Great Alaya of the universe, on the invisible world, on the parallel universes of the superior dimensions of space.

Concentrate your thought on the valkyries, gods of fire, air, water, and earth.

Agni is the god of fire. **Paralda** is the god of air. **Varuna** is the god of water. **Gob** is the god of the element earth. Through meditation you can enter into communication with the gods of the elements.

You must trace the rune Hagal on a blank paper, then after, concentrate your mind on any of the four principal gods of the elements. Call upon them so they can help you when it is necessary.

Final Commentary

How can we forget **Xochipilli**, the god of happiness, music, dance, and flowers among the Aztecs, and **Tlaloc**, the god of the rain, who is still gloriously shining among the Nahuas. This elemental god lives in the parallel universe of conscious will. "The human sacrifices were not my fault," he said when we recriminated him about it. Then he added, "I will return in the Aquarian age."

What can we say about **Ehecatl**, the god of wind? This elemental deva of the Aztecs was precisely the one who cooperated in the resurrection of Jesus, by inducing activity and movement into the body of the master.

We, the Gnostics, still render cult to the gods of the tender and ripe corn.

We know very well **Camazotz**, the Aztec bat god. This angel lives in the parallel universe of cosmic will, and works in the fourth dimension with the angels of death.

We love the elemental gods of the ancient Egypt of the pharaohs, and we will never forget the millenary Sphinx.

The rune Hagal and deep meditation will permit us to be in contact with those sparks, with those ineffable flames.

Chapter 38

The River Lethe

The Divine Mother Kundalini always accomplishes Her word. Therefore, I waited with supreme patience for the given day, date, and hour [mentioned in Chapter 35].

The Purgatorial region is very painful, and I wanted to leave from there; I was longing for my emancipation.

Caton, the angel of Purgatory, fights in those molecular regions for the freedom of souls.

This angel suffered greatly when he lived in this world. Any initiate knows that when in Utica, Africa, this being was a man who preferred death to a life under the chains of slavery.

I also wanted liberty, therefore I asked for it, and it was granted unto me. Each time that a soul abandons the Purgatorial region, an intense joy surges from within the heart of **Caton**.

So, the longed for moment arrived... Since I had known the temporal and eternal fire and had departed from rash ways and from narrowness, I had to encounter the Sun inside of my own soul.

Thus, I felt that from the unknown, something mysterious was forcing, straining the intimate atomic doors of my interior universe.

My fears were useless, vain was the resistance, "It" was compelling me, constraining me, pressing me, and finally (oh God of mine!) I felt myself transformed. The Cosmic Christ had entered within me.

But, my individuality? Where had it gone? What had happened to my vain human personality? Where was it?

Only remembrances of the Holy Land were coming into my memory: the humble birth in the stable of the world, the baptism in the river Jordan, the fast in the wilderness, the transfiguration, Jerusalem — the beloved city of the prophets, the human multitudes of those times, the doctors of the law, the Pharisees, the Sadducees, etc.

I floated in the environment surrounding the temple. I courageously advanced towards a table before which were seated the modern Caiaphases, the most high dignitaries of the Failing Church. They were vested with their sacerdotal habits and the cross hung from their necks. They were projecting, planning, tracing insidious and perfidious plans against me in secrecy.

"You thought that I would not return, but I am here again." This was the only thing that occurred to me to utter.

Moments later, the **Lord** had gone out of me, and I again felt myself an individual. Then, together with Litelantes, I rested for brief moments at the foot of my cross.

I cannot deny that lamentably the thorns of the heavy crosspiece were hurting me, and I had a brief discussion with Litelantes about it.

Afterwards, she and I advanced towards the platform of the temple. A master took the floor in order to say that **Christ** has no individuality, and that **He** incarnates and manifests **Himself** inside any **Man** (human being) who is properly prepared.

It is clear that the word **Man** is extremely demanding. Diogenes did not find a single **Man** in Athens.

The intellectual animal is not a **Man**. In order to become one, one needs to be dressed with the wedding garment of the soul, the famous **To Soma Heliakon**, the body, or better if we say, the bodies of the **Solar Man**.

Fortunately, I built those bodies of gold in the forge of the Cyclops, in the flaming forge of Vulcan.

Hercules had repeated all of his tasks, all of his labors, inside of me. He had to strangle all of the poisoned serpents that wanted to take his life when he was still a child. He had to decapitate the Hydra of Lerna, to clean the stable of Augeas, to kill the lion of Nemea, to take Cerberus the infernal dog out of the frightful Tartarus, etc.

Hercules, the Christ, practices what he teaches, and each time he incarnates inside of a **Man**, he repeats the whole of his cosmic drama. This is why the Lord is the Master of Masters.

It is written that the Son of Man has to descend into the atomic infernos of Nature.

It is written that the Son of Man has to ascend to heaven, after passing through the Purgatorial region.

The Son of Man has to carefully submerge himself within the waters of Lethe in order to reconquer innocence.

With great urgency, we need to forget the sinful and absurd past that is the origin of much bitterness.

Lethe and Eunoe are certainly, and without the least bit of doubt, a single river of clear and profound waters.

On one side, its waters delectably descend, singing upon its rocky bed, carrying the marvelous virtue that erases the memory of sin, the remembrances of "myself." Its name is Lethe.

The other very holy and sublime shore has the delectable enchantment of fortifying virtues, and its name is Eunoe.

It is obvious that the tenebrous remembrances of too many yesterdays must be erased, because to our own disgrace, they have the tendency of actualizing, projecting themselves into the future through the alley of the present.

In the name of truth, I have to say that the profound work within the waters of Lethe is frightfully difficult and more bitter than bile.

The matter of passing beyond the body, affections, and the mind is not easy. Too many beloved shadows live within time... The memories of desire persist, they refuse to die, they do not want to disappear.

But, what about sex? Maithuna? Sex yoga? Then what, oh God of mine? The twice-born already know very well that they cannot return into the flaming forge of Vulcan.

It is obvious that the Maithuna is vital, cardinal, and definitive in order to build the wedding garment of the soul, the To Soma Heliakon. However, any initiate knows that this is only the inferior work of initiation.

Sex is forbidden for the Son of Man. This is known by the gods, and as thus it is written.

First, we must work with the Third Logos in the Ninth Sphere until reaching the Second Birth (which the great Kabir Jesus spoke of to the rabbi Nicodemus).

Afterwards, we need to work with the Second Logos, and then sex is prohibited.

The error of many pseudo-esotericists and pseudo-occultists, monks, and anchorites consists of renouncing sex without having previously built the solar bodies in the forge of the Cyclops.

These sincere mistaken ones want to work with the Second Logos without previously having worked with the Third Logos. Behold, here is their mistake.

Definitive and radical sexual abstention is only commended for the Twice-born, for the Son of Man.

Whosoever is admitted into the temple of the Twice-born must dissolve the ego, must incinerate the seeds of the "I," and must bathe in the waters of Lethe. This is known by the gods, the sparks, the flames, the resplendent dragons of wisdom.

Truly, no one could pass beyond sex, the affections, and the mind, without having previously bathed within the waters of Lethe.

After the Second Birth, we need to tear the sexual Adamic Veil (or Veil of Isis) into pieces in order to enter into the great mysteries.

Children of the Earth!... Listen to your instructors, who are the Children of the Fire.

Adepts of the Light! You must invoke your Divine Mother Kundalini and then submerge yourselves into the profound waters of Lethe.

Chapter 39

The Pines — The Nymphs

Iris, divine, ineffable maiden, messenger goddess of winged feet, you are the one who protects initiate women who work in the flaming forge of Vulcan.

Was it not you, oh sublime beauty, who delivered the celestial message from Juno, goddess of initiate matrons, to bold Turnus, the warring Rutulian chief commander?

After the solemn libations, the war-like Turnus, as a new Achilles, was soon moving threateningly with his whole army across the open Trojan plain. This is how it is written and known by the divine and human.

However, the Trojans were neither tardy nor weak. They reunited themselves at once in the war room, and with a great clamor they streamed into the battle line.

Terrorizing, Dantesque, and dreadful was Turnus, who prowled round the Trojan walls in a fury, going one way and another. It was a strange destiny to repeat in Latium the same epic combats of defeated Troy.

Nevertheless, this time, because of Aeneas' absence, and in spite of being veterans of many wars, the Trojans did not commit themselves to a fair fight with the enemy on the level plain. For these were the orders they had received from Aeneas, the greatest of warriors, as he left them.

What later happened is known by the legend of the centuries... The fire, the flames, the blazing torches crackled threateningly.

The Rutulians, blazing with anger, wanted to burn Aeneas' fleet. But Cybele herself, the Divine Mother Kundalini, is said to have beseeched the help of the Cosmic Christ, great Jupiter, son of Cronos, and thus Jupiter helped the Trojans.

Fortunately, those ships were made with the sacred wood of pines, from trees gladly given to the Trojan warrior upon the holy mount of Ida, where the Christ (Jupiter) had his favorite forest.

Oh, the astonishment...! Oh, the marvel...! In an instant, each one of these mysterious ships, instead of burning as a fatal holocaust, was miraculously changed into a nymph of the immense sea.

Ah!... If only the human mind had not degenerated so greatly... Many times I, myself, have seen tender maidens dressed as brides, as if ready for their wedding celebration.

Yes, oh God! I have seen these innocent souls at the foot of each pine. Truth? Yes, these are plant elementals.

These are truly the elementals of the pines, each one of these Christmas trees has its own soul.

When will the Christ cultists [worshippers] once again establish their sanctuaries within the forest filled with pines?

Do these trees have powers? Who would dare to doubt it? Could perhaps the warriors of Turnus, the new Achilles, have turned the Trojan fleet into a holocaust?

If people would awaken consciousness, then they could converse face to face with the nymphs of the boisterous ocean.

If people would awaken consciousness, then they could talk with the elementals of the pines.

Nevertheless, oh what pain!... Oh God of mine!... These poor people are profoundly asleep.

Ah! If those who investigate in the field of occultism could truly comprehend the author of *The Metamorphosis of Plants* [by Goethe]. If they could understand Humboldt with his *Cosmos*. If truly they could intuit the *Timeaus* and *Critias* of Plato the Divine, then they would approach the amphitheater of cosmic science and they would enter into the mystery of the magic of plants.

If those who study occult anatomy could comprehend the mysteries of Devi Kundalini, if truly they would love Cybele and divine Jupiter, if they would work in the Ninth Sphere, then they would be admitted into the elemental paradises of Nature.

Let us now remember the chorus of the nymphs of Calypso, in the very occult work *The Adventures of Telemachus* by François Fénelon.

The fairies spread on the moss of a millenary rock a fine lace tablecloth. Its beautiful figure could be compared to those subtle textiles which are sometimes formed by the cirrus in the sky. Upon it were placed Atlantean-made dishes that had colors that brought remembrances of the Talaveranean zone (which was in fashion a few years earlier) from afar. They served them a meal of frugal appearance, but which was so nutritive that it seemed to fill all of them with happiness and youth.

Wheat, rye, honey syrup, corn, cocoa, walnut, kola nut, sopari bread, are what the Hindustani adepts give as a sign of alliance to their disciples. The honey, the non-fermented must, a thousand juices, and undescribable molasses constituted their dishes.

These were delicious dishes that not even Brillat-Savarin had ever tasted, and that neither Montino and Altimira could ever comprehend.

A certain fragrant liquor that was served in an agate cup, that was evoking memories of the Holy Grail, placed this group of brothers and sisters into a mysterious and strange state in the end.

They were joyful, happy, and filled with vigor and youth, capable of embarking without any fear into the most terrible adventure.

It is relevant to say that this group explored Atlantis and knew all the mysteries of that submerged continent.

I also knew two other marvelous nymphs when I was navigating on a sailboat in the Caribbean Sea.

They came to encounter us through the boisterous waves. They were of an incomparable beauty.

One of them, a delicate maiden, was the color of violets. She floated over the waters, sometimes walking with a rhythmical and innocent step, sweetly approaching, agile, and simple. She was without any animal quality, yet she had a lot of divinity. She looked rather like an Indian female with bare feet.

The other one was the marvelous color of coral. Within the cordial shape of her mouth, a strawberry had left its purplish red, and in the subtle delicate draw of that visage, her eyes shone.

The aurora dawned upon the ocean; I saw them, and when uttering the word of light, they spoke to me. Then, very slowly, they approached the beach and rose upon the cliffy rocks.

I became a friend of these two marvelous nymphs, and when I think of their powers and of those changed ships of Aeneas, I submerge myself into meditation and prayer.

Chapter 40
Rune Not (Nauthiz)

Truly, it is indispensable in this 1968-1969 Christmas Message to deeply study the famous rune Not.

Let us continue studying this matter of karma. Listen to me, beloved reader: One day (it does not matter which one), Raphael Ruiz Ochoa and my insignificant person were coming back from the picturesque city of Taxco, Guerrero, of the Republic of Mexico.

We were going to the Federal District (Capital of Mexico) in a ramshackle vehicle, which, due to the unbearable weight of years, roared frightfully with tremendous noise and clatter.

To see this old and decrepit vehicle running was intriguing. Frequently, like something Dantesque, it horrifyingly and dreadfully over-heated, and only my friend Raphael had the patience to deal with it.

Once in a while, we stopped in the shadow of some tree along the road in order to put water in the vehicle and to cool it a bit.

This was a duty for my friend Raphael, as I preferred to take advantage of those instants in order to submerge myself into profound meditation.

I now remember something very interesting. While seated near the road, out of that curious, very old vehicle, I saw some insignificant ants that assiduously and diligently were circulating everywhere.

Suddenly, I resolved to put order into my mind and to concentrate my attention exclusively on one of them.

Afterwards, I passed into meditation, and finally unto me came ecstasy, samadhi, or that which in Zen Buddhism is denominated satori.

What I experienced was extraordinary, marvelous, formidable. I verified the intimate relationship between the ant and that which Leibnitz named the Monad [Spirit].

Certainly, it is obvious to integrally comprehend that such a Directrix-Monad is not incarnated or inserted inside the body of the ant. It is clear that this Monad lives out of its physical body. However, it is connected to its dense vehicle by means of the silver cord.

That cord is the thread of life, the septuple Antakarana of the Hindustani. It is something magnetic and subtle, that has the power of extending or prolonging itself into the infinite.

Truly, the Monad of that insignificant ant, which was observed in detail by me, seemed to be a beautiful twelve year old girl. She was dressed with a white tunic and carried over her shoulders a dark, blue colored cape.

Much has been spoken about Marguerite Gautier, but this girl was more ineffable and beautiful. Her eyes were of an evocative beauty, her gestures like that of a prophetess. Upon her was the sacred fragrance of the altar. Her innocent smile was like that of the Mona Lisa, with lips that no one in heaven or earth would dare to kiss.

So, what did the girl say? Terrible things; she spoke to me about her karma, certainly very horrifying karma. We conversed very carefully, inside the vehicle; she entered in by herself and when seated, she invited me to conversation. I humbly seated myself beside her. "We, the ants," said this Monad, "have been punished by the lords of karma, and we suffer a lot."

Now it is opportune to remember the legends of the giant ants from Tibet, which are referred to by Herodotus and Pliny (Herodotus, *The Histories,* book XI; Pliny, *Natural History,* book III).

Of course, oh God of mine!... it would be difficult on the first attempt to imagine Lucifer as a bee, or the Titans as ants. But it is clear that these creatures also had their downfall. This downfall in itself was of the same nature as the error committed by Adam.

Many centuries before the first root race appeared upon the face of the Earth, those **non-human** creatures that today are named ants and bees lived on this world.

These creatures knew in depth good from evil and evil from good. Certainly, and in the name of truth, I have to say that they were old souls. They had evolved greatly, but never in life had they entered onto the path of the revolution of the consciousness.

It is obvious that evolution can never conduce anyone to the realization of the Innermost Self.

It is normal that every evolution is inevitably followed by a devolution. Every rise is followed by a decline; every ascension is followed by a descent.

These creatures came to renounce the idea of superior knowledge and of the esoteric circle of life. Thus, they established their faith on gibberish such as that of a Marxist-Leninist type, similar to that of the Soviet Union.

Their way of understanding was undoubtably more mistaken and more grave than that of Adam, therefore the result is shown before the sight of all the world.

Thus, this is what the ants and bees are: they are devolved, retarded, and regressed creatures.

These beings altered their own organisms; they horrifyingly modified them; they made their organisms retrocede in time, until reaching the present state they are in.

Maeterlinck, when referring to the civilization of the termites, wrote:

> "Their civilization, which is the most ancient amongst all, is the most curious, the most intelligent, the most complex and in a certain way, the most logical and the one which is the most adapted to the difficulties of existence among all the civilizations which have appeared before our own civilization upon the globe. From many points of view, this civilization, even when cruel, sinister, and often repulsive, is superior to that of the bee, to that of the common and current ant and to that of the human being.

> "Within the termite colony (or nest of white ants), the Communist gods convert themselves into insatiable Molochs. The more that is given unto them, the more they demand, and they persist in their demands until the individual is annihilated and his misery is complete. This frightful tyranny has not been parallelled in humanity, since among us humans, some people benefit at least, but in the termite colony not one benefits.

"Their discipline is more ferocious than that of the Carmelites or Threepences. Their voluntary submission to laws and regulations, which comes from who knows where, is such that it does not have a parallel in any human society. This new form of fatality maybe the most cruel of all the social fatalities which we, ourselves are walking towards. It is a society which has been added to those which we already know and that have already sufficiently preoccupied us. They do not rest, except in the very last of their dreams. Sickness is intolerable, and weakness carries with it its own death sentence. Their communism is taken to the limits of cannibalism and coprophagy.

"Demanding the sacrifice and misery of many for the benefit and happiness of no one, is all for the objective that one species of universal desperation, could be continuable, renovative and multipliable as long as the world is alive. These cities of insects which appeared on this planet before humans appeared, could serve almost as a caricature of ourselves, as a parody of the terrestrial paradise, towards which the majority of civilized countries walk."

Thus, Maeterlinck demonstrates in a concrete way the price of those Marxist-Leninist types of regimens.

They used to have wings, now they do not have them. They do not have eyes, since they have renounced them. They used to have sex, but they have sacrificed this, too.

To all of this, we have to add that before sacrificing their wings, their sight and their sex, these white ants (and all ants in general), had to sacrifice their intelligence.

If, in the beginning, an iron dictatorship was necessary to establish their abominable communism, afterwards everything became automatic, and their intelligence — once displaced by their mechanicity — became atrophied little by little.

Today, we are astonished when we contemplate a bee's honeycomb or an ant-hive, but we lament that they now lack intelligence, and that they have become mechanical.

Let us now talk about the forgiveness of sins. Can perhaps karma be forgiven?

We say that karma can be forgiven. When an inferior law is transcended by a superior law, the latter has in itself, without a doubt, the extraordinary power of washing away the first one.

Nevertheless, there are lost cases, such as that of the ants and bees. Such creatures, after having normal personalities, became devolved; they became deformed, and diminished themselves, until reaching their present state.

I owed karma from previous lives, but I was forgiven. An eminent special encounter with my Divine Mother Kundalini was announced to me. I knew that when arriving at a certain esoteric degree, I was going to be taken to her presence.

Certainly, the longed-for day arrived, and I was taken before her. A very exalted adept conducted me towards the sanctuary.

Oh God of mine! Once there... I cried... I prayed... I invoked my Beloved One. This cosmic event was extraordinary.

She, my Beloved Mother, came to me. It is impossible to explain what I felt. All of my dear mothers who I have had in all of my distinct reincarnations were represented in her.

However, she was beyond all of them... She was my Mother, yes, but perfect, ineffable, and terribly divine.

The Father had deposited within her all the grace of his wisdom. Christ (the Son) had saturated her with his love, and the Holy Spirit had conferred her with all of his igneous powers.

Thus, I could comprehend that in my Mother, all of wisdom, love, and power vividly expressed themselves.

We sat face to face. She was on one chair and I on another, and so, delectably, we conversed as son and mother.

How joyful... how happy I was when conversing with my Divine Mother! I had something to say, and when I spoke I did so with a voice which surprised my very own self. "I ask you to forgive me of all of the crimes I committed in previous lives, since you know that nowadays I would be incapable of falling into the same errors."

"I know it, my son," replied my Mother with a paradisiacal voice filled with infinite love.

"Not even for a mIlium dollars would I commit those errors again," I continued saying to my Divine Mother Kundalini.

"What is that about dollars, my son? Why are you saying that? Why are you talking like that?"

Then, oh God!... I felt embarrassed with myself... Confused, ashamed, and filled with pain, I answered, "Pardon me, Mother of mine, the problem is that this is the spoken way of that vain and illusory physical world where I live."

"I understand, my son," answered my Mother. So, with these words the Beloved One restored tranquility and peace unto me.

"Now, yes, Mother of mine, I ask you to bless me and forgive me." I spoke filled with ecstasy.

Terrific was the moment in which my Mother, on her knees, kneeled with infinite humbleness and, filled with wisdom, love, and power, blessed me when saying, "My son, you are forgiven."

"Allow me to kiss your feet, oh Mother of mine," I cried.

Then, oh God! — when I deposited my mystical kiss upon her sacred feet, she instructed me with a certain symbol that reminded me of the washing of feet in the Last Supper of the Lord.

I understood and comprehended everything in depth. I had already dissolved the pluralized "I" within the mineral regions, within the infernal worlds of Nature, but I needed to burn up the Satanic seeds within the inferior molecular world, or Purgatorial region. Then after, I had to bathe myself in the rivers of Lethe and Eunoe in order to erase the memories of evil and fortify virtues. Such a thing must be done before having the right to be confirmed in the Light.

Later, I found myself involved in a potentially painful scene, similar to one from my past life where I had committed a lamentable error. I was very close to being run down by a car within the Federal District, capital city of Mexico. I was completely convinced that I was already free of karma.

I studied my own book of karma in the superior worlds, and found all of its pages blank. I only found the name of a mountain written on one of the pages. I comprehended that later I have to live there.

"Is this a type of karma?" I asked unto the lords of karma.

"This is not a karma," they answered me. "You will go to live there for the good of the Great Cause."

Nonetheless, it is clear that this will not be mandatory for me; the liberty of choosing is granted unto me.

At present, I do not owe any karma, yet I have to pay tax unto the lords of the law. Everything has a price, and the right to live in this world must be paid. I pay with good deeds.

Therefore, I have presented to the consideration of my readers two cases: the irremediable karma, like that of bees and ants, and the forgiven karma.

Let us now talk of negotiations. Let us make it real with the rune Not. In Masonry, this symbol is taught only to masters, never to beginners.

Let us remember the sign for succor for those of the Third Degree, that is to say, for the masters: the interlaced hands are placed over the head, at the level of the forehead, with the palms facing outward, while pronouncing at the same time, "Around me, children of the widow!" or, in Hebrew, "**Elai Beni Al Manah.**"

All Masons must concur when hearing this cry, in order to aid the brother who is in misfortune and to grant him their protection in all cases and circumstances of life.

In Masonry, the rune Not is practiced with the head, and this rune has been, is, and will always be an "S.O.S.," a sign for help.

As a fact, the rune Not in itself signifies danger, but it is obvious that the power for intelligently avoiding this danger resides within the same rune.

Those who transit upon the path of the razor's edge are incessantly assaulted by the tenebrous ones, and so they suffer the unspeakable. Therefore, they can and must defend themselves with the rune Not.

We can beseech, ask for help, from Anubis and his forty-two judges of karma with this rune Not, in order for them to consider negotiations.

We must not complain because of karma, since it is negotiable. Whosoever has capital from good deeds can pay without the necessity of suffering.

Practice One

The practices of the rune Not take us to the performance of Pranayama, that is to say, to the wise and intelligent combination of solar and lunar atoms.

PRANAYAMA

You must profoundly inhale the vital air, the Prana, the life, through the right nostril, and exhale it through the left nostril while mentally counting up to twelve. Then after, inhale through the left nostril and exhale through the right one, and vice versa. Continue with this exercise for ten minutes. In this practice, you must control your nostrils with your index finger and your thumb.

Afterwards, the Gnostic student must sit down or lay down in dorsal decubitus (on his back, facing upwards). With his body relaxed, he must concentrate and try to remember his past lives.

Practice Two

In the case of requiring the assistance of Anubis, if you urgently need to negotiate with him, then you must open your arms to the sides. While in this position, you must form the rune by placing one arm at an angle of 135 degrees and the other arm at an angle of only 45 degrees.

RUNE NOT

Then, the arm which forms the angle of 45 degrees will move in order to form an angle of 135 degrees, and the other arm will move to form the angle of 45 degrees.

During this exercise, you must chant the mantras **NA**, **NE**, **NI**, **NO**, **NU**, while having your mind concentrated on Anubis, the chief of karma. In this manner, beseech him for the negotiation you wish, and ask him for the urgently needed help.

You must observe well the form of the rune Not, imitating with your arms this sign. The right and left arms must alternate in their movements.

PARSIFAL TEMPTED IN THE ENCHANTED GARDEN

Chapter 41
Parsifal

Let us talk about the Templar knights; let us converse a little bit about these loyal custodians of the Holy Grail. May the gods listen to us, may the Muses inspire us.

What could we say about the Castle of Monsalvat? Let us all sing the hymn of the Grail.

HYMN OF THE GRAIL

O feast of love undying, from day to day renewed, draw near, as for the last time, to taste this sacred food. Who revels in good deeds this holy feast still feeds: he dares approach the shrine to share this gift divine.

For sins of the world with thousand sorrows His sacred blood He offered; to the world's Redeemer with joyful heart, oh, how gladly my blood I proffer: He died, for sin atoning thus, He lives, by death He lives in us!

In faith and love, behold the dove, the Savior's shining token: take ye the wine, His blood divine, and bread of life here broken!

You men and gods! Lo and behold, the grail knights and their squires. All of them are dressed with white tunics and white cloaks, similar to the Templar knights... but, instead of the red tau [cross], the symbol of a white dove in soaring flight is rightfully displayed on their weapons and embroidered on their cloaks. This is an extraordinary symbol of the Third Logos, a living sign of the Holy Spirit, of Vulcan, that marvelous sexual force with which we can perform many prodigies and marvels.

Well... it would be helpful to penetrate within the deep meaning of Wagner's drama. In this drama, "Amfortas is a specific type of remorse, Titurel is the voice of the past, Klingsor is the black magician, Parsifal is redemption, Kundry is seduction, and Gurnemanz is tradition."

In the beginning, the marvelous trombones sound their solemn reveille, and Gurnemanz sinks to his knees with his two squires, joining them in silent morning prayer.

Two strong knights come from the Grail's castle with the evident purpose of exploring the path that Amfortas, the king of the sacred chalice, is going to follow.

The old successor of King Titurel comes earlier than he ever has, to bathe himself within the sacred waters of the lake. This is done with the desire of calming the strong pains that have afflicted him since the moment of his own disgrace, when he received a frightful thrust of a lance, a spear that Klingsor, the perverse black magician, wounded him with.

A sorrowful story is the one of Klingsor! Horrifying! He was a sincerely mistaken one, as many are in this day and age. He was living as a penitent in a frightful desert. He wanted to be a saint; thus, he became an enemy to all that could have sexual savor. He fought dreadfully against the animal passions, he wore bloody sackcloths upon his flagellated body, and he cried a lot. Nevertheless, everything was useless, since his lust, lasciviousness, and his secret impudence, in spite of all his efforts and sacrifices, were swallowing him alive.

Therefore (oh, dear God!), being impotent in eliminating his sexual passions, this unhappy man resolved to mutilate, to castrate himself with his own hands. Then after, he beseechingly extended his hands towards the Grail, but he was rejected with indignation by the guardian.

This disgraced one believed that by hating the Holy Spirit, by rejecting the Third Logos, by destroying the sexual organs, he could be admitted into the Castle of Monsalvat. The unhappy one thought that he could be admitted into the Order of the Holy Grail without the Maithuna, without previously achieving the Second Birth, and while being dressed with lunar rags. This wretched, unfortunate, and ill-starred knight supposed that one could enter to work with the Second Logos (the Christ) without previously having worked with the Third Logos (the Holy Spirit, the sexual fire).

To that end, the tenebrous, despairing Klingsor unjustly resolved to avenge himself against the noble knights of the

Holy Grail. Therefore, he transformed his penitent desert into a bewitched and fatal garden of voluptuous delights, and he filled it with exquisite and diabolical women, dangerously beautiful.

Thus, there in that delectable mansion, accompanied by his beauties, he lurked in secrecy for the Grail Knights in order to drag them into concupiscence, which inevitably conduces people towards the infernal worlds.

Whosoever allowed himself to be seduced by these provocative she-devils became his victim. Hence, this is how he succeeded in carrying many knights into perdition.

Amfortas, king of the Grail, fought this fatal, evil, venturesome Klingsor. The king wanted to put an end to this fatal, enchanted plague, but he, too, fell, surrendering to passion within the impudent arms of the lustful Kundry.

With such a formidable moment for Klingsor, he would have been foolish if he would have lost such an opportunity. Therefore, he audaciously snatched the sacred spear from the hands of Amfortas, then, smiling, he triumphantly withdrew.

Thus, this is the way in which Amfortas, the king of the Grail, lost the blessed spear with which Longinus pierced the side of the Lord upon Golgotha.

Amfortas, who is also pierced in his side with the frightful wound of remorse, suffers the unspeakable.

Kundry, a delectable woman of extraordinary beauty, also suffers with remorse; but she humbly serves the brethren of the Holy Grail.

Within the depth, you, Kundry, fatal woman, are nothing but an instrument of perfidy, under the service of that magician from darkness. You want to march along the path of light; yet, hypnotized, you fail.

Amfortas, while submerged within intimate, profound meditation, listens in ecstasy to the mysterious words of mystical meaning that come from the Grail:

> "Made wise through pity, the blameless fool (the innocent and chaste one), wait for him, the one I choose."

Suddenly, something extraordinary happens, something unusual. A great commotion stirs among the people of the Grail. Precisely at the shore of the lake, they have intercepted an ignorant boy, who, errant on those shores, has just wounded to death a swan, a sacred bird of immaculate whiteness.

But, why so much scandal? To Parsifal, this was an event that had just occurred in the past, which fortunately was washed clean within the precious waters of Lethe.

Who has not wounded the sacred swan to death? Who has not wounded the Third Logos? Who is the one who has not assassinated the miraculous Hamsa, the Holy Spirit? Who, because of fornication, has not assassinated the Phoenix Bird of paradise? Who has not sinned against the immortal Ibis? Who has not made the Holy Dove, living symbol of the sexual force, to bleed?

It is clear that Parsifal, after suffering greatly, reached total innocence. He is the son of Herzeleide, a poor woman from the forest. Really, he ignores mundane things, because he is protected by his innocence.

Klingsor's flower maidens are useless, as these joyless ones cannot seduce such an innocent one. Therefore, they flee defeated.

Useless become the seductive efforts of Herodias (Gundryggia, Kundry), as all of her arts fail. Thus, when looking at herself defeated, she cries, asking help from Klingsor, who in desperation and rage, hurls the sacred spear against Parsifal.

Nevertheless, Parsifal is protected by his innocence. Therefore, instead of piercing his body, the spear hangs over Parsifal's head for an instant. Then, the boy grasps the spear with his right hand, and swings this sharp weapon in the blessed sign of the cross. Finally, the Castle of Klingsor collapses and sinks into the abyss, converted into cosmic dust.

The best comes afterwards, as Parsifal, in company with his Guru Gurnemanz, enters into the Temple of Montserrat, Spain, Cataluña.

The doors of the temple are opened, and in solemn procession, all the knights of the Holy Grail enter the holy place.

In an orderly manner and with infinite veneration, they place themselves before two long, cloth covered tables, which are parallel to each other and with an empty space between them.

Delectable are those moments in which the mystical supper is celebrated, the cosmic banquet of the Pascal Lamb.

Extraordinary are those instants in which the bread and the wine of the transubstantiation are eaten and drank.

Gloriously shining during the ritual is the blessed chalice in which Joseph of Arimathea collected the blood that poured from the wounds of the Lord upon the Golgotha of all bitterness.

Ineffable moments of pleroma are those in which Parsifal miraculously heals the wound of Amfortas, by applying to his side the same blessed spear that previously had wounded him.

This spear is a formidable symbol. It is one hundred percent phallic; it is sexual in its integral form.

Amfortas fell because of sex. He dreadfully suffered with the pain of remorse. But, thanks to the sexual mysteries, he totally regenerated and healed himself.

The great Kabir Jesus said,

"If any man will come after me, let him deny himself, and take up his cross, and follow me." - Matthew 16:24

The knights of the Holy Grail did deny themselves; they dissolved the pluralized "I" by incinerating the satanic seeds, by bathing themselves within the waters of Lethe and Eunoe.

The knights of the Holy Grail worked in the flaming forge of Vulcan; they never ignored that the cross is the result of the insertion of the vertical beam inside the horizontal cteis.

The knights of the Holy Grail have sacrificed themselves for the sake of humanity; they have worked with infinite love in the Great Work of the Father.

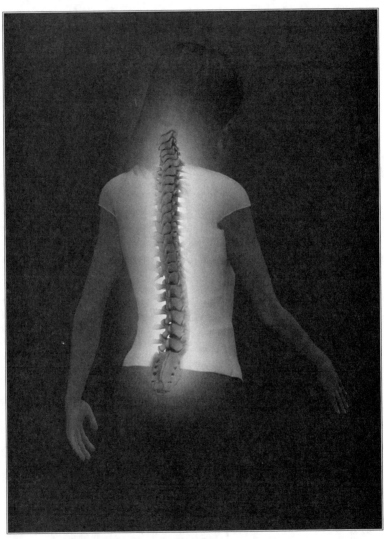

THE SPINAL COLUMN

Chapter 42
The Sacred Fire

The sexual energy polarizes itself in the two following ways: static or potential (Kundalini), and dynamic. These polarizations, known by all cultural and spiritual persons, are certainly active forces within the organism.

It is obvious that within the dorsal spine there are seven very special magnetic centers. Infinite igneous powers are found latent within them.

All of the multiplicity of divine powers enter into activity with the ascension of the sacred fire along the medullar canal.

The fundamental clue in order to awaken this sacred fire, the Kundalini, is certainly hidden within sex yoga, within Maithuna, within the sexual connection of the lingam-yoni, phallus-uterus, but without the ejaculation of the ens seminis (entity of semen). This is because the whole ens virtutis of the fire is enclosed within this semi-solid and semi-liquid substance.

Refrained desire makes the sexual energy flow inward and upward towards the brain.

When the solar and lunar atoms of the seminal system make contact in the coccyx near the Triveni, the base of the dorsal spine, then the sacred fire is awakened and begins its ascent through the medullar canal to the brain.

It is urgent to comprehend, it is necessary to know, that if the entity of semen is spilled, then the ascending fire descends one or more vertebrae, according with the magnitude of the fault.

The Kundalini, the divine fire, ascends slowly in accordance with the merits of the heart.

Those who walk upon the path of the razor's edge know very well by direct experience that the Divine Mother Kundalini, the sacred fire, conducts Shiva, the Holy Spirit, to the cerebral center, and finally into the heart temple.

No authentic esotericist would dare to deny that a static state always exists behind any activity.

We can undoubtedly find the fundamental static center of the human organism in the coccygeal bone (base of the dorsal spine).

This coccygeal chakra is in itself the Church of Ephesus of Christian esotericism. It is the root-support of the physical body and of all movements of vital forces within the interior of our organism.

We know by direct experience that in this specific center of the body, the igneous serpent of our magical powers is found coiled three and a half times. This is the serpentine annular fire that is marvellously developed in the body of the ascetic.

A very careful analysis of this magnetic coccygeal center permits us to comprehend that this in itself is consciousness. There is no doubt that this center possesses very special qualities.

The Kundalini, the contained power within this cited coccygeal center, is efficient and definitive for the awakening of the consciousness. It is obvious that this sacred fire can open the igneous wings of the Caduceus of Mercury upon the dorsal spine of the initiate. Thus, this is how we can consciously penetrate into any department of the kingdom.

The Hindustani adepts make a distinction between the supreme cosmic consciousness and its active energetic power, which is capable of penetrating within the most profound zones of our subconsciousness in order to truly awaken us.

The oriental wise men say that when cosmic consciousness is manifested as energy, it possesses two identical faces, the potential and the kinetic.

The Kundalini, the sexual fire, is without a doubt a Vedantic and Jehovistic truth that perfectly represents the whole universal process as a wise polarization in the consciousness itself.

To utilize this sacred fire, the igneous serpent of our magical powers, in order to awaken the consciousness, is an intimate, vital, and indispensable necessity.

The human being — or better if we say, the poor intellectual animal mistakenly called man — has his consciousness completely asleep. Therefore, he certainly is incapable of vividly experiencing that which is not of time, that which is the Reality.

The sacred fire possesses very special and effective virtues in order to take the poor human biped out of the unconscious state in which he is.

Whosoever develops this sacred fire with all of its seven degrees of power, obviously acquires certain faculties with which he can command the creatures of fire, air, water, and earth.

Nevertheless, it is urgent to comprehend that the sword, forged by Vulcan, must be incandescently tempered within the spermatic waters of the Styx lake.

Disgraceful is the one who spills the cup of Hermes.

> *"It had been good for that man if he had
> not been born."* — Matthew 26:24

Or,

> *"It were better for him that a millstone were
> hanged about his neck, and he were drowned
> in the depth of the sea."* — Matthew 18:6

Aeneas, the eminent Trojan hero, with his flaming sword on high and looking fixedly at the sun, uttered words while in prayer. Such words could only be comprehended by those who work in the magistery of fire. He put as his witness the Cosmic Christ, his blessed land which he invoked, also the all-powerful Father who dwells in secret, and Saturnian Juno Kundalini, the eternal spouse of the Third Logos.

He called to glorious Mars, lord of wars, and to all the elemental creatures of the fountains and rivers, to all the children of the fire, to all divinities of the blue sea. He even promised that if victory should chance befall to his enemy Turnus, he would withdraw defeated to the city of Evander. But, if victory were granted to him with Mars being in his favor, then he would not convert the Italians into slaves. He would only think to co-exist with them as friends, and that is all.

The following oath of the good King Latinus is very significant to all of those who work in the magistery of fire. When he looked up fixedly to the sun, and called as his witness the sacred fires that stand lit within us and the divinities, he said:

> "The day shall not come when men of Italy shall violate this treaty or break this peace, whatever chance will bring."

King Latinus put the same divinities to witness all his oaths: the earth, sea, and stars, the two children of Latona, the unmanifested Prakriti (Diana and Apollo), and Janus (Ianos) with his I.A.O., the three vowels which are chanted during the sexual trance of the Maithuna.

This great King Latinus did not forget in his prayer the terrible abode of Pluto and the infernal gods, those divine beings, those sacred individuals who renounced the happiness of Nirvana in order to live in the infernal worlds to fight for the decidedly lost ones.

All of these prayers, all of the supplications and oaths from the ancient classic world, certainly are incomprehensible without the sacred science of fire.

The advent of the fire within ourselves is the most formidable cosmic event. The fire transforms us radically.

The four letters written upon the cross of the redeemer of the world come into my memory in these instants: INRI. **Ignis natura renovatur integra**. "The fire renews Nature incessantly."

There, in the profound night of the centuries, in the ancient Egypt of the pharaohs, the great Kabir Jesus, while practicing Maithuna with a vestal of a pyramid, chanted the mantras **INRI, ENRE, ONRO, UNRU, ANRA**. He resounded each letter in a prolonged and profound way. It is obvious that each one of these mantras is divided into two esoteric syllables for its pronunciation.

We need to be swallowed by the serpent. It is urgent to convert ourselves into living flames; it is indispensable to achieve the Second Birth in order to enter into the kingdom.

Chapter 43

Rune Laf (Lagu, Laguz)

I was still very young, and she (the starry night) was named
Urania. So, on one of those nights (it does not matter which
one), I abandoned this physical body for a while.

How happy I felt while out of the dense body. There is no
better pleasure than feeling oneself as a detached soul. Past,
present, and future become an eternal now.

To enter within the parallel universes becomes relatively
easy when one has the consciousness awakened.

While in the parallel universe of the fifth dimension, I felt
the necessity of invoking a master, thus I cried with a great
voice, calling, beseeching, asking.

In an instant, it looked as if the whole universe was transformed; such is the power of the Word.

The silver cord has the power of infinitely elongating itself.
This is how souls can freely travel throughout the starry space.

So, I traveled a lot and arrived at the temple. Filled with
ecstasy, I advanced upon the mysterious path that conducts
the initiates to the doors of this very saintly place. I was then
unexpectedly attacked by a great beast, by a Mithraic bull,
which was dreadful in a great manner.

Without boasting of valor, I tell you, beloved reader, that
I did not feel fear. I confronted the animal in a resolute and
blunt way, holding it by its horns. Thus, I managed to sink it
down to the ground.

However, in those precise moments, something unusual
happened. Before my astonished consciousness, a chain of iron
dropped, and as if by magic, the terrible animal disappeared.

I intuitively comprehended everything in those moments.
Clearly, I needed to make myself free, to break the enslaving
chains, to eliminate the animal ego.

Afterwards, I continued on my way and entered through
the doors of the temple. I became inebriated by an exquisite
spiritual voluptuousness. Certainly, I would not change those
instants, not even for all the gold of the world.

What happened afterwards is well known by the gods, and now I write it for the humans.

I saw the chariot of the centuries, which was driven by three masters of the White Lodge, and a venerable elder was in this chariot of mystery.

How can I forget that face? That countenance? That appearance? That sublime perfection?

The forehead of that elder was certainly high and majestic, his nose straight and perfect, his lips fine and delicate, his ears small and recoiled, his beard white and with an aureole of light, and his hair of an immaculate whiteness was falling over his shoulders.

It is obvious that I could not stop inquiring about him, since he was terribly divine and formidable.

"His name is **Peter**," answered one of the hierophants who was driving the chariot of the centuries.

Then after... oh God of mine!... I abased myself on the ground before this elder of the centuries, and filled with infinite love and compassion, while speaking in the golden language, he blessed me.

Since then I have reflected a lot, and I will never be sorry for having taught humanity the gospel of **Peter**, the Maithuna, sex yoga.

Patar, **Peter**, said:

"Behold I lay in Sion a chief corner stone, elect, precious...

"Unto you therefore which believe he is precious: but unto them which be disobedient, the stone which the builders disallowed, the same is made the head of the corner.

"And a stone of stumbling, and a rock of offense." — 1 Peter 2:6, 7, 8

But then, what about the Holy Grail? Is it not perhaps the same initiatic stone?

The Grail is a precious stone that was brought to the Earth by the angels and entrusted to an initiatic fraternity for its custody. This fraternity was named the Grail Custodians.

Here we are then with the stone of Jacob, the sacred stone of the Scottish Liafail, the cubic stone of Yesod, which the Hebraic Kabbalists locate in the sexual organs.

The legitimate text from Wolfram von Eschenbach, related to this holy stone and to the White Brotherhood who wisely have custody of it, is as follows:

> "Those heroes are animated by a stone.
> Do not you know its august and pure essence?
> It is called Lapiz-Electrix [**Magnes**].
> Any marvel [**Magic**] can be performed through it.
> As the phoenix which is precipitated into the flames,
> It can be reborn from its own ashes.
> Because within the same flames it rejuvenates its plumage,
> thus rejuvenated, it glows more beautiful than before.
> Its power is such that any man,
> who, no matter how unhappy in his own state he might be,
> no matter his color, no matter his face, instead of dying as others,
> he no longer knows what age might be.
> And whether man or woman,
> they shall enjoy from this ineffable delight,
> which is to contemplate the **Stone**
> for more than two hundred years."

This initiatic stone is esoterically converted into the Hermes cup, into the sacred chalice.

Pedro, **Patar**, **Peter**, the initiatic Revelation, is within sex, and anything that is not through this way signifies a useless loss of time.

It becomes tremendously significant that as much in the north of America as well as in the same whole continent, we can find engraved on the stones the **Laftar**, or **rune Laf**, whose meaning is **"savior."**

It is obvious that we must build the church for the intimate Christ upon the living stone. Woe to those who build their interior temple upon the quicksand of theories. Rain will fall, rivers will run, and their house will crumble into the abyss, where only weeping and the gnashing of teeth are heard.

If we join two **Lafs** by their arms, then we have the letter m of matrimony.

It is clear and certain by all means that only by treading upon the path of the perfect matrimony can the wedding garment of the soul be attained. This garment is the perfect synthesis of the solar bodies.

Woe to those unhappy ones who present themselves at the banquet of the Lord without the wedding garment.

The command of the king is written:

"Bind him hand and foot, and take him away, and cast him into outer darkness; there shall be weeping and gnashing of teeth.

"For many are called, but few are chosen." — Matthew 22:13, 14

Practice

The practice that corresponds to this rune consists of going towards the Sun in the morning. In the moments of sunrise, adopt a mystical attitude, that is, lift the hands as shown by the rune. In this way, one implores unto It (the Sun, Christ) for esoteric help.

This practice must be performed on the 27th of each month.

RUNE LAF

Chapter 44
The Final Liberation

In the name of the truth, we have to affirm the necessity of renunciation. We need to pass through the Great Death, and this is only possible by totally liberating ourselves from the mind.

When Nature has been radically dominated, omnipotence and omniscience are the logical result.

When the Self-realized Gnostic renounces even the ideals of omnipotence and omniscience, the destruction of the true seed of evil, the one which brings us into the mahamanvantara (cosmic day) after the great pralaya (cosmic night) is precipitated.

It is obvious that whosoever has achieved the realization of the Innermost Self has the right to live in Nirvana, but if he renounces that happiness, he will continue upon the direct path that leads to the Absolute.

Nevertheless, many lateral paths exist, as well as tempting gods, who are many times more dangerous than human beings.

They tempt us, not because of evil, or jealousy, not even because of fear of losing their place, as many oriental authors mistakenly suppose, but because of compassion.

In these instants in which I write this chapter, something very interesting comes into my memory.

A certain day, after having made a Nirvanic renunciation, I was joyfully in my seventh principle (Atman), upon a precious balcony of an ineffable mansion.

It is clear that I was in Nirvana, the region of the Dharmasayas, the world of gods.

Suddenly, floating in that sacred space, many blessed Nirvanis approached me.

Certainly, seeing these ineffable beings dressed with their Dharmasaya tunics was admirable.

When seeing them, I could verify by direct experience that these beings are living flames with three wicks, and that they are immortal.

To that end, one of those ineffable ones took the floor in order to tell me, "My brother, why are you going through that very narrow, bitter, and hard path? Here in Nirvana, we are happy. Stay here with us!..."

"The human beings could not patronize me with their temptations; you gods will not do so, not even by a long shot. I go to the Absolute." That was my answer. Afterwards, I left that precious place with a firm and decided step.

The Gnostics who do not achieve absolute perfection die. Then, they are converted into gods. They commit the mistake of abandoning the great Direct Path; they undertake the lateral paths and acquire many powers. Afterwards, it is clear that they need to reincarnate anew in order to enter again into the Direct Path that will take them to the Absolute.

In order to attain the absolute quietude of the mind, it is indispensable to deflect the diverse forms of our mental content.

Direct knowledge grants us very beautiful qualities, but whosoever walks on the Direct Path must not be attached to such virtues.

Obtaining psychic powers never leads to any liberation. It is nothing but a search for vain enjoyments.

The possession of occult powers does not do anything but increase that which is mundane in us, which in the end makes this existence more bitter.

Even when almost achieving total liberation, numerous souls fail because they cannot absolutely renounce all their occult powers. Those beings submerge themselves for a short time within Nature in order to emerge anew as owners, chiefs, and lords.

There are thousands of gods of this type. They are divine and ineffable, but they do not have the right to enter into the Absolute.

There are many Self-realized ones who are submerged within Nature. Certainly, these brothers and sisters have desisted in this part of their perfection. While impeded for a certain time in reaching the end, they continue governing this or that part of the universe.

Certainly, the holy gods correspond to certain superior functions of Nature that are attained by different souls. However, in reality, they still have not achieved final liberation.

Radical, absolute liberation can be achieved only by renouncing the idea of converting ourselves into gods, and of becoming rulers of kalpas (cycles).

Success is close for the one who is extremely energetic. We need to be pitiless towards ourselves.

To renounce, and to die from instant to instant, is urgent. We can enter into the Absolute, but only based on many renunciations and deaths.

I talk to human beings based on my own direct experience. I am an avatar from **Ishvara**.

Really, **Ishvara** (the supreme master) is a very special Purusha who is exempted from sufferings, actions with results, and desires.

Imagine the Universal Spirit of Life as an ocean without beaches, without shores. Think for a moment of a wave that emerges in order to get lost anew within its liquid element. Then, this diamantine wave would be **Ishvara**.

Brahma, the ocean of the Spirit, manifests itself as **Ishvara**, who is the master of masters, the governor of the universe.

Within him, that omniscience (which in others only exists as a germ) becomes infinite.

He is the Master, even of the ancient masters, since he is not ever limited by time. The word which manifests him is **AUM**.

So, **Ishvara** came unto me, and he told me, "You must write books, messages, pamphlets, and **Tijitlis**."

"Lord," I exclaimed, "what does the word **Tijitlis** mean?"

The Lord answered, "To form the army for salvation, the Gnostic movement, the POSCLA." And then I comprehended.

Ishvara is the true prototype of perfection. Certainly, he is very much beyond the body, the mind, and the affections.

Nevertheless, truly I tell you, beloved Gnostics, that first you must achieve the Second Birth. You must die in yourselves and give even the last drop of blood for this suffering humanity.

Only thus can you tread upon the path of **John**, which is the Direct Path that will take you to the Absolute, beyond human beings and gods.

Do not commit the error of waiting for the law of evolution to conduct you to the final liberation.

This Direct Path is only possible through incessant, intimate revolutions.

Now you are only **imitatus**. In order to climb the three triangles, you must first convert yourselves into **adeptus**.

Angels, Archangels, and Principalities constitute the first triangle.

Powers, Virtues, and Dominions personify the second triangle.

Thrones, Cherubim, and Seraphim personify the third triangle.

That which has no name, that which is not of time, which is the Absolute, is very much beyond these three ineffable triangles.

Chapter 45

The Dream of the Consciousness

Beloved Gnostic disciples, with a lot of efforts and great love, we have arrived at the penultimate chapter of this 1968-1969 Christmas Message, and it is convenient for the good of the Great Cause to eliminate certain weeds that obstruct the way.

Something very grave exists in all of these matters. I want to emphatically refer to the dream of the consciousness.

The four gospels insist on the necessity of awakening, but disgracefully, people suppose that they have already awakened.

What is even worse is that there are certain types of individuals everywhere who, by the way, are certainly very psychic, yet they not only sleep, but moreover they dream that they are awake. These type of people call themselves (so to speak) "seers." They become very dangerous because they project their dreams, hallucinations, and madness upon others. Precisely, they accuse others of crimes they did not commit, and this is how they destroy homes.

It is obvious to understand that we are not speaking against legitimate clairvoyants. We are only referring to the hallucinating ones, to those sincerely mistaken ones who dream that they are awake.

Truly, with profound pain we have found that the cause of esoteric failure is the sleeping consciousness.

Really, many sincere, devout Gnostics who are lovers of the truth fail due to the lamentable state of their sleeping consciousness.

In ancient times, the Great Arcanum, Maithuna, sex yoga, was only taught to those neophytes who had awakened their consciousness. The hierophants knew very well that the sleeping disciples would sooner or later abandon the work in the Ninth Sphere.

What is worse is that these failing ones cheat themselves by thinking the best of themselves. Almost always, they fall as harlots into the arms of some new little school that will grant unto them some kind of consolation. Afterwards, they pronounce phrases like these, "I do not follow the Gnostic teachings, because they demand a couple. This is a matter for oneself, since liberation, the Great Work, is a matter that has to be searched for alone."

Naturally, the only cause of these words of self-consolation and self-consideration is their own self-justification.

If these poor people had their consciousness awake, then they could see their error; they would comprehend that they did not beget themselves alone, that they have a father and a mother, and that there was a coitus that gave them life.

If these poor people had their consciousness awake, then they could verify for themselves that as above, so below, and vice versa. They would directly experience the crude reality. They would be perfectly aware of the lamentable state in which they are. Thus, they would comprehend the necessity of Maithuna in order to build their solar bodies, the wedding garment for their souls. This is how they would achieve the Second Birth, which the great Kabir Jesus spoke about to the rabbi Nicodemus.

But such "wisdom taunting ones" are asleep, and truly, they are not capable of verifying for themselves that they are dressed with protoplasmic bodies, with lunar rags, that they are wretched and miserable.

The dreaming ones, the sleepy ones who suppose that they are awake, not only harm themselves, but moreover, they cause grave harm to their fellowmen.

Truly, I believe that the sincerely mistaken one, the sleepy one who dreams of being awake, the mythomaniac who believes himself to be super-transcended, the hallucinating one who qualifies himself as being illuminated, is used to doing very much harm to himself and to humanity. He does more harm than that inflicted by the one who never in his life entered into our studies.

We are talking in a very blunt language. However, you can be sure, beloved reader, that when many sleeping and hallucinating ones read these lines, instead of stopping for awhile in order to reflect, correct, and rectify themselves, they will only search for a way of incorporating my words into themselves with the evident purpose of supporting their madness.

To the disgrace of this poor human ant-hive, people carry within themselves an awful secretary, which always wrongly interprets the Gnostic teachings. We are referring to the pluralized "I," the "myself."

The most comical aspect of Mephistopheles (the ego) is the way in which he disguises himself as a "saint." It is clear that the ego is pleased when it is placed upon altars and is worshipped.

It becomes pathetic and evident to comprehend in depth that while the consciousness continues to be bottled up within the pluralized "I," not only will we sleep, but even worse, the consciousness will sometimes have the bad taste of dreaming of being awakened.

The worst genre of madness is the result of the combination of mythomania with hallucination.

The mythomaniac type of person is the one who boasts of being a god, who feels himself to be super-transcended, who wishes to be worshipped by all of the world.

When studying this chapter, these type of persons will accommodate my words to others, since they will think that they have already dissolved the "I" in themselves, even though they might have it more robust than a gorilla.

You must be very sure that when a sleeping mythomaniac works in the forge of the Cyclops, very soon they will abandon this work, and will say, "I already achieved the Second Birth. I am a liberated one. I have renounced Nirvana for the love of humanity. I am a god."

We have seen many ugly things within our beloved Gnostic movement. It is dreadful to see the mythomaniacs, the sleepy, hallucinated ones prophesying madness, slandering their neighbors, qualifying others as black magicians, etc. Certainly, this is dreadful.

Devils judging devils! All of these "perfection boasters" do not want to be aware that in this painful world in which we live, it is sometimes almost impossible to find a saint.

Every magician is more or less black. In no way can one be white while the demon, the pluralized "I," is inserted within the body.

The attitude of going everywhere saying that "such a fellow is a fallen one," is certainly a joke of very bad taste, since in this world all the people are fallen.

The attitude of slandering neighbors and destroying families with false prophesies is normal for hallucinating ones, for people who dream of being awakened.

Truly, if someone wants to awaken, then he has to have the resolution of dying from moment to moment. Let him practice deep meditation. Let him be liberated from his mind. Let him practice the Runes, such as we have taught them in this book.

Constantly, many letters from many sleepy ones are mailed to me at this patriarchal headquarters of the Gnostic movement, which say, "My wife, my friend, or such fellow, is very evolved, is a very old soul, etc." These poor, sleepy ones who talk like this, think that time and evolution can awaken them, can Self-realize them, can take them to the final liberation. These people do not want to comprehend that evolution and its twin sister devolution are exclusively two mechanical laws of Nature that work in a harmonious and coordinated way, in the whole of creation. When one awakens the consciousness, then one comprehends the necessity of emancipating oneself from these two laws and of entering the path of the revolution.

We want awakened people, firm and revolutionary. In no way do we accept incoherent, vague, imprecise, insipid, and inodorous phrases, etc.

We must live alert and vigilant as a watchman in an epoch of war. We want people who work with the three factors of the revolution of the consciousness. We lament the cases of too many sincere, mistaken ones, sleepy ones who only work with one factor, which, disgracefully, is many times wrongly done.

We need to comprehend what we are: poor, sleepy beasts, machines that are controlled by the ego.

Chapter 46
Rune Gibur (Gebo, Gyfur)

The discs or baked clay coins that are very abundant in the marvelous ruins of ancient Troy are engraved with Jain crosses or swastikas.

This invites us to think that the people of Shekelmesha, even when they were related to the Atlanteans, also carried the Aryan genes in their veins like the famous Yucatecan populace.

We must remember that the Aryan populace began about one mIlium years ago. The first of three Atlantean catastrophes happened 800,000 years ago, and the last one, as we already said in our former Christmas Message, happened about 11,000 years ago.

The swastika of Fusaiolas is a profoundly significant esoteric symbol. Such an ineffable sign actually glows over the head of the great serpent of Vishnu, and in the Shesta-Ananta of one thousand heads, whose habitat resides in Patala or the inferior region.

If we study this matter in depth, then we come to see that all of the ancient people always put the swastika at the head of their religious emblems. We also find Thor's hammer, the magical weapon forged by the pygmies against the giants, or pre-cosmic Titanic forces, who were in opposition to the law of universal harmony.

The sacred swastika is then the hammer that produces the tempests which the Ases or heavenly lords use. In the Macrocosm, its rectangular, elbowed arms clearly express without the least bit of doubt the incessant evolutions and devolutions of the seven cosmoses.

The swastika in the Microcosm represents the human being with his right arm aiming towards heaven and the left arm aiming towards the earth.

The swastika is an alchemical, cosmogonical, and anthropological sign with seven distinct interpretative clues. In short, it is (as a symbol of transcendental electricity) the Alpha and the Omega of the universal sexual force, from the Spirit to

SWASTIKA ON A BUDDHIST TEMPLE IN KOREA

matter. Therefore, whosoever grasps of all of its mystical significance remains free from **Maya** (illusion).

Without any doubt, the swastika is the electrical windmill of physicists. All of the mysteries of the lingam-yoni are enclosed within it.

The swastika in itself is the cross in movement (the rune Gebo in movement), that is to say, sex yoga, Maithuna, Sexual Magic.

Gnostics know very well that the ens seminis, which is contained within the endocrine sexual glands, is the Water of Life, the Fountain of Immortality, the Elixir of Longevity, the Nectar of Spirituality.

The realization of the Innermost Self is rooted exclusively in the medulla and the semen. Therefore, anything that is not through this way is lamentably a waste of time.

Everyone would like to submerge themselves within the current of sound in order to achieve the final liberation. Albeit, verily, verily, I say unto you, "Except you be born again, you cannot enter into the kingdom of heaven."

Truly, this matter about being born again in the sanctum regnum is something that belongs to the mysteries of the cross, of the swastika.

The god of life of Aztec Mexico carries the swastika-cross on his forehead, and the priests had it as an ornament over their sacred vestures.

It is obvious that without sexual alchemy, without the electric windmill, without the sacred mysteries of the swastika, the realization of the Innermost Self, the Second Birth which the great Kabir Jesus talked about to the rabbi Nicodemus becomes something more than impossible.

In Zen Buddhism from Japan, the onion with its distinct layers symbolizes the human being with his subtle bodies. In the occidental world, distinct schools of pseudo-esotericism and pseudo-occultism study those suprasensible vehicles. Zen monks emphasize the necessity of disintegrating, of reducing to dust, those subtle bodies, in order to achieve the final liberation. Zen philosophy conceptualizes that these subtle organisms are nothing but simple mental forms that must be dissolved.

It is evident that these internal bodies, which were studied by Mr. Leadbeater, Annie Besant, and many other authors, are nothing but lunar bodies, protoplasmic bodies that evolve until certain points that are perfectly defined by Nature. Then afterwards, they precipitate themselves into the devolving way until reaching the point of their original departure. Therefore, it is obvious that the lunar bodies have a beginning and an end. Thus, the Zen monks are not mistaken when they try to dissolve them.

But, let us go a little bit further; let us talk about the To Soma Heliakon, the wedding garment of the soul, the body of the solar man.

Remember the evangelical parable of the wedding feast:

> "...When the king came in to see the guests, he saw there
> a man which had not on a wedding garment, and he

*saith unto him, 'Friend, how cammest thou in hither not
having a wedding garment?'"* — Matthew 22:11,12

It is clear that he was speechless, since he was not prepared
to answer.

Terrible was the moment in which the king commanded
that he be bound by hand and foot, and he be taken away, in
order to be cast into the outer darkness, where only weeping
and gnashing of teeth are heard.

That the distinct, interpenetrating solar bodies constitute
in themselves the wedding garment of the soul is something
that must not surprise us.

What is fundamental, what is cardinal, is to build the solar
bodies, and this is only possible by transmuting the Sexual
Hydrogen Si-12.

It is obvious that based on incessant sexual trans-
mutations, we can perform the condensation of the hydrogen
of sex into the splendid and marvelous form of the Astral Solar
Body.

It is evident that with the hammer of the physicists, within the forge of the Cyclops (sex), we can crystallize the sexual
hydrogen into the paradisiacal body of the Solar Mind.

It is indisputable that by working until the maximum in
the Ninth Sphere, we can and must give form to the Solar
Body of Conscious Will.

Thus, only in such a way, by means of these alchemical
crystallizations, can we incarnate the divine Spirit within ourselves.

Thus, only in such a way, by working with the mysteries of
the sacred swastika, can we arrive at the Second Birth.

The absolute ignorance of these enunciated principles conducts thousands of mystical students towards the most grave
errors.

To ignore these fundamental postulations of Gnosticism
is very grave, because the result of such an attitude is that our
intelligence becomes bottled up inside of distinct dogmas and
theories, which are sometimes enchanting and fascinating, yet
absurd and stupid when we truly examine them in the light of
the tertium organum (the third canon of thought).

Max Heindel thinks that the wedding garment of the soul is the "Soma Psuchikon" that is constituted by the two superior ethers of the Vital Body, or Lingam Sarira of the Hindustani. This author (Heindel) believes that the Soma Psuchikon is attained by increasing the volume of these two superior ethers. This concept is very pretty, yet it is false, because these two ethers are not all that we need. It is urgent to build the superior existential bodies of the Being, that is to say, the solar vehicles, if what we truly want is to attain the Second Birth.

In no way can the solar bodies, the wedding garment of the soul, be built without the sexual mysteries of the rune Gibur (Gebo).

This rune is the letter G of Masonry. It is lamentable that the M.M. did not comprehend the profound significance of this mysterious letter.

The G is the swastika-cross, the Amen, the marvelous end found in all prayers.

G is also *gott* which signifies **God**. It is good to know that Gibraltar was named *Giburaltar* in the past, that is to say, the ara, the altar of the divine life from the Gibur.

People have already forgotten the runic practices, but fortunately the rune cross (Gebo) has not been forgotten yet.

When tracing the sacred sign of the swastika with the thumb, middle, and index fingers, we can defend ourselves from the tenebrous potencies. The columns of demons flee before the swastika.

It is written in previous chapters, yet we will never tire of repeating it:

"If any man will come after me, let him deny himself, and take up his cross, and follow me." — Matthew 16:24

Peter, when crucified with his head downwards towards the hard stone and with his feet vertically upwards, invites us to descend into the forge of the Cyclops, into the Ninth Sphere, in order to work with the fire and the water, which is the origin of worlds, beasts, human beings, and gods. Every authentic White Initiation begins here.

The infrasexuals protest against Sexual Alchemy, against the swastika. The infrasexuals are the degenerated, the declared enemies of the Third Logos.

If someone tells you that it is possible to achieve Self-realization without the Holy Cross, that is to say, without the sexual crossing of two people (wife and husband), then tell them that they lie.

If someone utters maledictions against sex and assures you that sex in itself is bestial and satanic, then tell them that they lie.

If someone tells you that to spill the cup of Hermes is necessary, and that this matter has not even the miniscular of consequences, then tell them that they lie.

If someone teaches you some beautiful doctrine which excludes sex, then tell them that they lie.

Woe to you sodomites, homosexuals, enemies of the opposite sex. For you... there will be only weeping and the gnashing of teeth.

Woe to those who call themselves Christians and who carry the cross hanging over their chest, yet they abhor Maithuna, sex yoga. For these hypocritical Pharisees, there will be only weeping and desperation.

Woe! Woe! Woe!

Final Salutations

Beloved Gnostic brothers and sisters,
I wish you a merry Christmas and a prosperous new year.
May the star of Bethlehem shine upon your way.

Practice these runes in order; you should start your runic exercises the 21st of March [read Chapter 3]. Dedicate the time that you wish to each rune.

Beloved reader, I beseech you, if you write, do not mail me adulations, praises, or compliments. Remember that all of those who betrayed us in the past were really tremendous adulators.

I want all of you to radically resolve to die in all of the levels of the mind.

Really, the way you are now, with that tremendous "I" very alive inside, you are only a failure.

Many complain that they cannot travel at will in the Astral Body. Let these people awaken their consciousness. Astral travel stops being a problem when one awakens consciousness. The sleepy ones are good for nothing.

In this 1968-1969 Christmas Message, I have delivered to you the whole science that you need in order to attain the awakening of the consciousness.

Do not commit the error of reading this book as when someone is reading the newspaper. You must profoundly study it for many years; thus you will live it, and will select it in the practical way.

I advise patience and serenity to those who complain because they do not achieve illumination.

Illumination comes to us when we dissolve the pluralized "I," when we truly have died in all the forty-nine regions of the subconsciousness.

Those who covet occult powers, those who utilize Maithuna as a pretext in order to seduce women (or men), will enter into the submerged devolution in the infernal worlds.

Work with the three factors of the revolution of the consciousness in an orderly and perfect way.

Do not commit the error of committing adultery and fornication.

You must abandon fluttering. Those who live fluttering around like butterflies from flower to flower — that is to say, from school to school — are really candidates for the abyss and the Second Death.

You must abandon all self-justification and self-consideration. You must convert yourselves into enemies of your own selves if truly what you want is to radically die. Thus, only in this way, will you attain illumination.

Beloved ones, start from zero. You must abandon mystical pride, mythomania, that tendency of considering yourselves super-transcended. All of you are nothing but poor intellectual animals who are sentenced to the penalty of living.

Thus, only in this way, by doing an inventory of yourselves, can you know what you really are.

Truly, you only possess the lunar bodies and the animal ego, that is all. Then, why do you fall into mythomania? Your soul, your Essence, is bottled up, asleep within the "I." Then, on what is your mystical pride based?

Be humble so you can reach wisdom, and after you reach wisdom, be even more humble.

"If any man will come after me, let him deny himself, and take up his cross, and follow me." — Matthew 16:24

Inverential Peace,
Samael Aun Weor

Glossary

Absolute: Abstract space; that which is without attributes or limitations. The Absolute has three aspects: the Ain, the Ain Soph, and the Ain Soph Aur. "The Absolute is the Being of all Beings. The Absolute is that which Is, which always has Been, and which always will Be. The Absolute is expressed as Absolute Abstract Movement and Repose. The Absolute is the cause of Spirit and of Matter, but It is neither Spirit nor Matter. The Absolute is beyond the mind; the mind cannot understand It. Therefore, we have to intuitively understand Its nature." - Samael Aun Weor, *Tarot and Kabbalah*

"In the Absolute we go beyond karma and the gods, beyond the law. The mind and the individual consciousness are only good for mortifying our lives. In the Absolute we do not have an individual mind or individual consciousness; there, we are the unconditioned, free and absolutely happy Being. The Absolute is life free in its movement, without conditions, limitless, without the mortifying fear of the law, life beyond spirit and matter, beyond karma and suffering, beyond thought, word and action, beyond silence and sound, beyond forms." - Samael Aun Weor, *The Major Mysteries*

Akashic Records: Permanent impressions held in nature of everything that has ever occurred, i.e. "the memory of nature." By means of awakening consciousness, it is possible to access past, present, and future events within these records.

"The Akasha is a subtle agent that penetrates and permeates the whole space. All the events of the Earth and its races, the life of Jesus etc., are depicted as an eternal and living film within the Akasha. [...] We already know that all movement is relative and that there is only one constant. This one is the velocity of light. Light travels at a certain constant velocity. With their lenses astronomers perceive stars that have already ceased to exist. What they see and even photograph of these stars is the memory, the Akasha. Many of these stars are so distant, that the light coming from them could have begun its journey before the formation of the world. This slowness of light, this constant, may in reality make the invention of certain special instruments with which the past can be seen possible. None of this is impossible. Thus, with a very special telescope, with a very special radio-television apparatus, it is possible to capture sounds and light, events and happenings that have occurred on our Earth since the formation of the world. [...] The devotee will be able to study the Akashic Records of Nature with the Astral Body and know all past, present and future events." - Samael Aun Weor, *The Perfect Matrimony*

Alaya: (Sanskrit, a, "not"; laya, from the verb-root li, "to dissolve"; hence Alaya means "the indissoluble." Also alaya-vijnana. In Tibetan: kunshi namshe) In the Mahayana Yogachara school, the ground consciousness or storehouse consciousness, the base consciousness of everything that exists, from which everything arises. It is said to contain the seeds or germs of experience. Alaya is a synonym of Ain Soph.

"Immense is the ineffable joy of those Diamond Souls who became lost within the great Alaya of the universe. [...] Alaya is the Anima Mundi of Plato, the Over-Soul of Emerson, submitted to incessant periodical changes. Alaya is in itself eternal and immutable; however, it suffers tremendous changes during the Mahamanvantaric manifestation. The Yogacharyas from the Mahayana school state that Alaya is the personification of the Illuminating Void. It is unquestionable that Alaya is the living foundation of the seven cosmos... [...] Alaya, even being eternal and immutable in its essence, reflects itself within every object of the universe, just as the moon does in the clear and tranquil water. [...] The cosmic consciousness, the great Alaya of the universe, must awaken within each human being. Nevertheless, we make emphasis of the necessity of not confusing the consciousness with the Absolute." - Samael Aun Weor, *Cosmic Teachings of a Lama*

Alchemy: Al (as a connotation of the Arabic word Allah: al-, the + ilah, God) means "The God." Also Al (Hebrew) for "highest" or El "God." Chem or Khem is from kimia which means "to fuse or cast a metal." Also from Khem, the ancient name of Egypt. The synthesis is Al-Kimia: "to fuse with the highest" or "to fuse with God." Alchemy is one of the oldest sciences in the world, and is the method to transmute our inner impurity into purity. It is also known in the East as Tantra.

Astral: This term is derived from pertaining to or proceeding from the stars, but in the esoteric knowledge it refers to the emotional aspect of the fifth dimension, which in Hebrew is called Hod. Related terms are below.

Astral Body: The body utilized by the consciousness in the fifth dimension or world of dreams. What is commonly called the Astral Body is not the true Astral Body, it is rather the Lunar Protoplasmatic Body, also known as the Kama Rupa (Sanskrit, "body of desires") or "dream body" (Tibetan rmi-lam-gyi lus). The true Astral Body is Solar (being superior to Lunar Nature) and must be created, as the Master Jesus indicated in the Gospel of John 3:5-6, "Except a man be born of water and of the Spirit, he cannot enter into the kingdom of God. That which is born of the flesh is flesh; and that which is born of the Spirit is spirit." The Solar Astral Body is created as a result of the Third Initiation of Major Mysteries (Serpents of Fire), and is perfected in the Third Serpent of Light. In Tibetan Buddhism, the Solar Astral Body is known as the illusory body (sgyu-lus). This body is related to the emotional center and to the sephirah Hod.

"Really, only those who have worked with the Maithuna (White Tantra) for many years can possess the Astral Body." - Samael Aun Weor, *The Elimination of Satan's Tail*

Baetylus: (Greek βαίτυλος; pl. baetyli) Also Bethel or Betyl. Any sacred stone that fell from heaven and contained the power of life, and thereafter used for worship and ritual. Every religion utilizes sacred stones in various forms, which have symbolic value, representing the Philosophical Stone: mercury.

Being: Our inner, divine Source, also called the Innermost or Monad, which is not easily definable in conceptual terms. The use of the term "Being" is important though, in relation to its roots:

From the Online Etymology Dictionary: "O.E. beon, beom, bion "be, exist, come to be, become," from P.Gmc. *beo-, *beu-. This "b-root" is from PIE base *bheu-, *bhu- "grow, come into being, become," and in addition to the words in English it yielded German present first and second person sing. (bin, bist, from O.H.G. bim "I am," bist "thou art"), L. perf. tenses of esse (fui "I was," etc.), O.C.S. byti "be," Gk. phu- "become," O.Ir. bi'u "I am," Lith. bu'ti "to be," Rus. byt' "to be," etc. It also is behind Skt. bhavah "becoming," bhavati "becomes, happens," bhumih "earth, world."

Black Lodge: An organization or intelligence that seeks to pull souls into attachment to desire-sensation and the awakening of the consciousness (negatively) that is trapped within desire (lust, anger, pride, envy, etc.).

"From the dawn of life, a great battle has raged between the powers of Light and the powers of Darkness. The secret root of that battle lies in sex. Gods and Demons live in eternal struggle. The Gods defend the doctrine of chastity. The Demons hate chastity. In sex is found the root of the conflict between Gods and Demons... There are Masters of the Great White Lodge. There are Masters of the Great Black Lodge. There are disciples of the Great White Lodge. There are disciples of the Great Black Lodge. The disciples of the Great White Lodge know how to move consciously and positively in the Astral Body. The disciples of the Great Black Lodge also know how to travel in the Astral Body... The White Magician worships the inner Christ. The Black Magician worships Satan. This is the I, the me, myself, the reincarnating ego. In fact, the I is the specter of the threshold itself. It continually reincarnates to satisfy desires. The I is memory. In the I are all the memories of our ancient personalities. The I is Ahriman, Lucifer, Satan." - Samael Aun Weor, *The Perfect Matrimony*

"Understand that every association of fornicators forms a black lodge, and each lodge or school of this kind has its boss or manager who they venerate as a saint or master." - Samael Aun Weor, *The Major Mysteries*

Black Magic: Magic comes from "mag," priest. Black magic is the science of the impure priesthood, or those who awaken the consciousness within the ego (pride, anger, lust, etc).

"Black Magic appeals to the mass mind. It appeals to the principles of our civilization. It offers something for nothing. As long as there is cupidity in the human heart, it will remain as a menace to the honesty and integrity of our race." - Manly P. Hall, from *Magic: a Treatise on Esoteric Ethics*

"The black magicians have their mysticism, and they always firmly believe that they walk on the good path. No black magician believes that he walks on the evil path. The path of black magic is a broad way filled with vices and pleasures." - Samael Aun Weor, *The Revolution of Beelzebub*

"Multitudes of schools of black magic exist, many of them with very venerable traditions that teach Sexual Magic with the spilling of semen. They have very beautiful theories that attract and captivate, and if the student falls in that seductive and delicious deceit, he becomes a black magician. Those black schools affirm to the four winds that they are white and that is why ignorant ones fall. Moreover, those schools talk of beauty, love, charity, wisdom, etc., etc. Naturally, in those circumstances the ignorant disciple attains the belief with firmness that such institutions are not evil and perverse. Remember good disciple, that the Abyss is full of sincerely mistaken ones and people of very good intentions..." - Samael Aun Weor, *Tarot and Kabbalah*

"Evilness is so fine in the world of the mind... Evilness is so delicate and subtle in the plane of cosmic understanding that in reality a lot of intuition is needed in order not to be cheated by the demons of the Mental World." - Samael Aun Weor, *Treatise of Sexual Alchemy*

"The intellect as the negative function of the mind is demoniacal. Everyone that enters into these studies, the first thing that they want is to dominate the mind of others. This is pure and legitimate black magic. No one has the right to violate the free will of others. No one has the right to exercise coaction upon the mind of others because this is black magic. The ones that are guilty of this grave error are all of those mistaken authors that are everywhere. All of those books of hypnotism, magnetism and suggestion are books of black magic. Whosoever does not know how to respect the free will of others is a black magician; those who perform mental works in order to violently dominate the mind of others convert themselves into perverse demons. These people separate themselves from the Innermost and they crumble into the Abyss." - Samael Aun Weor, *Tarot and Kabbalah*

"Black magic is not a fundamental art; it is the misuse of an art. Therefore it has no symbols of its own." - Manly P. Hall

Böns: The oldest religion in Tibet. It was largely overshadowed (some say persecuted) by the arrival of Buddhism. Samael Aun Weor had accepted the statements of earlier investigators which described the Bön religion as essentially black; but upon further investigation he discovered that they are not necessarily black, just extreme in some practices.

Buddhata: Derived from "buddhadatu or buddhadhatu" (Sanskrit), which means "essence of the Buddha," (from dhatu, "element, primary element, cause, mineral"). The term buddhadhatu appeared in Mahayana scripture as a reference to tathagatagarbha, the "embryo of the Buddha," also called Buddha Nature. In general use, this describes that element in us that has the potential to become a Buddha, an "awakened one."

Chakra: (Sanskrit) Literally, "wheel." The chakras are subtle centers of energetic transformation. There are hundreds of chakras in our hidden physiology, but seven primary ones related to the awakening of consciousness.

"The Chakras are centres of Shakti as vital force... The Chakras are not perceptible to the gross senses. Even if they were perceptible in the living body which they help to organise, they disappear with the disintegration of organism at death." - Swami Sivananda, *Kundalini Yoga*

"The chakras are points of connection through which the divine energy circulates from one to another vehicle of the human being." - Samael Aun Weor, *Aztec Christic Magic*

Chastity: Although modern usage has rendered the term chastity virtually meaningless to most people, its original meaning and usage clearly indicate "moral purity" upon the basis of "sexual purity." Contemporary usage implies "repression" or "abstinence," which have nothing to do with real chastity. True chastity is a rejection of impure sexuality. True chastity is pure sexuality, or the activity of sex in harmony with our true nature, as explained in the secret doctrine. Properly used, the word chastity refers to sexual fidelity or honor.

"The generative energy, which, when we are loose, dissipates and makes us unclean, when we are continent invigorates and inspires us. Chastity is the flowering of man; and what are called Genius, Heroism, Holiness, and the like, are but various fruits which succeed it." - Henry David Thoreau, *Walden*

Christ: Derived from the Greek Christos, "the Anointed One," and Krestos, whose esoteric meaning is "fire." The word Christ is a title, not a personal name.

"Indeed, Christ is a Sephirothic Crown (Kether, Chokmah and Binah) of incommensurable wisdom, whose purest atoms shine within Chokmah, the world of the Ophanim. Christ is not the Monad, Christ is not the Theosophical Septenary; Christ is not the Jivan-Atman. Christ is the Central Sun. Christ is the ray that unites us to the Absolute." - Samael Aun Weor, *Tarot and Kabbalah*

Church: (Greek ἐκκλησία ekklēsia, "place of assembly" especially in a religious sense. From a compound of ἐκ and a derivative of καλέω, thus meaning "to call forth.") 1. Traditionally, a place of worship. 2. Physiologically, energetic centers that allow energy from the superior worlds to connect to the physical world. The churches are only activated in those who have awakened them through raising the fire of the Holy Spirit (pentecost, Kundalini) upon the spinal column (the rod of Aaron). The conditions to awaken them are described in the book of Revelation.

"The seven most important glands of the human organism constitute the seven laboratories controlled by the Law of the Triangle. Each of these glands has an exponent in a chakra of the organism. Each one of the seven chakras is found located in intimate correlation with the seven churches of the spinal medulla. The seven churches of the dorsal spine control the seven chakras of the Grand Sympathetic Nervous System. The seven churches become intensely active with the ascent of the Kundalini along the medullar canal. The Kundalini dwells in the electrons. The Sages meditate on it; devotees adore it, and in homes where the Perfect Matrimony reigns, it is worked with practically." - Samael Aun Weor, *The Perfect Matrimony*

"The seven churches are within the Microcosmos and within the Macro-cosmos. The seven churches of the spinal medulla are united to the seven chakras or plexus of the Grand Sympathetic Nervous System by means of very fine nerves. The seven churches are similar to lotus flowers which are suspended from the famous Nadi Chitra. The canal of Shushumna is within the medullar canal. The canal of Nadi Chitra is within this canal of Shushumna. The seven beautiful and divine churches are suspended from this precious medullar canal." - Samael Aun Weor, *The Aquarian Message*

Consciousness: "Wherever there is life, there exists the consciousness. Con-sciousness is inherent to life as humidity is inherent to water." - Samael Aun Weor, *Fundamental Notions of Endocrinology and Criminology*

From various dictionaries: 1. The state of being conscious; knowledge of one's own existence, condition, sensations, mental operations, acts, etc. 2. Immediate knowledge or perception of the presence of any object, state, or sensation. 3. An alert cognitive state in which you are aware of yourself and your situation. In universal Gnosticism, the range of potential conscious-ness is allegorized in the Ladder of Jacob, upon which the angels ascend and descend. Thus there are higher and lower levels of consciousness, from the level of demons at the bottom, to highly realized angels in the heights.

"It is vital to understand and develop the conviction that consciousness has the potential to increase to an infinite degree." - The 14th Dalai Lama

"Light and consciousness are two phenomena of the same thing; to a lesser degree of consciousness, corresponds a lesser degree of light; to a greater degree of consciousness, a greater degree of light." - Samael Aun Weor, *The Esoteric Treatise of Hermetic Astrology*

Devolution: (Latin) From devolvere: backwards evolution, degeneration. The natural mechanical inclination for all matter and energy in nature to return towards their state of inert uniformity. Related to the Arcanum Ten: Retribution, the Wheel of Samsara. Devolution is the inverse process of evolution. As evolution is the complication of matter or energy, devolu-tion is the slow process of nature to simplify matter or energy by applying forces to it.

Through devolution protoplasmic matter and energy descend, degrade and increase in density within the infradimensions of nature to finally reach the center of the earth where these attain their ultimate state of inert uniformity.

Devolution transfers the psyche, moral values, consciousness, or psycho-logical responsibilities to inferior degradable organisms (Klipoth) through the surrendering of our psychological values to animal behaviors, espe-cially sexual degeneration.

Divine Mother: "Among the Aztecs, she was known as Tonantzin, among the Greeks as chaste Diana. In Egypt she was Isis, the Divine Mother, whose veil no mortal has lifted. There is no doubt at all that esoteric Christianity has never forsaken the worship of the Divine Mother Kundalini. Obviously she is Marah, or better said, RAM-IO, MARY. What orthodox religions did not specify, at least with regard to the exoteric or public circle, is the aspect of Isis in her individual human form. Clearly, it was taught only in secret to the Initiates that this Divine Mother exists individually within each human being. It cannot be emphasized enough that Mother-God, Rhea, Cybele, Adonia, or whatever we wish to call her, is a variant of our own individual Being in the here and now. Stated explicitly, each of us has our own particular, individual Divine Mother." - Samael Aun Weor, *The Great Rebellion*

"Devi Kundalini, the Consecrated Queen of Shiva, our personal Divine Cosmic Individual Mother, assumes five transcendental mystic aspects in every creature, which we must enumerate:

1. The unmanifested Prakriti

2. The chaste Diana, Isis, Tonantzin, Maria or better said Ram-Io

3. The terrible Hecate, Persephone, Coatlicue, queen of the infemos and death; terror of love and law

4. The special individual Mother Nature, creator and architect of our physical organism

5. The Elemental Enchantress to whom we owe every vital impulse, every instinct." - Samael Aun Weor, *The Mystery of the Golden Blossom*

Drukpa: (Also known variously as Druk-pa, Dugpa, Brugpa, Dag dugpa or Dad dugpa) The term Drukpa comes from from Dzongkha and Tibetan 'brug yul, which means "country of Bhutan," and is composed of Druk, "dragon," and pa, "person." In Asia, the word refers to the people of Bhutan, a country between India and Tibet.

Drukpa can also refer to a large sect of Buddhism which broke from the Kagyug-pa "the Ones of the Oral Tradition." They considered themselves as the heirs of the indian Gurus: their teaching, which goes back to Vajradhara, was conveyed through Dakini, from Naropa to Marpa and then to the ascetic and mystic poet Milarepa. Later on, Milarepa's disciples founded new monasteries, and new threads appeared, among which are the Karmapa and the Drukpa. All those schools form the Kagyug-pa order, in spite of episodic internal quarrels and extreme differences in practice. The Drukpa sect is recognized by their ceremonial large red hats, but it should be known that they are not the only "Red Hat" group (the Nyingmas, founded by Padmasambhava, also use red hats). The Drukpas have established a particular worship of the Dorje (Vajra, or thunderbolt, a symbol of the phallus).

Samael Aun Weor wrote repeatedly in many books that the "Drukpas" practice and teach Black Tantra, by means of the expelling of the sexual energy. If we analyze the word, it is clear that he is referring to "Black Dragons," or people who practice Black Tantra. He was not referring to all the people of Bhutan, or all members of the Buddhist Drukpa sect. Such a broad condemnation would be as ridiculous as the one made by all those who condemn all Jews for the crucifixion of Jesus.

"In 1387, with just reason, the Tibetan reformer Tsong Khapa cast into flames every book of necromancy that he found. As a result, some discontent Lamas formed an alliance with the aboriginal Bons, and today they form a powerful sect of black magic in the regions of Sikkim, Bhutan, and Nepal, submitting themselves to the most abominable black rites." - Samael Aun Weor, *The Revolution of Beelzebub*

Ego: The multiplicity of contradictory psychological elements that we have inside are in their sum the "ego." Each one is also called "an ego" or an "I." Every ego is a psychological defect which produces suffering. The ego is three (related to our Three Brains or three centers of psychological processing), seven (capital sins), and legion (in their infinite variations).

"The ego is the root of ignorance and pain." - Samael Aun Weor, *The Esoteric Treatise of Hermetic Astrology*

"The Being and the ego are incompatible. The Being and the ego are like water and oil. They can never be mixed... The annihilation of the psychic aggregates (egos) can be made possible only by radically comprehending our errors through meditation and by the evident Self-reflection of the Being." - Samael Aun Weor, *The Gnostic Bible: The Pistis Sophia Unveiled*

Elohim: [אלהים] An Hebrew term with a wide variety of meanings. In Christian translations of scripture, it is one of many words translated to the generic word "God," but whose actual meaning depends upon the context. For example:

1. In Kabbalah, אלהים is a name of God the relates to many levels of the Tree of Life. In the world of Atziluth, the word is related to divnities of the sephiroth Binah (Jehovah Elohim, mentioned especially in Genesis), Geburah, and Hod. In the world of Briah, it is related beings of Netzach and Hod.

2. El [אל] is "god," Eloah [אלה] is "goddess," therefore the plural Elohim refers to "gods and goddesses," and is commonly used to refer to Cosmo-creators or Dhyan-Choans.

3. אלה Elah or Eloah is "goddess." Yam [ים] is "sea" or "ocean." Therefore אלהים Elohim can be אלה-ים "the sea goddess" [i.e. Aphrodite, Stella Maris, etc.]

There are many more meanings of "Elohim." In general, Elohim refers to high aspects of divinity.

"Each one of us has his own interior Elohim. The interior Elohim is the Being of our Being. The interior Elohim is our Father-Mother. The interior Elohim is the ray that emanates from Aelohim." - Samael Aun Weor, *The Gnostic Bible: The Pistis Sophia Unveiled*

Evolution: "It is not possible for the true human being (the Self-realized Being) to appear through the mechanics of evolution. We know very well that evolution and its twin sister devolution are nothing else but two laws which constitute the mechanical axis of all Nature. One evolves to a certain perfectly defined point, and then the devolving process follows. Every ascent is followed by a descent and vice-versa." - Samael Aun Weor, *Treatise of Revolutionary Psychology*. "Evolution is a process of complication of energy." - Samael Aun Weor, *The Perfect Matrimony*

Eye of Dangma: Dangma is a Sanskrit term for "a purified soul," thus the Eye of Dangma is a reference to the spiritual sight of the elevated initiate. It is polyvoyance, the capacity to perceive all the dimensions of nature, and is rooted in the pineal gland. From Blavatsky's *The Secret Doctrine:* "In India it is called "The Eye of Siva," but beyond the great range it is known as "Dangma"s opened eye" in esoteric phraseology. Dangma means "a purified soul," one who has become a Jivanmukta, the highest adept, or rather a Mahatma. His "opened eye" is the inner spiritual eye of the seer, and the faculty which manifests through it is not clairvoyance as ordinarily understood, i.e., the power of seeing at a distance, but rather the faculty of spiritual intuition, through which direct and certain knowledge is obtainable. This faculty is intimately connected with the "third eye," which mythological tradition ascribes to certain races of men."

Fohat: (Theosophical/Tibetan) A term used by H.P. Blavatsky to represent the active (male) potency of the Shakti (female sexual power) in nature, the essence of cosmic electricity, vital force. As explained in *The Secret Doctrine*, "He (Fohat) is, metaphysically, the objectivised thought of the gods; the "Word made flesh" on a lower scale, and the messenger of Cosmic and human ideations: the active force in Universal Life.... In India, Fohat is connected with Vishnu and Surya in the early character of the (first) God; for Vishnu is not a high god in the Rig Veda. The name Vishnu is from the root vish, "to pervade," and Fohat is called the "Pervader" and the Manufacturer, because he shapes the atoms from crude material..." The term fohat has recently been linked with the Tibetan verb phro-wa and the noun spros-pa. These two terms are listed in Jäschke"s Tibetan-English Dictionary (1881) as, for phro-wa, "to proceed, issue, emanate from, to spread, in most cases from rays of light..." while for spros-pa he gives "business, employment, activity."

Fornication: Originally, the term fornication was derived from the Indo-European word gwher, whose meanings relate to heat and burning (the full explanation can be found online at http://sacred-sex.org/terminology/fornication). Fornication means to make the heat (solar fire) of the seed (sexual power) leave the body through voluntary orgasm. Any voluntary orgasm is fornication, whether between a married man and woman, or an unmarried man and woman, or through masturbation, or in any other case; this is explained by Moses: "A man from whom there is a discharge of semen, shall immerse all his flesh in water, and he shall remain unclean until evening. And any garment or any leather [object] which has semen on it, shall be immersed in water, and shall remain unclean until evening. A woman with whom a man cohabits, whereby there was [a discharge of] semen, they shall immerse in water, and they shall remain unclean until evening." - Leviticus 15:16-18

To fornicate is to spill the sexual energy through the orgasm. Those who "deny themselves" restrain the sexual energy, and "walk in the midst of the fire" without being burned. Those who restrain the sexual energy, who renounce the orgasm, remember God in themselves, and do not defile themselves with animal passion, "for the temple of God is holy, which temple ye are."

"Whosoever is born of God doth not commit sin; for his seed remaineth in him: and he cannot sin, because he is born of God." - 1 John 3:9

This is why neophytes always took a vow of sexual abstention, so that they could prepare themselves for marriage, in which they would have sexual relations but not release the sexual energy through the orgasm. This is why Paul advised:

"...they that have wives be as though they had none..." - I Corinthians 7:29

"A fornicator is an individual who has intensely accustomed his genital organs to copulate (with orgasm). Yet, if the same individual changes his custom of copulation to the custom of no copulation, then he transforms himself into a chaste person. We have as an example the astonishing case of Mary Magdalene, who was a famous prostitute. Mary Magdalene became the famous Saint Mary Magdalene, the repented prostitute. Mary Magdalene became the chaste disciple of Christ." - Samael Aun Weor, *The Revolution of Beelzebub*

Gnosis: (Greek) Knowledge.

1. The word Gnosis refers to the knowledge we acquire through our own experience, as opposed to knowledge that we are told or believe in. Gnosis - by whatever name in history or culture - is conscious, experiential knowledge, not merely intellectual or conceptual knowledge, belief, or theory. This term is synonymous with the Hebrew "daath" and the Sanskrit "jna."

2. The tradition that embodies the core wisdom or knowledge of humanity.

"Gnosis is the flame from which all religions sprouted, because in its depth Gnosis is religion. The word "religion" comes from the Latin word "religare," which implies "to link the Soul to God"; so Gnosis is the very pure flame from where all religions sprout, because Gnosis is knowledge, Gnosis is wisdom." - Samael Aun Weor from the lecture entitled The Esoteric Path

"The secret science of the Sufis and of the Whirling Dervishes is within Gnosis. The secret doctrine of Buddhism and of Taoism is within Gnosis. The sacred magic of the Nordics is within Gnosis. The wisdom of Hermes, Buddha, Confucius, Mohammed and Quetzalcoatl, etc., etc., is within Gnosis. Gnosis is the doctrine of Christ." - Samael Aun Weor, *The Revolution of Beelzebub*

Gnostic Church: (Greek) From γνῶσις, knowledge, and ἐκκλησία, assembly. Thus, strictly defined, the Gnostic Church is a body or gathering of knowledge. The Gnostic Church is the repository of the greatest knowledge in the universe. The Gnostic Church is comprised of all the perfect beings in existence, who are called gods, angels, buddhas, masters, etc. The Gnostic Church is not a physical entity, but exists in the internal worlds in the superior dimensions. The Gnostic Church utilizes whatever means are appropriate in the physical world in order to aid the elevation of humanity out of suffering. Throughout time, we have known that aid through the various religions, philosophies, teachers, etc. For a complete explanation of the Gnostic Church, study the online course The Sacraments of the Gnostic Church.

"In this course, we are going to explain the sacraments instituted since ancient times in the church of Christ, which has its latest roots in Egypt. Internally, the Holy Gnostic Church is situated in the superior dimensions. Yet, in this day and age, the Holy Gnostic Church has in the physical world a physical exponent in every Lumisial of our visible and invisible Gnostic organisations that form the gigantic Gnostic Movement. The Gnostic Church was instituted by the Master Jesus two thousand years ago in the Middle East, but is a church that has a history much longer than that. It is related with the mysteries of ancient Egypt that has its roots in Atlantis, which come from a Neptunian-Amentian epoch directly related with the World of Yesod, the fourth dimension and beyond. As you know, Gnosis comes from a Greek word for knowledge, and this doctrine of knowledge is related with the famous tree of knowledge of the book of Genesis..." - The Sacraments of the Gnostic Church

Hasnamuss: A term used by Gurdjieff in reference to a person with a divided consciousness: part of it is free and natural, and part is trapped in the ego. In synthesis, everyone who has ego is a Hasnamuss. Although there are many variations and kinds of Hasnamuss, there are generally describes four primary grades:

mortal: the common person

those with the Solar Astral body

those with the Solar Bodies created

fallen Angels

These are described in detail by Samael Aun Weor in his lecture "The Master Key."

"The Twice-born who does not reduce his Lunar Ego to cosmic dust converts himself into an abortion of the Cosmic Mother. He becomes a Marut, and there exist thousands of types of Maruts. Certain oriental sects and some Muslim tribes commit the lamentable error of rendering cult to all of those families of Maruts. Every Marut, every Hasnamuss has in fact two personalities: one White and another Black (one Solar and another Lunar). The Innermost, the Being dressed with the Solar Electronic Bodies, is the White Personality of the Hasnamuss, and the pluralized "I" dressed with the Protoplasmic Lunar Bodies is the Hasnamuss' Black Personality. Therefore, these Maruts have a double center of gravity." - Samael Aun Weor

Gurdjieff described these qualities of the Hasnamuss:

Every kind of depravity, conscious as well as unconscious
The feeling of self-satisfaction from leading others astray
The irresistible inclination to destroy the existence of other breathing creatures
The urge to become free from the necessity of actualizing the being-efforts demanded by Nature
The attempt by every kind of artificiality to conceal from others what in their opinion are one's physical defects
The calm self-contentment in the use of what is not personally deserved
The striving to be not what one is.

Although the origin of this term is uncertain and has interesting meanings when analyzed in Arabic, Hebrew, etc., in Sanskrit we find Hasnamuss can be derived from Ha: a Sanskrit particle expressing sorrow, dejection, pain; asna: voracious, eating, consuming; or, a stone; mus: mouse, thief

Herakles: Also Heracles or Hercules (Greek Ἡρακλῆς) from Hera, "protectress," (that has an intimate etymological relation with Eros - Love - the Son of the Divine Mother Aphrodite), related to heros "hero," originally "defender, protector." And kleos "glory or aura." Therefore Herakles means "the aura or glory of Hera" or the "aura or glory of Eros." The Greek symbol of the Christ.

Holy Spirit: The Christian name for the third aspect of the Holy Trinity, or "God." This force has other names in other religions. In Kabbalah, the third sephirah, Binah. In Buddhism, it is related to Nirmanakaya, the "body of formation" through which the inner Buddha works in the world.

"The Holy Spirit is the Fire of Pentecost or the fire of the Holy Spirit called Kundalini by the Hindus, the igneous serpent of our magical powers, Holy Fire symbolized by Gold..." - Samael Aun Weor, *The Perfect Matrimony*

"It has been said in The Divine Comedy with complete clarity that the Holy Spirit is the husband of the Divine Mother. Therefore, the Holy Spirit unfolds himself into his wife, into the Shakti of the Hindus. This must be known and understood. Some, when they see that the Third Logos is unfolded into the Divine Mother Kundalini, or Shakti, She that has many names, have believed that the Holy Spirit is feminine, and they have been mistaken. The Holy Spirit is masculine, but when He unfolds Himself into She, then the first ineffable Divine Couple is formed, the Creator Elohim, the Kabir, or Great Priest, the Ruach Elohim, that in accordance to Moses, cultivated the waters in the beginning of the world." - Samael Aun Weor, *Tarot and Kabbalah*

"The Primitive Gnostic Christians worshipped the lamb, the fish and the white dove as symbols of the Holy Spirit." - Samael Aun Weor, *The Perfect Matrimony* Innermost: "Our real Being is of a universal nature. Our real Being is neither a kind of superior nor inferior "I." Our real Being is impersonal, universal, divine. He transcends every concept of "I," me, myself, ego, etc., etc." - Samael Aun Weor, *The Perfect Matrimony*

Also known as Atman, the Spirit, Chesed, our own individual interior divine Father.

"The Innermost is the ardent flame of Horeb. In accordance with Moses, the Innermost is the Ruach Elohim (the Spirit of God) who sowed the waters in the beginning of the world. He is the Sun King, our Divine Monad, the Alter-Ego of Cicerone." - Samael Aun Weor, *The Revolution of Beelzebub*

Hyperborean Root Race: The second Root Race of this terrestrial humanity. A nation mentioned in Greek mythology. The name means "beyond the North Wind," thus they are supposed to have been somewhere north of Greece, but the name also means "beyond the mountains" and "those who carry (merchandise) across." Apollo was said to spend the winter months among them, and his mother Leto was presumed to have been born in their land. Perseus went there searching for the Gorgon, and Heracles chased the Cerynitian hind to their country. The writer Pindar represented them as a blessed people untouched by human afflictions. H. P. Blavatsky places their country around the North Pole, saying it was "The Land of the Eternal Sun," beyond Boreas, the god of winter. She asserts that this land was of a near tropical climate. In universal Gnosticism, they are known to be the Second Root Race of this Terrestrial humanity.

"The second Root Race was governed by Quetzalcoatl; this was the Hyperborean humanity. The degenerated people of the second Root Race converted themselves into monkeys; these are the ancestors of present monkeys. They reproduced themselves by budding, such as the plants do: from their trunk sprout many branches. They were wiped out by strong hurricanes." - Samael Aun Weor, *The Kabbalah of the Mayan Mysteries*

Initiation: In white magic, the process whereby the Innermost (the Inner Father) receives recognition, empowerment and greater responsibilities in the Internal Worlds, and little by little approaches His goal: complete Self-realization, or in other words, the return into the Absolute. White initiation NEVER applies to the "I" or our terrestrial personality.

"There are Nine Initiations of Minor Mysteries and seven great Initiations of Major Mysteries. The Innermost is the one who receives all of these Initiations. The Testament of Wisdom says: "Before the dawning of the false aurora upon the earth, the ones who survived the hurricane and the tempest were praising the Innermost, and the heralds of the aurora appeared unto them." The psychological "I" does not receives Initiations. The human personality does not receive anything. Nonetheless, the "I" of some Initiates becomes filled with pride when saying 'I am a Master, I have such Initiations.' Thus, this is how the "I" believes itself to be an Initiate and keeps reincarnating in order to "perfect itself", but, the "I" never ever perfects itself. The "I" only reincarnates in order to satisfy desires. That is all." - Samael Aun Weor, *The Aquarian Message*

Innermost: "That part of the Reality (God) within man that the Yogi seeks to attune himself to before attaining cosmic consciousness." - M, *The Dayspring of Youth*

"Our real Being is of a universal nature. Our real Being is neither a kind of superior nor inferior "I." Our real Being is impersonal, universal, divine. He transcends every concept of "I," me, myself, ego, etc., etc." - Samael Aun Weor, *The Perfect Matrimony*

Also known as Atman, the Spirit, Chesed, our own individual interior divine Father.

"The Innermost is the ardent flame of Horeb. In accordance with Moses, the Innermost is the Ruach Elohim (the Spirit of God) who sowed the waters in the beginning of the world. He is the Sun King, our Divine Monad, the Alter-Ego of Cicerone." - Samael Aun Weor, *The Revolution of Beelzebub*

Intellectual Animal: When the Intelligent Principle, the Monad, sends its spark of consciousness into Nature, that spark, the anima, enters into manifestation as a simple mineral. Gradually, over millions of years, the anima gathers experience and evolves up the chain of life until it perfects itself in the level of the mineral kingdom. It then graduates into the plant kingdom, and subsequently into the animal kingdom. With each ascension the spark receives new capacities and higher grades of complexity. In the animal kingdom it learns procreation by ejaculation. When that animal intelligence enters into the human kingdom, it receives a new capacity: reasoning, the intellect; it is now an anima with intellect: an Intellectual Animal. That spark must then perfect itself in the human kingdom in order to become a complete and perfect human being, an entity that has conquered and transcended everything that belongs to the lower kingdoms. Unfortunately, very few intellectual animals perfect themselves; most remain enslaved by their animal nature, and thus are reabsorbed by Nature, a process belonging to the devolving side of life and called by all the great religions "Hell" or the Second Death.

"The present manlike being is not yet human; he is merely an intellectual animal. It is a very grave error to call the legion of the "I" the "soul." In fact, what the manlike being has is the psychic material, the material for the soul within his Essence, but indeed, he does not have a Soul yet." - Samael Aun Weor, *The Revolution of the Dialectic*

Kabbalah: (Hebrew קבלה) Alternatively spelled Cabala, Qabalah from the Hebrew קבל KBLH or QBL, "to receive." An ancient esoteric teaching hidden from the uninitiated, whose branches and many forms have reached throughout the world. The true Kabbalah is the science and language of the Superior Worlds and is thus objective, complete and without flaw; it is said that "All enlightened beings agree," and their natural agreement is a function of the awakened consciousness. The Kabbalah is the language of that consciousness, thus disagreement regarding its meaning and interpretation is always due to the subjective elements in the psyche.

"The objective of studying the Kabbalah is to be skilled for work in the Internal Worlds... One that does not comprehend remains confused in the Internal Worlds. Kabbalah is the basis in order to understand the language of these worlds." - Samael Aun Weor, *Tarot and Kabbalah*

"In Kabbalah we have to constantly look at the Hebrew letters." - Samael
Aun Weor, *Tarot and Kabbalah*

Kundabuffer: The negatively polarized sexual energy.

"The Lord sent against the people the fiery snakes, and they bit the people,
and many people of Israel died. The people came to Moses and said, "We
have sinned, for we have spoken against the Lord and against you. Pray to
the Lord that He remove the snakes from us." So Moses prayed on behalf
of the people." - Numbers 21:6

"It is necessary to know that the Kundabuffer Organ is the negative
development of the fire. This is the descending serpent, which precipitates
itself from the coccyx downwards, towards the atomic infernos of the human being. The Kundabuffer Organ is the horrifying tail of Satan, which
is shown in the "body of desires" of the Intellectual Animal, who in the
present times is falsely called man." - Samael Aun Weor, *The Elimination of
Satan's Tail*

"The diabolic type whose seduction is here, there and everywhere under
the pretext of working in the Ninth Sphere, who abandons his wife because
he thinks she will not be useful to him for the work in the fiery forge of
Vulcan, instead of awakening Kundalini, will awaken the abominable
Kundabuffer organ. A certain Initiate, whose name will not be mentioned
in this treatise, commits the error of attributing to the Kundalini all the
sinister qualities of the Kundabuffer organ... When the fire is cast downwards from the chakra of the coccyx, the tail of Satan appears; the abominable Kundabuffer organ. The hypnotic power of the organ of Witches'
Sabbath holds the human multitude asleep and depraved. Those who
commit the crime of practicing Black Tantra (Sexual Magic with seminal
ejaculation) clearly awaken and develop the organ of all fatalities. Those
who betray their guru or master, even if practicing White Tantra (without
seminal ejaculation), will obviously activate the organ of all evils. Such
sinister power opens the seven doorways of the lower abdomen (the seven
infernal chakras) and converts us into terribly perverse demons." - Samael
Aun Weor, *The Mystery of the Golden Blossom*

Kundalini: "Kundalini, the serpent power or mystic fire, is the primordial
energy or Sakti that lies dormant or sleeping in the Muladhara Chakra, the
centre of the body. It is called the serpentine or annular power on account
of serpentine form. It is an electric fiery occult power, the great pristine
force which underlies all organic and inorganic matter. Kundalini is the
cosmic power in individual bodies. It is not a material force like electricity,
magnetism, centripetal or centrifugal force. It is a spiritual potential Sakti
or cosmic power. In reality it has no form. [...] O Divine Mother Kundalini,
the Divine Cosmic Energy that is hidden in men! Thou art Kali, Durga,
Adisakti, Rajarajeswari, Tripurasundari, Maha-Lakshmi, Maha-Sarasvati!
Thou hast put on all these names and forms. Thou hast manifested as
Prana, electricity, force, magnetism, cohesion, gravitation in this universe.
This whole universe rests in Thy bosom. Crores of salutations unto thee.
O Mother of this world! Lead me on to open the Sushumna Nadi and

take Thee along the Chakras to Sahasrara Chakra and to merge myself in Thee and Thy consort, Lord Siva. Kundalini Yoga is that Yoga which treats of Kundalini Sakti, the six centres of spiritual energy (Shat Chakras), the arousing of the sleeping Kundalini Sakti and its union with Lord Siva in Sahasrara Chakra, at the crown of the head. This is an exact science. This is also known as Laya Yoga. The six centres are pierced (Chakra Bheda) by the passing of Kundalini Sakti to the top of the head. 'Kundala' means 'coiled'. Her form is like a coiled serpent. Hence the name Kundalini." - Swami Sivananda, *Kundalini Yoga*

"Kundalini is a compound word: Kunda reminds us of the abominable "Kundabuffer organ," and lini is an Atlantean term meaning termination. Kundalini means "the termination of the abominable Kundabuffer organ." In this case, it is imperative not to confuse Kundalini with Kundabuffer." - Samael Aun Weor, *The Great Rebellion*

These two forces, one positive and ascending, and one negative and descending, are symbolized in the Bible in the book of Numbers (the story of the Serpent of Brass). The Kundalini is "The power of life."- from the Theosophical Glossary. The Sexual Fire that is at the base of all life.

"The ascent of the Kundalini along the spinal cord is achieved very slowly in accordance with the merits of the heart. The fires of the heart control the miraculous development of the Sacred Serpent. Devi Kundalini is not something mechanical as many suppose; the igneous serpent is only awakened with genuine love between husband and wife, and it will never rise up along the medullar canal of adulterers." - Samael Aun Weor, *The Mystery of the Golden Blossom*

"The decisive factor in the progress, development and evolution of the Kundalini is ethics." - Samael Aun Weor, *The Revolution of Beelzebub*

"Until not too long ago, the majority of spiritualists believed that on awakening the Kundalini, the latter instantaneously rose to the head and the initiate was automatically united with his Innermost or Internal God, instantly, and converted into Mahatma. How comfortable! How comfortably all these theosophists, Rosicrucians and spiritualists, etc., imagined High Initiation." - Samael Aun Weor, *The Zodiacal Course*

"There are seven bodies of the Being. Each body has its "cerebrospinal" nervous system, its medulla and Kundalini. Each body is a complete organism. There are, therefore, seven bodies, seven medullae and seven Kundalinis. The ascension of each of the seven Kundalinis is slow and difficult. Each canyon or vertebra represents determined occult powers and this is why the conquest of each canyon undergoes terrible tests." - Samael Aun Weor, *The Zodiacal Course*

Lethe: (Greek) Λήθη, "forgetfulness, oblivion."

1. A symbolic "river" in the underworld, which the dead drink of in order to forget their past.

2. The spirit (daimona) of forgetfulness and oblivion, also associated with the underworld river Lethe.

"After having incinerated the seeds of the "Ego" through the purification of our corruption in Purgatory, the Initiate then bathes in the rivers Lethe [forgetfulness] and Eunoe. [...] The dissolution of the ego is necessary because the ego is nothing but an addition of tenebrous entities. We have arrived at the conclusion that every human being must dissolve the ego, burn the seeds of the ego, and be bathed in the waters of Lethe in order to be finished with the memories of the past. Then after the Confirmation in the Light, one is welcomed into the White Brotherhood; there one signs papers and is warned that one must be careful." - Samael Aun Weor, *Tarot and Kabbalah*

Logos: (Greek) means Verb or Word. In Greek and Hebrew metaphysics, the unifying principle of the world. The Logos is the manifested deity of every nation and people; the outward expression or the effect of the cause which is ever concealed. (Speech is the "logos" of thought). The Logos has three aspects, known universally as the Trinity or Trimurti. The First Logos is the Father, Brahma. The Second Logos is the Son, Vishnu. The Third Logos is the Holy Spirit, Shiva. One who incarnates the Logos becomes a Logos.

"The Logos is not an individual. The Logos is an army of ineffable beings." - Samael Aun Weor, *Fundamental Notions of Endocrinology and Criminology*

Mahamanvantara: (Sanskrit) "The Great Day." A period of universal activity, as opposed to a Mahapralaya, a cosmic night or period of rest.

"Truthfully, the quantities of years assigned to a cosmic day are symbolic. The cosmic night arrives when the ingathering of the perfect souls is complete, which means, when the cosmic day is absolutely perfected." - Samael Aun Weor, *The Gnostic Bible: The Pistis Sophia Unveiled*

"I was absorbed within the Absolute at the end of that Lunar Mahamanvantara, which endured 311,040,000,000,000 years, or, in other words, an age of Brahma." - Samael Aun Weor, *The Revolution of Beelzebub*

Maithuna: The Sanskrit word maithuna is used in Hindu Tantras (esoteric scriptures) to refer to the sacrament (sacred ritual) of sexual union between husband and wife. Maithuna or Mithuna has various appearances in scripture:

Mithuna: paired, forming a pair; copulation; the zodiacal sign of Gemini in Vedic Astrology, which is depicted as a man and woman in a sexual embrace

Mithunaya: to unite sexually

Mithuni: to become paired, couple or united sexually

By means of the original Tantric Maithuna, after being prepared psychologically and spiritually and initiated by a genuine teacher (guru), the couple learns how to utilize their love and spiritual aspiration in order to transform their natural sexual forces to purify the mind, eliminate psychological defects, and awaken the latent powers of the consciousness. The man represents Shiva, the masculine aspect of the creative divine, and the woman represents Shakti, the feminine aspect and the source of the power of creation. This method was kept in strictest secrecy for thousands of years in order to preserve it in its pure form, and to prevent crude-minded people from deviating the teaching, other people, or harming themselves. Nonetheless, some degenerated traditions (popularly called "left-hand" traditions, or black magic) interpret Maithuna or sacramental sexuality according to their state of degeneration, and use these sacred teachings to justify their lust, desire, orgies, and other types of deviations from pure, genuine Tantra.

Krishna: "And I am the strength of the strong, devoid of lust and attachment. O best of the Bharatas, I am sex not contrary to dharma." (Bhagavad Gita 7.11)

"The Tantric student must be endowed with purity, faith, devotion, dedication to Guru, dispassion, humility, courage, cosmic love, truthfulness, non-covetousness, and contentment. Absence of these qualities in the practitioner means a gross abuse of Shaktism. Sexual intercourse by a man with a woman who is not lawful to him is a sin. The Vaidika Dharma is very strict on this point. It forbids not merely actual Maithuna but Ashtanga or eightfold Maithuna namely Smaranam (thinking upon it), Kirtanam (talking of it), Keli (play with women), Prekshanam (making eyes at women), Guhya-bhashanam (talking in private with women), Sankalpa (wish or resolve for sexual union), Adhyavasaya (determination towards it), Kriyanishpatti (actual accomplishment of the sexual act). A Tantric can have copulation with his wife. He calls his wife his Shakti. Wife is a house-goddess Griha-lakshmi or Griha-devata united to her husband by the sacramental Samskara of marriage. She should not be regarded as an object of enjoyment. She is his partner in life (Ardhangini). The union of a man and his wife is a veritable sacred scriptural rite." - Swami Sivananda, *Tantra Yoga*

Mantra: (Sanskrit, literally "mind protection") A sacred word or sound. The use of sacred words and sounds is universal throughout all religions and mystical traditions, because the root of all creation is in the Great Breath or the Word, the Logos. "In the beginning was the Word..."

Maya: (Sanskrit, literally "not That," meaning appearance, illusion, deception) Can indicate 1) the illusory nature of existence, 2) the womb of the Divine Mother, or 3) the Divine Mother Herself.

Meditation: "When the esotericist submerges himself into meditation, what he seeks is information." - Samael Aun Weor

"It is urgent to know how to meditate in order to comprehend any psychic aggregate, or in other words, any psychological defect. It is indispensable to know how to work with all our heart and with all our soul, if we want the elimination to occur." - Samael Aun Weor, *The Gnostic Bible: The Pistis Sophia Unveiled*

"1. The Gnostic must first attain the ability to stop the course of his thoughts, the capacity to not think. Indeed, only the one who achieves that capacity will hear the Voice of the Silence.

"2. When the Gnostic disciple attains the capacity to not think, then he must learn to concentrate his thoughts on only one thing.

"3. The third step is correct meditation. This brings the first flashes of the new consciousness into the mind.

"4. The fourth step is contemplation, ecstasy or Samadhi. This is the state of Turiya (perfect clairvoyance). - Samael Aun Weor, *The Perfect Matrimony*

Mental Body: One of the seven bodies of the human being. Related to Netzach, the seventh sephirah of the Tree of Life; corresponds to the fifth dimension. In Egyptian mysticism, it is called Ba. In Hinduism, is it called vijnanmayakosha or kama manas (some Hindu teachers think the mental body is "manomayakosha," but that is the astral body).

"The mental body is a material organism, yet it is not the physical organism. The mental body has its ultra-biology and its internal pathology, which is completely unknown to the present men of science." - Samael Aun Weor, *The Revolution of Beelzebub*

Monad: From Latin monas, "unity; a unit" and Greek monas "unit," from monos "alone." The Monad is the Being, the Innermost, our own inner Spirit. In Kabbalah, the Monad is represented by the sephiroth Chesed, Geburah, and Tiphereth. In Sanskrit, this corresponds to Atman-Buddhi-Manas.

"We must distinguish between Monads and Souls. A Monad, in other words, a Spirit, is; a Soul is acquired. Distinguish between the Monad of a world and the Soul of a world; between the Monad of a human and the Soul of a human; between the Monad of an ant and the Soul of an ant. The human organism, in final synthesis, is constituted by billions and trillions of infinitesimal Monads. There are several types and orders of primary elements of all existence, of every organism, in the manner of germs of all the phenomena of nature; we can call the latter Monads, employing the term of Leibnitz, in the absence of a more descriptive term to indicate the simplicity of the simplest existence. An atom, as a vehicle of action, corresponds to each of these genii or Monads. The Monads attract each other, combine, transform themselves, giving form to every organism, world, micro-organism, etc. Hierarchies exist among the Monads; the Inferior Monads must obey the Superior ones that is the Law. Inferior Monads belong to the Superior ones. All the trillions of Monads that animate the human organism have to obey the owner, the chief, the Principal Monad. The regulating Monad, the Primordial Monad permits the activity of all of its subordinates inside the human organism, until the time indicated by the Law of Karma." - Samael Aun Weor, *The Esoteric Treatise of Hermetic Astrology*

"(The number) one is the Monad, the Unity, Iod-Heve or Jehovah, the Father who is in secret. It is the Divine Triad that is not incarnated within

a Master who has not killed the ego. He is Osiris, the same God, the Word."
- Samael Aun Weor, *Tarot and Kabbalah*

"When spoken of, the Monad is referred to as Osiris. He is the one that has to Self-realize Himself... Our own particular Monad needs us and we need it. Once, while speaking with my Monad, my Monad told me, 'I am self-realizing Thee; what I am doing, I am doing for Thee.' Otherwise, why are we living? The Monad wants to Self-realize and that is why we are here. This is our objective." - Samael Aun Weor, *Tarot and Kabbalah*

"The Monads or Vital Genii are not exclusive to the physical organism; within the atoms of the Internal Bodies there are found imprisoned many orders and categories of living Monads. The existence of any physical or suprasensible, Angelic or Diabolical, Solar or Lunar body, has billions and trillions of Monads as their foundation." - Samael Aun Weor, *The Esoteric Treatise of Hermetic Astrology*

Ninth Sphere: In Kabbalah, a reference to the sephirah Yesod of the Tree of Life (Kabbalah). When you place the Tree of Life over your body, you see that Yesod is related to your sexual organs.

"The Ninth Sphere of the Kabbalah is sex." - Samael Aun Weor, *The Perfect Matrimony*

The Ninth Sphere also refers to the sephirah Yesod and to the lowest sphere of the Klipoth.

"The great Master Hilarion IX said that in ancient times, to descend into the Ninth Sphere was the maximum ordeal for the supreme dignity of the Hierophant. Hermes, Buddha, Jesus Christ, Dante, Zoroaster, Mohammed, Rama, Krishna, Pythagoras, Plato and many others, had to descend into the Ninth Sphere in order to work with the fire and the water which is the origin of worlds, beasts, human beings and Gods. Every authentic white initiation begins here." - Samael Aun Weor, *The Aquarian Message*

Nirvana: (Sanskrit निर्वाण, "extinction" or "cessation"; Tibetan: nyangde, literally "the state beyond sorrow") In general use, the word nirvana refers to the permanent cessation of suffering and its causes, and therefore refers to a state of consciousness rather than a place. Yet, the term can also apply to heavenly realms, whose vibration is related to the cessation of suffering. In other words, if your mind-stream has liberated itself from the causes of suffering, it will naturally vibrate at the level of Nirvana (heaven).

"When the Soul fuses with the Inner Master, then it becomes free from Nature and enters into the supreme happiness of absolute existence. This state of happiness is called Nirvana. Nirvana can be attained through millions of births and deaths, but it can also be attained by means of a shorter path; this is the path of "initiation." The Initiate can reach Nirvana in one single life if he so wants it." - Samael Aun Weor, *The Zodiacal Course*

"Nirvana is a region of Nature where the ineffable happiness of the fire reigns. The Nirvanic plane has seven sub-planes. A resplendent hall exists in each one of these seven sub-planes of Nirvanic matter where the Nirmanakayas study their mysteries. This is why they call their sub-planes "halls" and not merely "sub-planes" as the Theosophists do. The Nirvanis say: "We are in the first hall of Nirvana or in the second hall of Nirvana, or in the third, or in the fourth, or fifth, or sixth, or in the seventh hall of Nirvana." To describe the ineffable joy of Nirvana is impossible. There, the music of the spheres reigns and the soul is enchanted within a state of bliss, which is impossible to describe with words." - Samael Aun Weor, *The Revolution of Beelzebub*

Prajna: (Sanskrit, "discriminative awareness," "consciousness" or "wisdom." In Tibetan, shes rab) Literally "perfect knowledge."

In Hinduism: The third of the four states of the consciousness of Atman. In the Mandukya Upanishad, Prajna is described as a state of blissful, cognizant, dreamless sleep.

In Buddhism: This term is defined by its context; it can mean intuitive wisdom, understanding, intelligence, discrimination, or judgment. In Buddhist philosophy, prajna describes the faculty of discriminative awareness that can see the true nature - the emptiness or void - of all things. Prajna is the highest paramita (conscious attitude or virtue).

Sahaja Maithuna: (Sanskrit) Sahaja, "natural." Maithuna, "sacramental intercourse"

Samadhi: (Sanskrit) Literally means "union" or "combination" and its Tibetan equivilent means "adhering to that which is profound and definitive," or ting nge dzin, meaning "To hold unwaveringly, so there is no movement." Related terms include satori, ecstasy, manteia, etc. Samadhi is a state of consciousness. In the west, the term is used to describe an ecstatic state of consciousness in which the Essence escapes the painful limitations of the mind (the "I") and therefore experiences what is real: the Being, the Great Reality. There are many levels of Samadhi. In the sutras and tantras the term Samadhi has a much broader application whose precise interpretation depends upon which school and teaching is using it.

"Ecstasy is not a nebulous state, but a transcendental state of wonderment, which is associated with perfect mental clarity." - Samael Aun Weor, *The Elimination of Satan's Tail*

Second Birth: The creation of the soul as taught by Jesus to Nicodemus:

"There was a man of the Pharisees, named Nicodemus, a ruler of the Jews: The same came to Jesus by night, and said unto him, Rabbi, we know that thou art a teacher come from God: for no man can do these miracles that thou doest, except God be with him. Jesus answered and said unto him, Verily, verily, I say unto thee, Except a man be born again, he cannot see the kingdom of God. Nicodemus saith unto him, How can a man be born when he is old? can he enter the second time into his mother's womb, and be born? Jesus answered, Verily, verily, I say unto thee, Except a man be born of water and of the Spirit, he cannot enter into the kingdom of God. That which is born of the flesh is flesh; and that which is born of the Spirit is spirit." - John 3:1-6

"In Gnosticism and Esotericism, one understands as Second Birth the fabrication of the Solar Bodies and the Incarnation of the Being." - Samael Aun Weor, *The Esoteric Treatise of Hermetic Astrology*

"To incarnate the Divine Immortal Triad (Atman-Buddhi-Manas) signifies the Second Birth, which means to come out of the Ninth Sphere. The child who is born comes out from the womb. Whosoever is born within the Superior Worlds comes out of the Ninth Sphere (Sex). Whosoever reaches the Second Birth is admitted into the temple of the Twice Born. Whosoever reaches the Second Birth has to renounce sex for all eternity. The Sexual Act is absolutely forbidden for the Twice Born. Whosoever violates this law will lose his Solar Bodies and will fall into the Valley of Bitterness." - Samael Aun Weor, *The Doomed Aryan Race*

In order to incarnate the Monad (the Triad) one must first create the Solar Bodies, which is only possible through White Tantra.

Second Death: A mechanical process in nature experienced by those souls who within the allotted time fail to reach union with their inner divinity (i.e. known as self-realization, liberation, religare, yoga, moksha, etc). The Second Death is the complete dissolution of the ego (karma, defects, sins) in the infernal regions of nature, which after unimaginable quantities of suffering, proportional to the density of the psyche, in the end purifies the Essence (consciousness) so that it may try again to perfect itself and reach the union with the Being.

"He that overcometh (the sexual passion) shall inherit all things; and I will be his God (I will incarnate myself within him), and he shall be my son (because he is a Christified one), But the fearful (the tenebrous, cowards, unbelievers), and unbelieving, and the abominable, and murderers, and whoremongers, and sorcerers, and idolaters, and all liars, shall have their part in the lake which burneth with fire and brimstone: which is the second death. (Revelation 21) This lake which burns with fire and brimstone is the lake of carnal passion. This lake is related with the lower animal depths of the human being and its atomic region is the abyss. The tenebrous slowly disintegrate themselves within the abyss until they die. This is the second death." - Samael Aun Weor, *The Aquarian Message*

"When the bridge called Antakarana,which communicates the divine triad with its inferior essence is broken, the inferior essence (trapped into the ego) is left separated and is sunk into the abyss of destructive forces, where it (its ego) disintegrates little by little. This is the Second Death of which the Apocalypse speaks; this is the state of consciousness called Avitchi." - Samael Aun Weor, *The Zodiacal Course*

"The Second Death is really painful. The ego feels as if it has been divided in different parts, the fingers fall off, its arms, its legs. It suffers through a tremendous breakdown." - Samael Aun Weor, from the lecture *The Mysteries of Life and Death*

Self-realization: The achievement of perfect knowledge. This phrase is better stated as, "The realization of the Innermost Self," or "The realization of the true nature of self." At the ultimate level, this is the experiential, conscious knowledge of the Absolute, which is synonymous with Emptiness, Shunyata, or Non-being.

Semen: In the esoteric tradition of pure sexuality, the word semen refers to the sexual energy of the organism, whether male or female. This is because male and female both carry the "seed" within: in order to create, the two "seeds" must be combined. In common usage: "The smaller, usually motile male reproductive cell of most organisms that reproduce sexually." English semen originally meant 'seed of male animals' in the 14th century, and it was not applied to human males until the 18th century. It came from Latin semen, "seed of plants," from serere `to sow.' The Latin goes back to the Indo-European root *se-, source of seed, disseminate, season, seminar, and seminal. The word seminary (used for religious schools) is derived from semen and originally meant 'seedbed.' That the semen is the source of all virtue is known from the word "seminal," derived from the Latin "semen," and which is defined as "highly original and influencing the development of future events: a seminal artist; seminal ideas."

"According to Yogic science, semen exists in a subtle form throughout the whole body. It is found in a subtle state in all the cells of the body. It is withdrawn and elaborated into a gross form in the sexual organ under the influence of the sexual will and sexual excitement. An Oordhvareta Yogi (one who has stored up the seminal energy in the brain after sublimating the same into spiritual energy) not only converts the semen into Ojas, but checks through his Yogic power, through purity in thought, word and deed, the very formation of semen by the secretory cells or testes or seeds. This is a great secret." - Sri Swami Sivananda, *Brahmacharya* (Celibacy)

Sexual Magic: The word magic is derived from the ancient word magos "one of the members of the learned and priestly class," from O.Pers. magush, possibly from PIE *magh- "to be able, to have power." [Quoted from On-line Etymology Dictionary].

"All of us possess some electrical and magnetic forces within, and, just like a magnet, we exert a force of attraction and repulsion... Between lovers that magnetic force is particularly powerful and its action has a far-reaching effect." - Samael Aun Weor, *The Mystery of the Golden Blossom*

Sexual magic refers to an ancient science that has been known and protected by the purest, most spiritually advanced human beings, whose purpose and goal is the harnessing and perfection of our sexual forces. A more accurate translation of sexual magic would be "sexual priesthood." In ancient times, the priest was always accompanied by a priestess, for they represent the divine forces at the base of all creation: the masculine and feminine, the Yab-Yum, Ying-Yang, Father-Mother: the Elohim. Unfortunately, the term "sexual magic" has been grossly misinterpreted by mistaken persons such as Aleister Crowley, who advocated a host of degenerated practices, all of which belong solely to the lowest and most perverse mentality and lead only to the enslavement of the consciousness, the worship of lust and desire, and the decay of humanity. True, upright, heavenly sexual magic is the natural harnessing of our latent forces, making them active and harmonious with nature and the divine, and which leads to the perfection of the human being.

"People are filled with horror when they hear about sexual magic; however, they are not filled with horror when they give themselves to all kinds of sexual perversion and to all kinds of carnal passion." - Samael Aun Weor, *The Perfect Matrimony*

Solar Bodies: The physical, vital, astral, mental, and causal bodies that are created through the beginning stages of Alchemy/Tantra and that provide a basis for existence in their corresponding levels of nature, just as the physical body does in the physical world. These bodies or vehicles are superior due to being created out of Solar (Christic) Energy, as opposed to the inferior, lunar bodies we receive from nature. Also known as the Wedding Garment (Christianity), the Merkabah (Kabbalah), To Soma Heliakon (Greek), and Sahu (Egyptian).

"All the Masters of the White Lodge, the Angels, Archangels, Thrones, Seraphim, Virtues, etc., etc., etc. are garbed with the Solar Bodies. Only those who have Solar Bodies have the Being incarnated. Only someone who possesses the Being is an authentic Human Being." - Samael Aun Weor, *The Esoteric Treatise of Hermetic Astrology*

Tantra: The word Tantra is Sanskrit and literally means, "a continuum, or unbroken stream [of energy]." The term Tantra refers first (1) to the continuum of vital energy that sustains all existence, and second (2) to the class of knowledge and practices that harnesses that vital energy, thereby transforming the practitioner. Tantra is publicly known in two forms: from India, related to Hinduism; from Tibet, related to Buddhism. Each have their own scriptures, schools, traditions, and practices, which vary widely. And, in spite of the opinions—and financial interests—of many people, the term Tantra is not immediately synonymous with sex, spiritual powers, or materialism. For thousands of years the teachings of Tantra had been protected and isolated in order to preserve their purity and to protect the naive from harming themselves. Now that much of Tantra has been made public, it has been completely disfigured by the passions, desires, and ambitions of misguided people. The vast majority of teachings of Tantra have degenerated completely and are now dangerous. One should study extensively before taking on any teachings or practice of Tantra. This has been emphasized by all truly authentic traditions of Tantra:

"Tantra Yoga had been one of the potent powers for the spiritual regeneration of the Hindus. When practised by the ignorant, unenlightened, and unqualified persons, it has led to certain abuses; and there is no denying that some degraded forms of Saktism have sought nothing but magic, immorality, and occult powers. - Swami Sivananda

Genuine Tantra is an exceptional method of purifying the consciousness of all egotistical elements: lust, pride, envy, gluttony, laziness, etc., but it is not easy or accomplished overnight, and requires great temperance, intelligence, education, and dedication. Real Tantra depends completely on robust and perfect ethics.

"[Buddha] Shakyamuni did not teach that people with loose ethics will succeed in Tantra. That is not the way leading to the city of nirvana. How could these evil churls succeed in Tantra? How could people with loose ethics go to the upper realms? They will not go to a high rebirth; they will not have supreme happiness." - *The Manjushri Root Tantra*

Success in Tantra is determined by the ethical discipline that leads up to it.

There are many varieties of Tantra, but they can be classified in three types: White, Grey and Black. These are differentiated by examination of the results they produce.

White Tantra: those schools that produce beings who are clean of all egotistical desire, anger, lust, envy, etc. Such beings are known as Buddhas, Masters, Angels, Devas, etc.

Grey Tantra: those schools who want to be White but do not renounce Black methods. They are caught in the middle.

Black Tantra: those schools that produce beings who sustain and develop the causes of suffering, namely lust, anger, greed, pride, etc. Such beings are called demons, sorcerers, Maruts, Asuras, etc.

Wedding Garment: From a parable of Jesus: "Then saith he to his servants, The wedding is ready, but they which were bidden were not worthy. Go ye therefore into the highways, and as many as ye shall find, bid to the marriage. So those servants went out into the highways, and gathered together all as many as they found, both bad and good: and the wedding was furnished with guests. And when the king came in to see the guests, he saw there a man which had not on a wedding garment: And he saith unto him, Friend, how camest thou in hither not having a wedding garment? And he was speechless. Then said the king to the servants, Bind him hand and foot, and take him away, and cast him into outer darkness; there shall be weeping and gnashing of teeth. For many are called, but few are chosen." - Matthew 22

"Let us now concentrate on the constitution of the human being. In order to be a human being in the most complete sense of the word, first of all it is necessary to have or possess Solar Bodies. We have been talking a lot about the Egyptian Sahu, which is the same Wedding Garment from that parable in which one man came to be seated at the table of the Lord without the Wedding Garment. Then the Master commanded that he be cast into the darkness. So then, without a Wedding Garment or Solar Bodies we also cannot enter into the Kingdom of the Heavens. It is logical that whosoever does not possess the Solar Bodies is dressed with the Lunar Bodies, which are cold, spectral, diabolic, and tenebrous bodies. An Anima (Latin for "soul") dressed with Lunar Bodies is not a Human Being, but is an Intellectual Animal, which is a Superior Animal (Anima). The mistake of humanity is to believe that they are already Human Beings, but they are not. Let us remember the story of Diogenes and his lantern; he was looking for a Man (Human Being) and he did not find one. Only Kout Humi, the Master Morya, Saint Germain, etc. are Human Beings; what we have abundantly in this present time are Intellectual Animals. The first body which must be built in the Forge of the Cyclops is the Astral Body. Thus, we become Immortals in the World of 24 Laws. Afterwards, we need to build the Mental Body, which is ruled by 12 Laws. Whosoever builds the Mental Body is Immortal in the World of 12 Laws. Afterwards, one must build the Body of Conscious Will, and become Immortal in the World of 6 Laws. [...] This famous garment is the Egyptian Sahu or the Greek "To Soma Heliakon," in other words, the Body of Gold of the Solar Man. This is the Wedding Garment required in order to attend the Banquet of the Pascal Lamb. It is necessary and essential to understand that in order to have the Body of Gold of the Solar Man, the Great Alliance is necessary, that is, the work in the Ninth Sphere between man and woman." - Samael Aun Weor, *Tarot and Kabbalah*

White Brotherhood or Lodge: That ancient collection of pure souls who maintain the highest and most sacred of sciences: White Magic or White Tantra. It is called White due to its purity and cleanliness. This "Brotherhood" or "Lodge" includes human beings of the highest order from every race, culture, creed and religion, and of both sexes.

Yoga: (Sanskrit) "union." Similar to the Latin "religare," the root of the word "religion." In Tibetan, it is "rnal-'byor" which means "union with the fundamental nature of reality."

"The word YOGA comes from the root Yuj which means to join, and in its spiritual sense, it is that process by which the human spirit is brought into near and conscious communion with, or is merged in, the Divine Spirit, according as the nature of the human spirit is held to be separate from (Dvaita, Visishtadvaita) or one with (Advaita) the Divine Spirit." - Swami Sivananda, *Kundalini Yoga*

"Patanjali defines Yoga as the suspension of all the functions of the mind. As such, any book on Yoga, which does not deal with these three aspects of the subject, viz., mind, its functions and the method of suspending them, can he safely laid aside as unreliable and incomplete." - Swami Sivananda, *Practical Lessons In Yoga*

"The word yoga means in general to join one's mind with an actual fact..." - The 14th Dalai Lama

"All of the seven schools of Yoga are within Gnosis, yet they are in a synthesized and absolutely practical way. There is Tantric Hatha Yoga in the practices of the Maithuna (Sexual Magic). There is practical Raja Yoga in the work with the chakras. There is Gnana / Jnana Yoga in our practices and mental disciplines which we have cultivated in secrecy for millions of years. We have Bhakti Yoga in our prayers and Rituals. We have Laya Yoga in our meditation and respiratory exercises. Samadhi exists in our practices with the Maithuna and during our deep meditations. We live the path of

Karma Yoga in our upright actions, in our upright thoughts, in our upright feelings, etc." - Samael Aun Weor, *The Revolution of Beelzebub*

"The Yoga that we require today is actually ancient Gnostic Christian Yoga, which absolutely rejects the idea of Hatha Yoga. We do not recommend Hatha Yoga simply because, spiritually speaking, the acrobatics of this discipline are fruitless; they should be left to the acrobats of the circus." - Samael Aun Weor, *The Yellow Book*

"Yoga has been taught very badly in the Western World. Multitudes of pseudo-sapient Yogis have spread the false belief that the true Yogi must be an infrasexual (an enemy of sex). Some of these false yogis have never even visited India; they are infrasexual pseudo-yogis. These ignoramuses believe that they are going to achieve in-depth realization only with the yogic exercises, such as asanas, pranayamas, etc.Not only do they have such false beliefs, but what is worse is that they propagate them; thus, they misguide many people away from the difficult, straight, and narrow door that leads unto the light. No authentically Initiated Yogi from India would ever think that he could achieve his inner self-realization with pranayamas or asanas, etc. Any legitimate Yogi from India knows very well that such yogic exercises are only co-assistants that are very useful for their health and for the development of their powers, etc. Only the Westerners and pseudo-yogis have within their minds the belief that they can achieve Self-realization with such exercises. Sexual Magic is practiced very secretly within the Ashrams of India. Any True Yogi Initiate from India works with the Arcanum A.Z.F. This is taught by the Great Yogis from India that have visited the Western world, and if it has not been taught by these great, Initiated Hindustani Yogis, if it has not been published in their books of Yoga, it was in order to avoid scandals. You can be absolutely sure that the Yogis who do not practice Sexual Magic will never achieve birth in the Superior Worlds. Thus, whosoever affirms the contrary is a liar, an impostor." - Samael Aun Weor, *Alchemy and Kabbalah in the Tarot*

Index

Abbot, 162
Abel, 119
Abiff, 125
Abortion, 138, 223
Abraham, 12, 76, 78
Absolute, 33, 40, 45, 55-56, 58, 62,
    70, 82, 84, 91, 94, 106, 152,
    197-200, 208, 213-214, 217,
    225, 229, 232, 235
Abstention, 168, 222
Abstract Absolute Space, 45, 55-56
Abyss, 4, 12, 24-26, 43, 49, 52-54,
    106, 128, 130, 147, 156, 186,
    195, 212, 216, 234
Achaemenides, 71
Achamoth, 85, 135
Acheans, 15, 59, 87, 102
Acheron, 98, 100, 139
Achilles, 24, 98, 128, 151, 169-170
Acrobat, 28, 149, 239
Act, 121-122, 230, 234
Action, 34, 82, 130, 199, 213, 231,
    235, 239
Active, 34, 89, 189-190, 217, 221,
    236
Activity, 9, 14, 33, 70, 81, 95, 148,
    164, 189, 217, 221, 229, 231
Actors, 130
Adam, 78, 107, 119, 121, 139, 156,
    174-175
Adam Kadmon, 156
Adam Sollus, 119
Adam-Eve, 119, 122
Adamic Veil, 79, 168
Adept, 89, 177, 221
Adepthood, 116
Adepts, 12, 112, 168, 171, 190
Adeptus, 200
Adhaesit, 153
Aditi, 90, 135
Adonia, 135, 219
Adriatic Sea, 35
Adshanti, 135

Adulterers, 103, 228
Adultery, 212
Advent, 42, 192
Adversities, 98
Aegis, 16
Aeneadae, 23
Aeolus, 4
Affections, 67, 81-83, 106, 135, 167-
    168, 199
Africa, 165
African, 85
Agamemnon, 102
Agate, 171
Age, 16, 49, 64, 90-91, 93-94, 103,
    111, 113, 117, 120-121, 126,
    131, 148, 164, 184, 195, 223,
    229
Age of Bronze, 103
Age of Gold, 120
Ages, 27, 36, 89, 129, 145, 157
Aggregates, 20, 25, 135-136, 139,
    220
Agni, 164
Agrippa, 144
Ahamkara Bhava, 135
Ain, 55-58, 92, 213-214
Ain Soph, 55-58, 92, 213-214
Ain Soph Paranishpana, 57
Air, 7, 13, 23, 37, 47, 49, 63, 90, 99,
    116, 120, 142, 147, 163-164,
    180, 191
Ajax, 102
Akasha, 12, 213
Akashic Records of Nature, 89, 213
Aladdin, 41
Alaya, 89, 163, 213-214
Alchemical, 205, 208
Alchemists, 41, 97
Alchemy, 27, 57, 207, 210, 214, 216,
    236, 239
Alecto, 125-128
Alert, 93, 204, 218
Alexander, 62
Alexis, 62

Alive, 16, 59, 115, 129, 176, 184, 211
Alliance, 87, 171, 220, 238
Alpha, 205
Altar, 11, 15, 17, 24, 39-41, 87, 100,
    103, 121, 157-158, 174, 209
Altars, 86, 203
Altimira, 171
Amata, 127
Ambassador of England, 7
Amber, 35
Ambiplasma, 45
Amen, 209
America, 7, 195
Amesha-Spentas, 89
Amfortas, 79, 183-185, 187
Amphora, 85
Amrita Nadi, 118
Anacreon, 105
Analysis, 8, 13, 19, 20-21, 27, 45, 82,
    190, 219, 224
Ananta, 205
Anathemas, 19
Anatomy, 112, 148, 170
Ancestors, 35, 37, 48, 225
Ancestry, 129
Anchises, 4, 18, 38, 134
Anchorites, 168
Androgynes, 119
Andromache, 59-60
Andros, 35
Angel, 18, 51, 107, 116, 145, 152,
    162, 164-165
Angel Israel, 51
Angel of Purgatory, 152, 165
Angels, 38, 59, 76, 78, 90, 146, 164,
    194, 200, 218, 223, 236-237
Angels of Death, 164
Anger, 5, 16, 48, 153, 169, 215, 237
Angola, 105
Angry, 103, 159-160
Anima, 153, 214, 226, 237
Animal, 11, 26, 49, 52, 55, 67, 87, 90,
    97, 135, 166, 171, 184, 190,
    193, 212, 218, 222, 226-227,
    234, 237
Animals, 26, 56, 161, 212, 226, 235,
    238

Animas, 158
Anna, 86, 88
Annihilated, 175
Annihilation, 106, 220
Ant, 173-175, 231
Antakarana, 174, 234
Anthropological, 205
Anti-matter, 8, 21, 43-45, 56
Anti-hydrogen, 45
Antioch, 145
Anti-particles, 43
Anti-plasma, 45
Anti-proton, 43, 45
Antiquity, 72
Anti-stars, 43, 45, 56
Antitheses, 69, 84, 111, 135
Antithesis, 84-85, 122
Antonomasia, 52
Antony, 144
Ants, 173-177, 179
Anubis, 131-132, 144, 179-181
Anvil, 142
Apocalypse, 91, 126, 234
Apocalyptic, 17
Apollo, 11, 15, 35-38, 48, 59-60, 86,
    97-98, 122, 192, 225
Apuleius, 112
Aquarian, 9, 49, 164, 218, 225, 232,
    234
Aquarian Age, 164
Aquarius, 1
Ar, 39, 41-42, 78
Ara, 209
Aramaic, 77
Arcadia, 24, 120
Arcadians, 159
Arcanum, 105, 111, 148, 201, 218,
    239
Arcanum Six, 111
Archangels, 59, 200, 236
Archer, 85
Archivists of Destiny, 133
Archon, 131-132
Ardent, 98, 107, 225-226
Argentine, 142
Aries, 78
Ark, 12, 149

Arm, 13, 104, 133, 180-181, 205
Armed, 48
Armies, 16, 142
Armor, 15, 88, 142-143, 145
Armored, 144
Arms, 5, 13-14, 17, 30, 38, 52, 66, 80,
    92, 100, 117-118, 133, 141-
    143, 180-181, 185, 196, 201,
    205, 234
Army, 16, 34, 47, 169, 199, 229
Aroma, 4, 107
Arousing, 126, 228
Arrogance, 25, 40, 53, 142, 152
Art, 4, 110, 141, 150, 215-216, 227,
    233
Artemis, 36
Arts, 52, 186
Aryan, 73, 119, 160, 205, 234
Ascanius, 16, 18, 143, 159
Ascend, 51, 99, 103, 167, 218
Ascendancy, 129
Ascended, 97, 101
Ascending, 40, 118, 189, 228
Ascends, 189
Ascension, 175, 189, 226, 228
Ascent, 189, 217, 221, 228
Ascetic, 148, 190, 219
Asceticism, 107
Ascetics, 1
Ases, 205
Ash Wednesday, 105
Ashes, 6, 59, 102, 148, 195
Asia, 1, 36, 219
Asleep, 52, 65, 86, 128, 151, 156,
    170, 190, 202, 212, 227
Aspera, 79
Assassin, 59
Assassinated, 36, 54, 186
Assassins, 103
Astaroth, 85, 87
Astonishment, 27, 31, 57, 59, 77, 170
Astral, 12, 57, 64, 131, 137, 145, 208,
    211, 213-215, 223, 231, 236,
    238
Astral Body, 57, 131, 137, 145, 211,
    213-215, 223, 231, 238
Astral Light, 12

Astral Solar Body, 208
Astrologers, 132
Astrological, 158
Astrology, 62, 218, 220, 229, 231-
    232, 234, 236
Atalanta, 85
Atash-behram, 11
Atheists, 103
Athens, 62, 166
Atlantean, 72, 79, 119, 157-158, 205,
    228
Atlantean Deluge, 72
Atlantean Root Race, 79
Atlantean-made, 171
Atlanteans, 75, 205
Atlantic Ocean, 73, 119
Atlantis, 4, 103, 119, 155-156, 171,
    223
Atma-Vidya, 136
Atman, 20, 197, 225-226, 233
Atman-Buddhi-Manas, 27, 231, 234
Atmosphere, 145
Atom, 19-20, 31, 33, 55-57, 92, 112,
    231
Atomic, 19, 31, 55-57, 84, 112, 165,
    167, 227, 234
Atoms, 8, 19-20, 31, 34, 56-57, 80,
    142, 180, 189, 217, 221, 232
Atrophied, 176
Attention, 81-82, 94, 173
Attila, 25
Augeas, 155, 166
August, 15, 95, 97, 195
Augustus Caesar, 144
Aulis, 87
AUM, 199
Aura, 144, 224
Aureole, 194
Auric, 142-143, 156
Aurora, 172, 225
Austria, 7, 129
Automatic, 176
Automatism, 69
Autumn, 96
Avarice, 53, 103, 153
Avatar, 199

Averno, 79, 99-100, 139, 141, 144, 151
Awake, 96, 201-202
Awaken, 12, 14, 65-66, 80, 117-118, 133, 135-136, 148, 170, 189-190, 204, 211, 214-215, 217, 227, 229
Awakened, 60, 189, 193, 201, 203-204, 216-217, 226, 228
Awakening, 13, 62, 65-66, 69, 83-84, 93, 95, 116, 133, 190, 201, 211, 213, 215-216, 227-228
Awakens, 12, 204, 211
Aware, 202-203, 218
Awoke, 127, 160
Axiom, 120
Aztaroth, 131-132
Aztec, 64-65, 116, 156, 164, 207, 217
Aztec Bat God, 164
Bacchanals, 105
Bacchante, 127
Bacchic, 61
Bacchus, 127
Balm, 65
Baltic, 35
Bamian, 72
Banks, 128, 159-161
Banquet, 47, 155, 187, 196, 238
Baptism, 165
Bar, 77-80
Barbaric, 15, 62, 90
Barinto, 160-161
Bat, 164
Bathe, 168, 178, 184, 187
Bathed, 53, 168, 229
Bathurst, 7
Battle, 5, 17, 24, 35, 59, 84, 102, 126, 169, 215
Beach, 48, 161, 163, 172, 199
Beam, 147, 187
Beast, 67, 97, 112, 126, 193
Beasts, 25, 100, 109, 155, 204, 209, 232
Beauties, 185
Beautiful, 15, 19, 35-36, 47, 49, 63, 80, 86, 113, 127, 130, 157,

171, 174, 185, 195, 198, 210, 216, 218
Beauty, 16, 62, 85-86, 148, 152, 155, 161, 169, 171, 174, 185, 216
Bed, 13, 88, 96, 154, 167
Bees, 174-177, 179
Beggar, 25
Begged, 23, 36, 88, 99, 141
Beginners, 163, 179
Beginning, 20, 27, 31, 38, 95, 118, 160, 176, 184, 207, 224-226, 230, 236
Being, 3, 12, 20-21, 27-30, 33, 40-41, 44, 53, 55, 64-65, 69, 72, 77, 79, 84-85, 88, 92, 95, 106, 111-112, 121, 126, 134-135, 141-142, 147, 149, 156, 158, 165-166, 169, 175, 178, 184, 190-191, 202-205, 207, 209, 211, 213-215, 217-220, 222-224, 226-229, 231, 233-234, 236-238
Belief, 69, 216, 222, 239
Believe, 15, 112, 138, 149, 194, 202, 215, 222, 237, 239
Believed, 31, 38, 87, 130, 147, 158, 184, 224, 228
Believes, 202, 209, 215, 225
Believeth, 41, 137
Bells, 63
Belly, 153
Berkeley, 43
Bestial, 25, 88, 107, 125, 154, 210
Bethlehem, 211
Betray, 53, 145, 156, 211, 227
Bewitched, 105, 110, 185
Bhava, 135
Bible, 72, 91, 220, 228-230
Bipolarity, 27
Bird, 49, 63, 112, 151, 161, 186
Birth, 99, 102, 138, 149, 163, 165, 167-168, 184, 192, 199, 202-203, 207-209, 233-234, 239
Bitterness, 16, 65, 69, 132, 167, 187, 234
Bituminous, 161

Black, 23, 28, 41, 49-50, 52, 74, 86-
   87, 98, 105, 111-112, 117,
   120, 122, 131, 145-146, 149,
   183-184, 203-204, 215-216,
   219-220, 223, 227, 230, 237
Black Lodge, 131, 215
Black Magic, 28, 149, 215-216, 220,
   230
Black Magician, 122, 183-184, 215-
   216
Black Moon, 111
Blame, 16
Blameless, 185
Blavatsky, 11, 48, 72-75, 221, 225
Blessed, 5, 18, 23, 28, 38-39, 41, 64,
   94, 153-154, 158, 178, 185-
   187, 191, 194, 197, 225
Blind, 15, 71, 74, 112, 126, 132, 147
Blood, 15, 23, 25, 48, 53, 66, 85-87,
   98, 100, 102, 107-108, 129,
   183, 187, 200
Blood-red, 142
Blood-soaked, 100
Bloody, 35, 143, 184
Blossoms, 107
Blue, 39, 160, 174, 191
Blue-greenish, 122
Boat, 50, 100, 139, 151, 161, 163
Bodhisattvas, 40, 54, 147
Bodies, 26, 28, 37, 57-58, 65, 101,
   142, 144, 148-149, 158, 166,
   168, 196, 202, 207-209, 212,
   223, 227-228, 231-232, 234,
   236-237
Bones, 108-109, 190
Bonfires, 128
Boniface, 153
Born, 12, 33, 52, 79, 103, 117, 120-
   121, 159, 191, 207, 214, 222,
   225, 233-234
Bosom, 5, 8, 41, 56, 74, 129, 227
Bottled, 69-70, 97, 106, 108, 129,
   203, 208, 212
Bottom, 82, 105, 149, 156, 160, 218
Bottomless, 12, 106
Boulder, 39, 75, 147, 156
Brahma, 69, 91, 199, 229

Brahman, 4
Brain, 12, 118, 189, 235
Brazen, 12
Bread, 146, 171, 183, 187
Breast, 36, 48, 125, 152
Breastplate, 142
Breath, 13, 86, 163, 230
Breathing, 36, 118, 224
Brendan, 160, 162
Briareus, 100
Bride, 87, 170
Brihaspati, 157
Brillat-Savarin, 171
Brimham, 75
Brittany, 73-74
Brontes, 142
Bronze, 15, 37, 48, 103, 142
Brother, 93, 156-157, 179, 198
Brotherhood, 1, 131, 145, 195, 229,
   238
Brothers, 71, 79, 90-92, 100, 103,
   108, 117, 125-126, 137, 142-
   144, 171, 198, 211
Bruno Pontecorvo, 9
Brute Stone, 91
Brutus, 125
Buddha, 5, 54, 77, 93, 102, 125, 135,
   216, 222, 224, 232, 237
Buddhata, 55, 84, 133, 144, 216
Buddhic, 29, 69
Buddhism, 55, 173, 207, 214, 216,
   219, 222, 224, 233, 236
Buddhist, 69, 106, 206, 219, 233
Buddhists, 94
Build, 36, 48, 57, 88, 118, 148-149,
   158, 167, 195, 202, 208-209,
   238
Builder, 34
Builders, 41, 91, 194
Bull, 23, 193
Bullocks, 48
Burn, 3, 88, 151, 169, 178, 229
Burned, 3, 18, 37, 78, 94, 222
Burning, 12, 88, 95, 170, 221
Butterflies, 84, 152, 212
C. O. N. H., 57
Cabala, 49, 226

Cabin, 121
Cadaver, 139, 154
Caduceus, 11, 158, 190
Caesar, 62, 144
Caiaphas, 125, 166
Cain, 119
Calixto, 109
Calm, 109, 224
Calming, 4, 184
Calmness, 70
Calypso, 170
Camazotz, 164
Canal, 145, 189, 217-218, 228
Cannibalism, 176
Capaneus, 25
Capital, 20, 63, 69, 113, 132, 144,
    173, 178, 180, 220
Capital of Mexico, 63, 173
Car, 34, 178
Carbon, 20, 57
Caribbean Sea, 171
Carmelites, 176
Carnac, 73-75
Carnal, 107, 153, 234, 236
Carthage, 5-6, 87
Cartujo, 162
Cassandra, 15, 38
Cassius, 125
Castle, 183-184, 186
Castrate, 184
Cat, 93
Cataibates, 12
Cataluña, 186
Catastrophes, 205
Cathedral, 63-65
Cato, 144
Caton, 165
Cattle, 48
Caucasus, 87
Causal World, 103
Cause, 28, 47, 82, 131, 179, 201-202,
    213, 216, 229
Caused, 37, 57, 85, 106
Causes, 8, 31, 53, 153, 232, 237
Causing, 127
Cave, 48, 59-60, 71-72, 75, 100, 102,
    108

Cavern, 62, 71, 97, 142
Cedars, 72
Celaeno, 47-48, 50
Celebrated, 24, 62, 156, 161-162, 187
Celebration, 170
Celestial, 158, 169
Celibate, 148
Cemeteries, 11
Centaurs, 22, 24
Center, 31, 34, 40, 56, 84, 97, 112,
    138, 141, 189-190, 214, 218,
    223
Centers, 136, 189, 216-217, 220
Central Asia, 1
Central Sun, 51, 217
Centuries, 12, 17-18, 23-24, 35-36,
    38, 47, 58, 61, 64, 75, 85, 93,
    98, 109, 121, 130, 145, 153,
    169, 174, 192, 194
Century, 11, 31, 72, 112, 129-130,
    160, 235
Cerastes, 125
Cerberus, 100, 102, 155, 166
Cerebral, 189
Ceremonies, 86, 121
Ceres, 17, 86, 141
Chain, 89, 193, 226
Chains, 54, 103, 165, 193
Chakra, 4, 12, 56, 190, 216-217,
    227-228
Chalice, 41, 85, 184, 187, 195
Chamber, 127, 157
Chan, 95
Chance, 25, 34, 131, 191-192
Change, 44, 62, 111, 193
Changeable, 83
Changed, 59, 127, 170, 172
Changing, 89
Channels, 118
Chant, 42, 94, 163, 181, 192
Chao Chou, 96
Chaos, 26, 88
Chapultepec, 101
Chariot, 7, 37, 58, 194
Charity, 3, 216
Charon, 49-50, 100, 139, 151
Charybdis, 60

Chaste, 28, 49, 107, 144, 185, 218-219, 222
Che Chiang, 95
Chechere, 148
Chela, 64-65, 115
Cherubim, 59, 200
Chiang Ning, 95
Chief, 41, 77, 158, 169, 181, 194, 231
Chiefs, 198
Child, 5, 17, 27, 74, 92, 129, 132, 155, 166, 234
Children, 7, 64, 78-80, 121, 131, 155, 168, 179, 191-192
Children of God, 80
Chimaera, 100
Chin Tien, 95
Chindin, 94
Chinese, 8-9, 70, 72, 93-96
Chiromancers, 132
Chiron, 24
Chitta, 82
Chosen, 18, 75, 196, 237
Chrestos, 77
Christ, 13-14, 17, 23, 41, 51, 77-79, 101, 104, 146, 155, 165-166, 169-170, 177, 184, 191, 195-196, 215, 217, 222-224, 232
Christ Will, 104
Christian, 157, 190, 220, 224, 239
Christianity, 59, 218, 236
Christians, 210, 224
Christic, 57, 80, 108, 217, 236
Christic Atoms, 80
Christic Mind, 57
Christified, 41, 234
Christmas, 1, 11, 111-112, 115, 119, 135, 161-162, 170, 173, 201, 205, 211
Christmas Message, 1, 115, 119, 173, 201, 205, 211
Christos, 77, 217
Chrysalid, 11
Chrysalises, 152
Church, 39, 79, 166, 190, 195, 217, 222-223
Churches, 79, 217-218
Circe, 109-113

Circle, 125, 142, 162, 175, 219
Circulation, 14, 66, 173, 217
Circumstances, 179, 216
Cities, 18, 36, 121, 141, 160, 176
Citizen, 6
City, 7, 12, 18, 23, 36-37, 39, 48, 62-64, 87, 91, 98, 103, 110, 113, 144, 156, 159, 165, 173, 178, 191, 237
City of Light, 39
Civilization, 90, 175, 215
Clairvoyants, 201
Clarity, 8, 25, 41, 72, 121, 135, 224, 233
Clean, 63, 152, 155, 166, 186, 237
Clemency, 106
Cleopatra, 144
Cloe, 106
Cloth, 103, 187
Cloth of Veronica, 103
Clothes, 95, 139
Cnossus, 37
Coaticlue, 97
Coccygeal, 190
Coccyx, 112, 145, 189, 227
Cocoa, 171
Cocytus, 128
Cohesion, 135, 227
Coiled, 190, 228
Coitus, 202
Cold, 64, 89, 91, 237
College, 1, 62, 117, 130
Color, 13, 19, 152, 160, 171, 195
Coloration, 157
Colored, 161, 174
Colors, 120, 171
Colossal, 73, 156
Colossus, 71
Colossuses, 121
Column, 11, 188, 217
Columns, 156, 209
Combat, 142, 169
Combination, 82-83, 180, 203, 233
Combinations, 121
Command, 87, 146, 191, 196
Commanded, 37-38, 47, 86, 99, 208, 237

Communion, 51, 238
Communism, 175-176
Compassion, 3, 62, 65, 194, 197
Comprehended, 30, 70, 93, 95, 105-
    107, 113, 138-139, 178-179,
    191, 193, 199
Comprehends, 152, 158, 204
Comprehension, 136, 138-139
Concentrate, 30, 104, 163-164, 173,
    180-181, 231, 237
Concept, 7, 33, 43, 209, 224, 226
Conception, 89
Concepts, 67
Conceptualizes, 207
Concupiscence, 185
Condemnation, 50, 219
Condemned, 53, 89, 148-149
Confuse, 15, 228
Confused, 64, 137, 178, 226
Confusion, 9
Conjuration, 122
Conjure, 4
Conscious, 12-13, 34, 40, 57, 69, 81,
    103, 116-117, 164, 208, 218,
    222, 224, 233, 235, 238
Conscious Will, 57, 103, 116-117,
    164, 208, 238
Consciously, 13, 131, 190, 215
Consciousness, 12-14, 28, 60, 62,
    64-67, 69-70, 80, 83-84, 86,
    93, 95, 100, 116-118, 133,
    135-136, 170, 175, 190, 193,
    201-204, 211, 213-216, 218,
    223, 225-226, 229, 231-236
Conservation of Parity, 8
Constellation, 40, 78, 116
Consummated, 120
Contemplate, 82, 176, 195
Contemplation, 70, 81, 231
Continent, 72, 119, 122, 145, 157,
    171, 195, 217
Continents, 73, 119
Copper, 43
Copulation, 121, 222, 229-230
Coral, 171
Corn, 24, 120, 164, 171
Cosmic Christ, 17, 23, 165, 169, 191

Cosmic Day, 34, 44-45, 58, 67, 89,
    92, 197, 229
Cosmic Drama, 125, 166
Cosmic Egg, 31, 33
Cosmic Justice, 52, 54
Cosmic Language, 120
Cosmic Mother, 17, 111, 138, 141,
    223
Cosmic Night, 57, 92, 197, 229
Cosmic Science, 170
Cosmic Space, 90, 135
Cosmic Will, 164
Cosmobiology, 11
Cosmocreators, 34, 220
Cosmogenesis, 21, 34, 43
Cosmogonical, 205
Cosmogonies, 21
Cosmos, 4, 20, 33, 170, 214
Cosmoses, 20, 67, 205
Countries, 18, 41, 176
Country, 23-24, 27, 35, 53, 65, 97-99,
    121, 146, 160, 219, 225
Couple, 122, 202, 224, 229
Covet, 6, 211
Cow, 47-49
Create, 19, 234-235
Created, 11, 19, 44, 62, 119, 214,
    223, 236
Creation, 20, 44, 204, 230, 233, 235
Creative, 56, 116, 229
Creator, 3, 20, 219, 224
Creator Logos, 20
Cremated, 148
Crematorium, 22, 24
Cretans, 36
Crete, 36-38, 97
Creusa, 16, 18
Crime, 5, 135, 227
Crimes, 54, 103, 177, 201
Criminal, 22, 24
Critias, 170
Crocodiles, 147
Cronos, 169
Crosier, 153
Cross, 41, 77, 99, 147, 166, 183, 186-
    187, 192, 206-207, 209-210,
    212

Crosses, 205
Crossing, 9, 99, 162, 210
Crowned, 62, 103
Crucified, 91, 209
Crucifixion, 51, 219
Crypt, 156-158
Crystal, 63
Crystallization, 33, 44-45, 67, 123,
    208
Crystals, 63
Cteis, 187
Cubic, 91, 195
Cubic Stone of Yesod, 195
Cult, 91, 103, 120, 160, 163-164, 223
Cultists, 170
Cumae, 60-62, 98
Cunning, 71, 109, 113
Cup, 86, 105, 109, 171, 191, 195, 210
Cup of Hermes, 191, 210
Cupbearer, 151
Cupid, 49, 85-87, 122
Cybele, 11, 37, 135, 141, 169-170,
    219
Cycles, 89-90, 160, 199
Cyclopean, 73, 121, 156
Cyclops, 5, 60, 140-143, 149, 158,
    161-162, 166, 168, 203, 208-
    209, 238
Daedalus, 97
Dance, 75, 127, 144, 164
Dangma, 89, 221
Dante, 4, 24, 46, 49, 102, 125, 150,
    153, 232
Dantesque, 47, 169, 173
Dardanus, 36, 38, 47, 87
Darkness, 1, 18, 25, 44, 47, 91, 98,
    115, 155, 162, 185, 196, 208,
    215, 237
Daughter, 2-3, 16, 90, 109, 125-128,
    131-132, 141
Dawn, 27, 34, 39, 43, 45, 58, 92, 157,
    215
Days, 7, 33, 47, 56, 93, 101, 113, 138,
    162
Dead, 24, 40, 50, 59, 94, 96-99, 105,
    139, 228

Death, 25-26, 37, 40, 50, 62, 77-78,
    87-88, 91, 94, 98-99, 108-109,
    125-126, 128, 131-132, 138,
    148, 164-165, 176, 183, 186,
    197, 212, 217, 219, 226, 234
Deaths, 199, 232
Debt, 18, 131-132
Decapitate, 166
Deceased, 100
Deceit, 108, 216
December, 63
Deeds, 94, 133, 155, 179-180, 183
Defect, 136, 138-139, 153-154, 220,
    230
Defects, 55, 123, 136, 139, 224, 229,
    234
Deformed, 71, 73, 75, 177
Degenerated, 170, 210, 225, 230,
    235-236
Degree, 34, 177, 179, 218
Degrees, 31, 34, 138, 180-181, 191
Deities, 24
Deity, 18, 49, 60, 119, 229
Dejanira, 52, 156
Delilah, 52, 156
Delos, 35-36
Delphi, 12, 83
Delphic, 61
Deluge, 72
Demigods, 65
Demon, 100, 112, 124-126, 131, 145-
    146, 204
Demon of Desire, 124-125
Demon of Evil Will, 124, 126
Demons, 91, 209, 215-216, 218, 227,
    237
Dense, 39, 56, 174, 193
Density, 26, 31, 218, 234
Descend, 51-52, 58, 98-99, 102-103,
    141, 167, 209, 218, 232
Descendants, 38, 47, 72
Descended, 12, 35, 99, 145, 148, 156,
    159
Descendents, 51
Descending, 5, 49, 52-53, 64, 80,
    149, 157-158, 160, 227-228
Descends, 142, 189

Descent, 26, 51, 102, 175, 221
Descents, 151
Desire, 40, 82, 85, 88, 103-104, 122, 124-125, 155, 167, 184, 189, 215, 230, 235, 237
Desires, 70, 86, 125, 199, 214-215, 225, 227, 236
Destiny, 88, 133, 169
Destroy, 78, 108, 141, 201, 224
Destroyed, 72, 88
Destroyer, 71, 109, 141
Destroying, 53, 184, 204
Destruction, 38, 45, 62, 87, 197
Destructive, 85, 234
Detached, 39, 193
Detachment, 132
Deus Inversus, 98
Deva, 116, 160, 164
Devamatri, 90, 111, 135
Devas, 65, 117, 159, 237
Develop, 103, 112, 148, 218, 227, 237
Developed, 11, 19, 90, 190
Developing, 104, 122, 145
Development, 21, 89, 227-228, 235, 239
Develops, 191
Devi, 12, 92, 134-135, 137, 170, 219, 228
Devi Kundalini, 12, 92, 134-135, 137, 170, 219, 228
Devic College, 117
Devil, 55, 126, 136, 139, 203
Devolution, 25, 49-50, 79, 89, 175, 177, 204-205, 211, 218, 220
Devolving, 26, 49, 160, 207, 220, 226
Devotion, 17, 101, 230
Devour, 44, 53, 79, 90, 147
Devouring, 52, 71, 156
Dharmasaya, 197
Diamantine, 149, 199
Diamonds, 149
Diana, 28, 49, 72, 192, 218-219
Dido, 5, 85-88, 100, 102
Dimension, 7-9, 20, 28, 49, 111-112, 131, 137, 163-164, 193, 214, 223, 231

Dimensions, 8, 18, 32, 34, 67, 163, 221, 223
Diogenes, 166, 237
Dionysus, 86
Dioscuri, 11
Direct, 19-20, 45, 67, 69, 93, 106, 189-190, 197-200, 221
Direct Path, 197-198, 200
Disappear, 167, 217
Disappeared, 7, 16, 33, 94, 193
Disciple, 41, 64, 115, 131, 160, 216, 222, 231
Disciples, 29, 161, 163, 171, 201, 215, 219
Discipline, 95, 107, 176, 237, 239
Disciplines, 20, 147, 238
Discord, 19, 100, 125, 128
Discs, 205
Diseases, 100
Disincarnated, 28
Disintegrate, 9, 57, 207, 234
Dissolution, 97, 107, 139, 151, 229, 234
Dissolve, 77, 99, 107, 138, 168, 207, 211, 213, 229
Dissolved, 67, 94, 151, 163, 178, 187, 203, 207
Divination, 75
Divine Language, 39, 77
Divine Mother, 2-6, 15-17, 27-28, 30, 37, 88, 92, 97, 118, 134-135, 137-139, 141-142, 154, 163, 165, 168-169, 177-178, 189, 218-219, 224, 227, 230
Divinity, 25, 171, 191-192, 220, 234
Divorce, 146
Doctors, 165
Doctrine, 1, 11, 26, 29-30, 65, 72-75, 79, 90, 119, 128, 210, 215, 217, 221-223
Dodona, 35
Dog, 24, 166
Dogma, 19, 208
Dogstar, 37
Dollars, 178
Dolorosa, 139, 151
Dominions, 59-60, 200

Don Juan, 113
Donkey, 68, 112-113
Door, 17, 39, 95, 98, 101, 117, 137,
    147, 239
Doors, 39, 50, 56, 97, 99, 101, 127,
    146, 165, 186, 193
Dorn, 101, 103-104, 118
Dorsal, 12, 180, 189-190, 217
Double, 45, 93, 138, 223
Doubt, 19-20, 25, 27-29, 33-34, 40,
    60, 69, 96, 118, 123, 162, 167,
    170, 177, 190, 205-206, 218
Dove, 183, 186, 224
Dragon, 95, 126, 131, 219
Drama, 17, 125, 130, 166, 183
Dream, 85-86, 115, 159, 201, 203-
    204, 214
Dreaming, 65, 87, 202-203
Dreams, 100, 115, 176, 201-202, 214
Drink, 4, 79, 93, 109, 228
Drowsiness, 82-83
Druid, 62
Drukpas, 112, 219
Drunk, 110, 103, 113
Dualism, 68-70, 84
Durga, 111, 227
Duty, 41, 85, 92-93, 95, 173
Dwarf, 156
Dysentery, 94
Eagle, 12, 16, 149, 151
Ears, 148, 161, 194
Earth, 3, 9, 12, 23, 25-27, 31, 36, 44,
    49, 51, 68, 73, 77-79, 89-91,
    98, 100, 103-104, 120, 122,
    126, 141-142, 147, 152, 157,
    163-164, 168, 174, 191-192,
    194, 205, 213, 215, 218, 225
Earthquake, 75, 98
East, 49, 62, 104, 214, 223
Easter, 62
Easter Island, 72
Easter Mass, 161
Easter Resurrection, 161-162
Ecclesiasticum, 105
Ecstasy, 28, 30, 39, 51, 56, 62, 82-84,
    91, 98, 106-108, 173, 178,
    185, 193, 231, 233

Eden, 111, 120-122, 155, 163
Education, 129, 237
Effigies, 18, 139
Effort, 57, 142
Efforts, 75, 93, 138, 145, 184, 186,
    201
Egg, 31, 33-34, 93
Ego, 24-26, 65, 97, 99, 105-108, 115,
    123, 136, 138-139, 151, 163,
    168, 193, 203-204, 212, 215,
    220, 223-224, 226, 229, 232,
    234
Egypt, 10, 61, 75, 117, 131, 146-148,
    156, 164, 192, 214, 218, 223
Egyptian, 1, 12, 27, 41, 146, 231,
    236-238
Ehecatl, 116-117, 164
Einstein, 21, 31, 33
Ejaculation, 121, 145, 148, 189,
    226-227
El, 162, 214, 220
Elai Beni Al Manah, 179
Elder, 15, 23, 56, 59, 64-65, 93, 160,
    194
Elderly, 17-18, 36
Elders, 64, 77, 93, 96
Electric, 20, 34, 207, 227
Electrical, 8, 45, 206, 235
Electricity, 112, 135, 205, 221, 227
Electron, 20
Element, 49, 69, 93, 106, 164, 199,
    216
Elemental, 8, 116-117, 142, 160, 164,
    170, 191, 219
Elementals, 26, 116, 159, 170
Elements, 4, 21, 24-25, 45, 78, 108,
    164, 220, 226, 231, 236
Eleusinian Mystery, 61
Elias, 51, 75
Elijah, 75
Eliminate, 24, 83, 97, 108, 123, 135,
    137, 139, 154-155, 184, 193,
    201, 229
Elimination, 136, 138-139, 214, 227,
    230, 233
Elixir of Longevity, 206
Elmo, 11

Elohim, 51, 119, 220, 224-226, 235
Emanate, 49, 55, 220-221
Emancipate, 69, 83-84, 204
Emancipation, 81, 165
Emblems, 205
Emerson, 89, 214
Emissions, 9
Emotion, 81, 123, 136
Emotionalism, 52
Endocrine, 149, 206
Endor, 61
Enemies, 37, 90, 103, 141, 159, 210,
    212
Enemy, 16, 29, 60, 112, 125, 139,
    169, 184, 191, 239
Energetic, 29, 40, 190, 199, 216-217
Energies, 34, 118
Energy, 8, 31, 33-34, 43-44, 104, 116,
    189-190, 217-219, 221-222,
    227-228, 235-236
Engineers, 34
England, 7
Enochs, 119
Ens Seminis, 145, 148, 189, 206
Ens Virtutis, 189
Envy, 53, 103, 107, 215, 236-237
Ephesus, 61, 190
Epiphany, 161
Epoch, 60, 120-121, 129-132, 138,
    145, 148, 157, 204, 223
Epochs, 33, 90, 121
Erda, 163
Erebus, 88
Eritrea, 61-62
Eros, 49, 85, 224
Erotic, 115, 142
Error, 40, 88, 121, 129, 138, 145,
    152, 168, 174, 178, 200, 202,
    211-212, 216, 223, 226-227
Errors, 137, 152, 177-178, 208, 220
Eschenbach, 195
Essence, 25, 55, 66, 69-70, 83-84, 92,
    195, 212, 214, 216, 221, 226,
    233-234
Eternal, 4, 12, 27, 33, 39, 49, 56, 65,
    69, 85, 91-92, 98, 103, 109,
    111, 122, 135, 138, 148, 160,

    163, 165, 191, 193, 213-215,
    225
Eternal Feminine, 49, 138, 148
Eternal Mother Space, 27, 49, 85,
    91-92, 98, 111, 122, 135
Eternity, 3, 44, 234
Ethereal, 72
Ethers, 209
Euboea, 35
Eunoe, 167, 178, 187, 229
Eusebius, 74
Evadne, 102
Evander, 155, 159, 191
Evangelical, 207
Eve, 121
Evil, 50, 53, 59, 69, 88, 94, 103-104,
    107-109, 112, 123-127, 130,
    133, 151, 154, 174, 178, 185,
    197, 215-216, 237
Evil Will, 103-104, 124, 126
Evocative, 85, 174
Evoker, 158, 171
Evolution, 90, 175, 200, 204-205,
    207, 218, 220-221, 228
Evolved, 89, 174, 204
Exercise, 104, 180-181, 216
Exercises, 12-13, 80, 149, 211, 238-
    239
Exert, 141, 235
Exhale, 14, 118, 180
Experience, 19-21, 45, 51-52, 56-57,
    67, 69-70, 84, 93-94, 106,
    108, 156, 189-190, 197, 199,
    202, 214, 222, 226
Experienced, 51, 56, 69, 84, 106, 173,
    234
Eye, 71, 89, 221
Eye of Dangma, 89, 221
Eye of Shiva, 89
Eyes, 4, 16, 56, 64, 82, 107, 122, 130,
    160-161, 171, 174, 176, 230
Factor, 125, 204, 228
Factors, 204, 211
Facts, 33, 69, 111, 116
Fah, 10-11, 13-14, 117
Fail, 102, 138, 185-186, 198, 201,
    234

Failed, 138
Failing, 79, 138, 166, 201
Failing Church, 79, 166
Failure, 84, 131, 138, 152, 201, 211
Fairies, 171
Faith, 14, 35, 95, 118, 160, 163, 175, 183, 230
Faithful, 102
Falconnet, 74
Fall, 3, 25, 37, 141, 146, 195, 201, 212, 216, 234
Fallen, 54, 145, 204, 223
Falling, 16, 60, 120, 177, 194
Falls, 5, 52, 82, 216
False, 27, 53, 126, 204, 209, 225, 239
Fame, 61, 109, 126
Families, 204, 223
Family, 17-18, 36, 38, 67, 87, 129-130
Fantasy, 116
Fate, 15, 49, 59, 62, 86-87, 141
Father, 4, 15-18, 29, 36-39, 41, 48-49, 51-52, 73, 78, 87, 91, 97-100, 104, 118, 126, 131, 149, 177, 187, 191, 202, 225-226, 229, 231
Fatherland, 74
Fault, 65, 164, 189
Faults, 138
Fear, 20, 40, 53, 102, 106, 120, 150-151, 165, 171, 193, 197, 213
Fecundate, 12-13
Feel, 69, 108, 129, 132-133, 193
Feeling, 39-40, 81, 129, 193, 224
Feelings, 129, 239
Feels, 56, 203, 234
Feet, 30, 40, 72, 93, 95, 104, 109, 113, 117, 152, 169, 171, 178, 209
Fell, 17, 24, 35, 90, 97, 106, 129, 145, 185, 187, 214
Female, 119, 125, 171, 221, 235
Feminine, 27, 49, 99, 130, 138, 148-149, 224, 230, 235
Fetus, 141
Fiat, 97
Fifteen, 121

Fifth, 1, 28, 48-49, 73, 94, 105, 119, 131, 137, 158, 193, 214, 231, 233
Fifth Gospel, 1, 105
Fight, 51, 143, 153-154, 169, 192
Fighting, 102
Fights, 165
Filthy, 47-48, 50, 52, 115, 154
Final Initiation, 52
Final Liberation, 197, 199-200, 204, 206-207
Fire, 11-12, 17, 23, 36, 38, 41-42, 60, 71, 78-79, 85-86, 88, 90, 112, 120, 126, 142, 147-148, 151, 153, 155, 163-165, 168-169, 184, 189-192, 209, 214, 217, 221-222, 224, 227-228, 232, 234
Fires, 11-12, 14, 141-142, 192, 228
First, 15-16, 21, 35-36, 44, 55, 60, 72, 79, 87, 97-98, 107, 117-119, 143, 149, 151, 155-157, 160, 167, 174, 177, 199-200, 205, 215-216, 221, 224, 229, 231, 233-234, 236-238
First Race, 72
Fish, 28, 161, 224
Five, 35, 48, 51, 72-73, 119, 123, 125, 135, 157-158, 219
Flame, 4, 11, 17, 28, 35, 38, 44, 86, 90, 145, 151, 222, 225-226
Flames, 13, 16, 25, 66, 99, 159, 164, 168-169, 192, 195, 197, 220
Flaming, 12, 25, 28, 39, 52, 54, 57, 122, 140-142, 147-148, 156, 166-167, 169, 187, 191
Flaming Forge of Vulcan, 28, 57, 141, 156, 166-167, 169, 187
Floated, 7, 166, 171
Floating, 145, 197
Flower, 3-4, 85, 93, 186, 212
Flowers, 102, 105, 161, 164, 218
Fohat, 11, 13, 34, 65, 123, 221
Fohatic, 112, 123, 126
Force, 4, 11, 25, 34, 39, 45, 112, 118, 126, 135, 183, 186, 205, 216, 221, 224, 227, 235

Forces, 8, 13-14, 20, 34, 39, 45, 47,
    55, 57, 80, 118, 142, 148,
    157, 189-190, 205, 218, 228-
    229, 234-236
Forehead, 17, 53, 85, 152, 179, 194,
    207
Forest, 59, 72, 97, 120, 169-170, 186
Forge, 25, 28, 57, 140-143, 149, 156,
    158, 162, 166-169, 187, 203,
    208-209, 227, 238
Forged, 142, 191, 205
Forget, 5, 57, 61, 87-88, 147, 156,
    163-164, 167, 192, 194, 228
Forgetfulness, 94, 228-229
Forgetting, 135
Forgive, 177-178
Forgiven, 41, 176-179
Forgiveness, 153, 176
Fornication, 122, 186, 212, 221
Fornicators, 103, 215
Forty, 162
Forty-nine, 70, 83, 115, 155, 211
Forty-two, 132, 179
Foundation, 21, 33, 45, 64, 82, 94,
    115, 126, 149, 214, 232
Foundations, 16, 44, 59, 126
Fountain of Immortality, 206
Fountains, 191
Four, 1, 15, 24, 57-58, 93, 119, 148,
    157, 164, 192, 201, 216, 223,
    233
Fourth, 8-9, 49, 72, 90, 111-112, 119,
    157, 163-164, 223, 231, 233
Fourth Coordinate, 112
Fourth Dimension, 8-9, 49, 111-112,
    163-164, 223
Fourth Round, 90
Fourth Vertical, 112
Fowls, 48-49, 90, 112
Frogs, 126
Fruit, 53, 90, 107, 120
Fruits, 162, 217
Fuel, 88
Funeral, 24, 35, 88, 109, 127
Furies, 5, 47-48, 88, 100, 103, 107,
    124-127, 144
Fury, 125, 127-128, 169

Future, 39, 44, 60, 72, 120, 167, 193,
    213, 235
Fénelon, 170
G, 83, 209, 215
G of Masonry, 209
Gaea, 49
Galactite, 41
Galaxies, 8, 20, 31, 33-34, 45
Galaxy, 21, 33, 39, 56
Gamma, 43
Ganges, 65, 122
Garden, 63, 122, 182, 185
Garden of Eden, 122
Gardens, 63
Garment, 149, 158, 166-167, 196,
    202, 207-209, 221, 236-238
Gauls, 144
Gaur, 75
Gautier, 174
Gebo, 205-206, 209
Gemblours, 162
General, 16-17, 176, 216, 220, 232,
    238
Generation, 34, 72, 143
Generative, 11, 217
Generosity, 3, 64
Genes, 205
Genesis, 57, 121-122, 220, 223
Genie, 100, 131, 152
Genii, 18, 38, 231-232
Genius, 31, 217
George Lemaitre, 31
Germ, 44, 199
Germans, 11
Germany, 7
Gestated, 5, 27, 92
Gestation, 89
Giant, 65, 71, 73, 75, 100, 174
Giants, 72-73, 75, 120, 205
Gibborim, 72
Gibraltar, 209
Gibur, 205, 207, 209
Gideon, 153
Girl, 5, 107, 130-132, 174
Girls, 47
Gland, 12, 56, 121, 221
Glands, 118, 149, 206, 217

Gluttons, 103, 153
Gluttony, 100, 107, 236
Gnomes, 26, 116
Gnosis, 90, 222-223, 238
Gnostic, 1, 4, 57, 81, 90, 103, 115,
    117, 125, 133, 180, 197, 199,
    201-204, 211, 220, 222-224,
    229-231, 239
Gnostic Lumisials, 81
Gnostic Movement, 90, 115, 199,
    203-204, 223
Gnostic Ritual, 4
Gnosticism, 7, 9, 70, 208, 218, 225,
    234
Gnostics, 12, 19, 33, 42, 164, 198-
    199, 201, 206
Goat, 100
Gob, 164
Goddess, 4, 16, 28, 37, 59, 85-87,
    109, 117, 122, 126, 141, 144,
    154-155, 160, 169, 220
Goethe, 170
Gold, 6, 18, 39, 77, 88-89, 105, 120,
    140, 142, 145, 149, 151, 153,
    156-157, 166, 193, 224, 238
Golden, 19, 27, 59, 77, 99, 109, 144,
    194, 219, 227-228, 235
Golden Child, 27
Golgotha, 51-52, 185, 187
Goose, 144
Gorgons, 11, 100, 125
Gorilla, 203
Gospel, 1, 105, 194, 214
Gospels, 1, 201
Gossip, 90
Grail, 1, 79-80, 171, 183-187, 194
Grail Knights, 183, 185
Grain, 9, 118
Grandfather, 17
Grapevines, 86
Gravitation, 45, 84, 135, 227
Gravity, 138, 223
Great Alaya, 89, 163, 214
Great Arcanum, 148, 201
Great Cause, 179, 201
Great Day, 67, 91-92, 126, 229
Great Death, 62, 197

Great Law, 132
Great Mysteries, 41, 137, 147, 168
Great Night, 91
Great Pralaya, 57, 91, 197
Great Work, 29, 41, 54, 97, 148-149,
    187, 202
Grecian, 83
Greece, 141, 225
Greed, 24, 237
Greedy, 103
Greek, 12, 16, 62, 98, 107, 127, 214,
    217, 222-225, 228-229, 231,
    236, 238
Greeks, 23, 28, 35, 38, 60-61, 151,
    218
Green, 60, 107, 125
Gryphon, 161
Guardian, 18, 48, 64, 126, 137-138,
    147, 184
Guilt, 48, 103, 216
Gundryggia, 52, 186
Gurnemanz, 183-184, 186
Guru, 93, 116, 148, 186, 227, 229-
    230
Guru-deva, 28-30
Gymnastics, 149
Hagal, 159, 161, 163-164
Hallucination, 201-204
Hammer, 158, 205, 208
Hamsa, 186
Happiness, 13, 28, 68-69, 82, 95,
    106, 153, 164, 171, 176, 192,
    197, 232, 237
Happy, 25, 40, 56, 171, 177, 193,
    198, 213
Harpies, 46-50, 100, 112
Harpy, 47, 52, 112-113, 163
Hated, 16
Hatha Yoga, 12, 28, 149, 238-239
Hatred, 53, 63, 107, 126, 184
Healed, 12, 41, 54, 65, 132, 187
Heart, 4, 14, 36, 38-40, 56, 59, 63, 65,
    85, 87-88, 98, 105, 109, 118-
    119, 125-127, 163, 165, 183,
    189, 215, 228, 230
Heart Temple, 189
Hearts, 85, 148, 153

Heaven, 4-5, 12, 43-44, 49, 51, 60, 87,
    97, 104, 107, 113, 142, 160,
    167, 174, 205, 207, 214, 232
Heavenly, 17, 58, 68, 152, 205, 232,
    235
Heavenly Man, 58
Heavens, 78, 237
Hebe, 85
Hebrew, 157, 179, 214, 220, 222,
    224, 226-227, 229
Hebrews, 153
Hector, 59
Hecuba, 15
Heindel, 209
Hekate, 28, 49, 88, 97, 111
Helen, 15
Helenus, 59-61
Heliakon, 166-167, 207, 236, 238
Heliopolis, 62
Hell, 98-100, 162, 226
Hellenes, 23
Heraclius, 75
Herbs, 88, 109
Hercules, 52, 99-100, 155-158, 166,
    224
Hermaphrodite, 41, 119-120
Hermaphroditus, 85
Hermes, 11, 77, 102, 158, 191, 195,
    210, 222, 232
Hermit, 108, 162
Herod, 155
Herodias, 52, 186
Herodotus, 35, 174
Herzeleide, 186
Hesperia, 38, 47, 60, 109
Heva, 85, 111, 135
Hierarch, 131-132, 137
Hieratic, 137, 147
Hieroglyphic, 49, 121
Hindustani, 12, 26, 49, 67, 171, 174,
    190, 209, 239
Hiram Abiff, 125
Histories, 35, 174
History, 23, 36, 78, 174, 222-223
Holocaust, 18, 170
Holy Grail, 1, 80, 171, 183-187, 194
Holy Land, 165

Holy Mary, 111-112
Holy Mount of Ida, 169
Holy Sepulchre, 51-52
Holy Spirit, 12, 142-143, 177, 183-
    184, 186, 189, 217, 224, 229
Holy Stone, 195
Holy Week, 161-162
Home, 5, 17, 37-38, 55, 65, 159-160
Homer, 25
Homes, 18, 201, 217
Homo Nosce Te Ipsum, 83
Homosexuals, 103, 210
Honey, 120, 171
Honeycomb, 176
Honeymoon, 121
Honor, 1, 36, 79, 98, 109, 126, 129,
    145, 149, 155, 160, 217
Hoof, 48
Hoofprints, 62
Hope, 3, 5, 36
Hoped, 23
Hopeless, 53
Hopes, 17
Horizontal, 99, 187
Horizontally, 122
Horns, 193
Horse, 15, 62
Horses, 7
Horus, 92
Hsu Chou, 96
Hsueh Yen, 96
Hsüan-tsang, 72
Hua Tou, 95
Hubble, 31
Humanity, 1, 4, 28, 45, 73, 79, 90, 99,
    106, 119, 121-122, 133, 137,
    141, 149, 163, 175, 187, 194,
    200, 202-203, 222-223, 225,
    235, 237
Humans, 40, 135, 175-176, 194
Humble, 3, 39-40, 165, 212
Humbled, 64, 178
Humbly, 101, 174, 185
Humboldt, 170
Humility, 93, 230
Hundred, 15, 36, 40, 52, 71-72, 88,
    97-98, 100, 103, 187, 195

Hundredfold, 90
Hundreds, 31, 216
Hurricane, 27, 60, 93, 147, 225
Hurricane-like, 142
Hurricane-wind, 97
Husband, 53, 59, 85, 130, 141, 148,
    152, 210, 224, 228-230
Hydra, 100, 125, 155, 166
Hydrogen, 20, 43, 45, 57, 149, 208
Hyperborean, 35-36, 72, 119, 225
Hyperoche, 35
Hypnotized, 185
Hypocritical, 53, 103, 210
Hypotheses, 9, 67
Hypothesis, 7, 9, 33-34
Hyrcanian, 87
I. A. O., 79, 90, 97, 127, 192
Ianos, 127, 192
Iarbas, 85
Iasius, 38
Ibidem, 75
Ibis, 186
Icarus, 97
Ida, 17, 23, 36-37, 118, 169
Idaeus, 102
Idea, 9, 70, 175, 199, 239
Ideals, 197
Ideas, 127, 235
Idomeneus, 37
Igneous, 12, 66, 145, 177, 189-190,
    224, 228
Ignipotent, 142
Ignis Natura Renovatur Integra, 12,
    41, 192
Ignorance, 118, 208, 220
Ignorant, 6, 186, 216, 236
Ilex, 159
Ilium, 6, 16, 23
Illuminated, 4, 44, 60, 70, 92-93,
    106, 119, 162, 202, 214
Illuminated Void, 106
Illumination, 62, 70, 83, 95, 108,
    136, 211-212
Illusion, 63, 67, 206, 230
Illusory, 20, 67, 178, 214, 230
Imagine, 14, 31, 118, 174, 199
Imitates, 93

Imitating, 181
Imitatus, 200
Immaculate, 5, 122, 186, 194
Immolate, 86, 88, 100, 105
Immortal, 27, 43, 186, 197, 234, 238
Immortality, 206
Immortalizes, 72
Imperishable, 11-12
Impersonalization, 106
Impotent, 184
Impudence, 122, 184-185
Incarnate, 78, 149, 156, 208, 234
Incarnated, 1, 56, 65, 77, 144, 157,
    173, 231, 236
Incarnates, 166, 229
Incense, 94-95
India, 48, 56, 118, 219, 221, 236, 239
Indian, 171, 219
Individual, 106, 121, 166, 175, 213,
    219, 222, 225-227, 229
Individuality, 65, 77, 106, 165-166
Individually, 83, 219
Individuals, 120, 153, 192, 201
Inebriation, 51, 71
Inferior, 34, 49, 151-152, 167, 177-
    178, 205, 218, 224, 226, 231,
    234, 236
Inferior Molecular World, 151-152,
    178
Infernal, 22, 24, 49, 52-53, 100, 155,
    166, 178, 185, 192, 211, 227,
    234
Infernal Gods, 192
Infernal Worlds, 22, 24, 49, 53, 100,
    178, 185, 192, 211
Inferno, 22, 26, 46, 142
Infernos, 28, 84, 112, 125, 167, 227
Infraconscious, 70, 84
Infradimensions, 8, 139, 218
Infrasexuals, 210
Inhalation, 4, 13, 118, 163, 180
Initiate, 52, 99, 146, 152, 156, 158,
    165, 167, 169, 190, 221, 225,
    227-229, 232, 239
Initiated, 87, 92, 95, 229, 239
Initiates, 35, 52, 60-61, 120, 148,
    156, 158, 193, 219, 225

Initiatic, 12, 62, 79, 90, 147, 157, 194-195
Initiatic Colleges, 62
Initiatic Stone, 79, 90, 194-195
Initiation, 52, 62, 99, 105, 167, 209, 214, 225, 228, 232
Innermost, 5, 27, 29, 84, 97, 128, 133, 135, 141, 175, 197, 206-207, 215-216, 223-226, 228, 231, 234
Innocence, 167, 186
Innocent, 7, 35, 48, 53, 86, 108, 120, 155, 170-171, 174, 185-186
INRI, 41, 192
Insects, 176
Insobertha, 135
Instinct, 115, 119, 123, 136, 155, 219
Intellect, 4, 67, 69, 81-83, 97, 123, 136, 216, 226
Intellectual, 11, 55-56, 67-70, 83-84, 90, 94, 135, 166, 190, 212, 222, 226-227, 237-238
Intelligence, 7, 176, 208, 215, 226, 233
Intelligent, 20, 34, 175, 180, 226
Intelligently, 77, 80, 93, 104, 179
Intimate Christ, 51, 79, 195
Introvert, 82
Intuit, 170
Intuitive, 40, 233
Intuitively, 154, 193, 213
Inverential Peace, 1, 212
Invisible, 6, 79, 163, 223
Invocations, 54
Invoke, 87, 168
Invoked, 36, 87-88, 177, 191
Invoking, 48-49, 193
IO, 135, 157
Iod-Havah, 119
Iohanes, 1
Ionian, 47
Ireland, 62, 162
Iris, 169
Iron, 24, 103, 141-142, 176, 193
Isa, 27
Isaiah, 63
Ishvara, 199

Isis, 1, 4, 27-28, 30, 79, 92, 135, 141, 168, 218-219
Island, 36-37, 47, 49, 72, 79, 109, 119, 151, 160-1632
Israel, 51, 73, 227
Israelites, 11-12
Italian, 9, 126-127, 160
Italians, 38, 191
Italic Peninsula, 35
Italus, 38
Italy, 48, 98, 192
Ithaca, 60, 71
Iztaccihuatl, 63
Jackal, 131
Jacob, 1, 51, 195, 218
Jagrenat, 155
Jahve, 145-146
Jain, 205
Jano, 79, 90
Janus, 1, 127-128, 192
Japan, 207
Javelins, 48
Jealousy, 52, 127, 197
Jerusalem, 68, 146, 165
Jesus, 41, 69, 77, 102, 111, 116, 146, 156, 164, 167, 187, 192, 202, 207, 213-214, 219, 223, 232-233, 237
Jewels, 36, 89
Jinn, 48, 65, 78, 120, 160
Jinn Temple, 65
Jinns, 1, 18, 38, 49, 90, 128
John, 69, 119, 200, 214, 222, 233
Jordan, 165
Joseph of Arimathea, 187
Jove, 25
Joy, 3, 41, 57, 64, 165, 214, 233
Joyful, 99, 163, 171, 177, 183
Joyfully, 7, 28, 39, 41, 197
Judas, 125
Judge, 100, 132-133, 153
Judges, 53, 132-133, 179
Judging, 203
Judgment, 54, 133, 233
Judo, 13-14
Juices, 171
July, 94

Juno, 60, 85-88, 126, 160, 169, 191
Jupiter, 4, 15-17, 23, 36-37, 73, 87,
     99, 141, 157, 169-170
Justice, 25, 52, 54, 122, 132, 144
K-meson, 8-9
Kabbalah, 52, 102, 148, 157, 213,
     216-217, 220, 224-227, 229,
     231-232, 236, 238-239
Kabbalists, 195
Kabir, 57, 69, 116, 146, 156, 167,
     187, 192, 202, 207, 224
Kalayoni, 122
Kali, 85, 87, 111-112, 117, 122, 155,
     227
Kali Astaroth, 85, 87
Kali Yuga, 111
Kalpas, 199
Kaom, 130
Karma, 15, 38, 130-133, 173-174,
     176-181, 213, 231, 234, 239
Karmic, 18
Kaum, 145-149
Khafra, 146
Khayyám, 105
Khem, 27, 146, 214
Kinetic, 190
King Evander, 155, 159
King Helenus, 59-61
King Herod, 155
King Latinum, 60
King Latinus, 126-128, 191-192
King of Libya, 85
King Priam, 15
King Titurel, 184
Kingdom, 1, 25-26, 28, 36-37, 45,
     48, 50, 52-53, 56, 77, 98, 108,
     139, 190, 192, 207, 214, 226,
     233, 237
Kingdom of Heaven, 207
Kingdoms, 36-37, 67, 146, 226
Kings, 25, 75-76, 78, 126, 141, 144
Kiss, 4, 40, 52, 107, 117, 174, 178
Klingsor, 183-186
Knees, 101, 110, 178, 184
Knights, 1, 79-80, 183-187
Koan, 96
Kola, 171

Korea, 206
Krishna, 26, 65, 77, 102, 122-123,
     230, 232
Ku, 95
Kundabuffer, 111-112, 122-123, 126,
     145, 227-228
Kundalini, 4, 12-13, 15-17, 27, 30,
     37, 51, 92, 97, 118, 134-137,
     139, 141-142, 154, 163, 165,
     168-170, 177-178, 189-191,
     217-219, 224, 227-228, 238
Kundry, 79, 183, 185-186
Labyrinth, 97, 149
Ladder, 40, 51, 218
Laf, 193, 195, 196
Lake, 82-83, 184, 186, 191, 234
Lamb, 160, 187, 224, 238
Lance, 184
Language, 9, 39, 77, 101, 120, 194,
     202, 226
Laodamia, 102
Laodicea, 35
Laomedon, 48
Lapidem, 75
Lapis, 73
Lapiz-Electrix, 1, 195
Larvae, 154
Larynx, 56
Lasciviousness, 184
Last Supper, 178
Latin, 1, 62, 79, 98, 159, 218, 222,
     231, 235, 237-238
Latinum, 60
Latinus, 126-128, 191-192
Latium, 109, 126-127, 159, 169
Latona, 192
Laurentians, 142
Laurentines, 159
Lavinia, 127-128
Lavinium, 98
Law, 8, 24, 28, 39, 65, 79, 99, 130-
     133, 144, 152, 165, 177, 179,
     200, 205, 213, 217, 219, 231,
     234
Law of Eternal Return, 65
Law of Karma, 132, 231
Law of Recurrence, 79, 130

Law of Universal Harmony, 205
Laws, 8, 21, 34, 157, 176, 204, 220,
    238
Lawyers, 132
Laziness, 153, 236
Lazio, 18, 38, 71, 87
Lazy, 103
Lead, 140, 142, 149, 227, 235
Leadbeater, 207
Legion, 125-126, 139, 220, 226
Leibnitz, 173, 231
Lemaitre, 31, 34
Lemnos, 61
Lemuria, 72, 119-121, 145
Lemurians, 35, 121
Lerna, 100, 166
Lernaean Hydra, 155
Lethe, 165, 167-168, 178, 186-187,
    228-229
Levi, 12
Liafail, 75, 195
Liberate, 67, 69, 133
Liberated, 25-26, 31, 59, 69, 83, 93,
    203-204, 232
Liberates, 69
Liberating, 69, 84, 133, 197
Liberation, 69, 81, 84, 197-200, 202,
    204, 206-207, 234
Liberty, 165, 179
Libya, 85
Lie, 109, 159, 210
Lies, 36, 215, 227
Light, 1, 8-9, 12-14, 17, 23, 33, 39,
    43-44, 49, 59-60, 62, 85, 90-
    92, 94, 96, 102-104, 106, 115,
    131, 147, 155, 157, 160-161,
    168, 172, 178, 185, 194, 208,
    213-215, 218, 221, 229, 239
Lighting, 16, 52, 128
Lightkeeper, 121
Lightning, 11, 40-41, 51-52, 54, 142,
    151
Lights of Saint Elmo, 11
Lilith, 85, 111
Limbo, 100
Limbus, 158
Linen, 147

Lingam, 41, 206, 209
Lingam Sarira, 209
Lingam-Yoni, 148, 189
Lion, 37, 71, 155, 166
Lips, 4, 15, 71, 77, 86, 94, 107, 148,
    152, 174, 194
Liquor, 115, 171
Litelantes, 101, 130-131, 166
Logic, 21, 69
Logical, 7-8, 175, 197, 237
Logos, 4, 20, 77, 111, 142-143, 155,
    163, 167-168, 183-184, 186,
    191, 210, 224, 229-230
Longevity, 206
Longinus, 185
Lotus, 56, 89, 92, 218
Love, 3-4, 12, 14, 16, 24, 28, 39, 53,
    60, 85, 87, 100-101, 107-108,
    117-118, 126, 129-130, 137,
    139, 141, 148, 164, 170, 177-
    178, 183, 187, 194, 201, 203,
    216, 219, 224, 228-230
Loved, 37, 100, 145
Lover, 108, 113
Lovers, 201, 235
Loving, 4, 16, 57, 92
Loving-kindness, 3
Lucid, 13, 94, 101
Lucifer, 86, 125-126, 157, 174, 215
Luciferic, 79, 112, 122-123, 125, 155,
    157
Lucifers, 91, 145
Luke, 52, 78
Lumisial, 81, 95, 148, 223
Lunar, 26, 65, 78-79, 88-91, 101, 121,
    123, 126, 180, 184, 189, 202,
    207, 212, 214, 223, 229, 232,
    236-237
Lunar Apocalypse, 91
Lunar Chain, 89
Lunar Mahamanvantara, 91, 229
Lunar Race, 78
Lust, 107, 122, 153, 184-185, 215,
    230, 235-237
Lustral, 17, 87
Lycanthropy, 111-113
Lying, 139, 154, 159

Lyre, 99, 120, 159
M, 49, 125, 156, 196, 209, 225
M. M., 125, 156, 209
Ma, 14
Machine, 55, 123, 135-136, 204
Macrocosm, 205
Madness, 86, 88, 201, 203
Maeterlinck, 175-176
Magdalene, 79, 222
Magi, 156
Magic, 16, 28, 62, 104, 115, 122, 130,
    145, 149, 158, 170, 193, 195,
    206, 215-217, 220, 222, 225,
    227, 230, 235-236, 238-239
Magical, 6, 8, 12-13, 41, 54, 60, 73,
    80, 88, 99, 122, 137, 145,
    190, 205, 224
Magician, 122, 183-185, 204, 215-
    216
Magicians, 203, 215
Magnes, 1, 195
Magnetic, 20, 45, 56, 112, 135, 174,
    189-190, 235
Maha-Lakshmi, 135, 227
Maha-Saraswati, 135
Mahabharata, 157
Mahakasyapa, 93
Mahamanvantara, 33-34, 44-45, 57-
    58, 89, 91, 145, 197, 229
Mahapralaya, 33, 91, 229
Mahatmas, 62
Maiden, 169, 171
Maidens, 36, 47, 49, 158, 170, 186
Maithuna, 13, 29, 51, 90, 104, 114-
    116, 121, 142, 145, 148-149,
    167, 184, 189, 192, 194,
    201-202, 206, 210-211, 214,
    229-230, 233, 238
Major, 62, 157, 213-215, 225
Major Brother, 157
Major Mysteries, 62, 213-215, 225
Male, 119, 132, 148, 221, 235
Maliaco Gulf, 35
Man, 3, 11-12, 19, 23, 28-29, 31, 36,
    47, 49, 58, 60, 71, 77-79, 83,
    85, 88, 96-98, 105, 113, 119,
    126, 129, 131, 135, 145-147,

154-155, 165-168, 184, 187,
    190-191, 195, 207, 209, 212,
    214, 217, 221, 225, 227, 229-
    230, 233, 237-238
Manah, 179
Mandatory, 179
Mangroves, 107
Mankind, 72
Mantra, 14, 30, 41-42, 66, 93-95, 230
Mantras, 80, 133, 163, 181, 192
Mantric, 104
Man-woman, 27
Mara, 5, 125-126
Marguerite Gautier, 174
Marriage, 88, 126, 148, 222, 230, 237
Married, 59, 128-129, 221
Mars, 157, 191
Martian, 144
Marxist-Leninist, 175-176
Mary, 79, 111-112, 135, 218, 222
Mary Magdalene, 79, 222
Masculine, 99, 149, 224, 229, 235
Masculine-feminine, 27
Masonry, 179, 209
Masons, 1, 179
Mass, 8, 20, 33, 43, 156, 161, 215
Masses, 53
Master, 4, 26, 29, 40, 56, 65, 93,
    95-96, 99, 101, 122, 145-
    146, 148, 164, 166, 193, 199,
    214-215, 223, 225, 227, 232,
    237-238
Master of Masters, 166, 199
Masters, 45, 62, 79, 166, 179, 194,
    199, 215, 223, 236-237
Mastery, 97, 100
Mater Dolorosa, 139, 151
Mathematical, 27, 31
Mathematician, 33
Mathematics, 20, 34
Matricides, 53
Matrimony, 111, 149, 196, 213, 215,
    217, 221, 224, 226, 231-232,
    236
Matripadma, 135
Matrons, 144, 169

Matter, 8-9, 19, 21, 33-34, 44-45,
    56-57, 65, 67, 69, 89, 97, 112,
    115, 120, 129, 131, 135, 137-
    138, 145, 167, 173, 193, 195,
    202, 205-207, 210, 213, 218,
    227, 232
Matthew, 52, 99, 118, 146, 187, 191,
    196, 208-209, 212, 237
Maya, 67, 206, 230
Mayan, 156, 225
Mechanical, 20, 132, 176, 204, 218,
    220, 228, 234
Mechanicity, 69, 132, 176
Mechanics, 19, 34, 220
Mechanism, 45, 68
Medicine, 62, 115
Medieval, 1, 41
Meditate, 30, 89, 118, 163, 217, 230
Meditating, 39, 64, 95
Meditation, 13, 29, 51, 56, 67, 69,
    81-83, 93-96, 138, 164, 172-
    173, 185, 204, 220, 230-231,
    238
Medulla, 99, 206, 217-218, 228
Medullar, 145, 189, 217-218, 228
Medusa, 125
Megaera, 125
Melchizedek, 76, 78-79
Memento Homo, 105
Memories, 88, 167, 171, 178, 215,
    229
Memory, 1, 5, 11, 24, 31, 39, 41, 61,
    72, 85, 105, 120, 129, 146,
    151, 165, 167, 192, 197, 213,
    215
Memphis, 61-62
Men, 4, 7-8, 15, 17, 33, 36-37, 43, 48,
    60-61, 64, 71, 75, 77, 80, 87,
    89, 100, 107, 109-111, 115-
    116, 126-127, 142, 144, 148,
    158, 160, 162, 183, 190, 192,
    211, 221, 227, 231
Meng Shan, 93-96
Mental, 67, 70, 81-82, 84, 94, 198,
    207, 216, 218, 231, 233, 236,
    238
Mentally, 94, 180

Mephistopheles, 203
Mercabah, 58
Mercury, 11, 13, 87, 158, 190, 215
Mercy, 5, 152
Merits, 101, 189, 228
Merloc, 160
Mernoc, 161
Message, 1, 115, 119, 169, 173, 201,
    205, 211, 218, 225, 232, 234
Messages, 11, 111-112, 135, 199
Messenger, 34, 59, 87, 157, 169, 221
Messer Marchese, 153
Metal, 147, 157, 214
Metallic, 15, 147
Metamorphosis, 112, 170
Metaphysical, 9
Meteors, 11
Metropolitan Cathedral, 63
Mexico, 1, 12, 63-64, 101, 113, 116,
    156, 173, 178, 207
Microcosm, 205
Microcosmic, 28
Microcosmos, 90, 218
Microphysics, 21
Midas, 153
Middle, 36, 129, 209, 223, 237
Middle Ages, 129
Midnight, 63, 95
Militant Church, 79
Military, 62, 104, 121
Milk, 24, 120, 143-144
Milky Way, 39
Mind, 20, 29, 31, 38, 40-41, 56-57,
    67-70, 81-84, 87, 93-94, 103,
    105-106, 115, 119, 124-125,
    127, 135-136, 151, 153, 155,
    160, 164, 167-168, 170, 173,
    181, 197-199, 204, 208, 211,
    213, 215-216, 229-231, 233,
    238
Minds, 45, 48, 239
Mineral, 25-26, 45, 50, 56, 67, 103,
    139, 178, 216, 226
Mineral Kingdom, 25-26, 45, 50, 56,
    139, 226
Minerva, 16, 144
Minos, 100

Minotaur, 97
Miracles, 126, 233
Miraculous, 186, 228
Miraculously, 132, 170, 187
Mirror, 8, 49
Mithra, 61, 193
Mo Chao, 70
Molecular, 135, 151-152, 165, 178
Molecules, 8, 20
Molochs, 175
Mona Lisa, 174
Monad, 5, 27, 173-174, 215, 217,
    225-226, 231-232, 234
Monadic, 91
Monastery, 95, 162
Monk, 94-95, 160
Monks, 161, 168, 207
Monsalvat, 79, 183-184
Montserrat, 186
Moon, 23, 39, 44, 49, 60, 62, 67, 89-
    91, 109, 111, 157, 214
Morning, 42, 122, 184, 196
Mortal, 3-4, 16, 28, 53, 126, 218, 223
Mortals, 3, 6, 63, 68, 100
Moses, 12, 77, 221, 224-227
Mother, 2-8, 15-17, 27-28, 30, 36-37,
    49, 85, 88-92, 97-98, 111,
    118, 122, 129-130, 134-135,
    137-139, 141-143, 151, 154,
    163, 165, 168-169, 177-178,
    189, 202, 218-219, 223-225,
    227, 230, 233
Mother Kundalini, 4, 15-17, 27,
    30, 37, 97, 118, 135, 137,
    139, 141-142, 154, 163, 165,
    168-169, 177-178, 189, 218,
    224, 227
Mother Space, 8, 27, 49, 85, 88, 91-
    92, 98, 111, 122, 135
Mother-death, 28
Mothers, 177
Mount Ida, 17, 36
Mount Oeta, 52, 156
Mount Wilson, 31
Mountain, 23, 71, 91, 97-98, 105,
    118, 146, 162, 179
Mountains, 63-64, 93, 127, 225

Mouse, 93, 224
Movement, 20, 44, 90, 115-116, 118,
    123, 136, 164, 199, 203-204,
    206, 213, 223, 233
Movements, 19, 118, 181, 190
Mu, 72, 119, 122, 145
Mud, 68, 117, 122, 152
Muddy, 50, 139
Multidimensionally, 21
Multiple, 12, 21, 78, 100, 121
Multipliable, 176
Multiplicity, 24, 189, 220
Multiplied, 33
Multiplying, 7, 107, 121
Muse, 85, 135, 159, 183
Music, 64, 164, 233
Mustard, 118
Mutant, 11
Mycenae, 59
Myrtles, 105
Mysteries, 7, 18, 41, 51, 61-62, 89,
    103, 132, 137, 145-147,
    149, 157, 168, 170-171, 187,
    206-209, 213-215, 223, 225,
    232, 234
Mysterium, 62
Mystery, 5, 39, 61, 137, 144, 170,
    194, 219, 227-228, 235
Mythomania, 203, 212
Mythomaniac, 202-203
Nadi, 118, 218, 227
Nahua, 156, 164
Nauthiz, 173
Nebo, 77
Negation, 69
Negative, 28, 43, 45, 49, 85, 111, 123,
    126, 157, 216, 227-228
Negotiations, 132, 179, 180-181
Nemea, 155, 166
Neophyte, 65, 147, 201, 222
Neptune, 4-5, 16, 47, 109, 144
Nereus, 141
Nerves, 108, 118, 218
Nervous, 118, 217-218, 228
Nessus, 52, 156
Neutral, 45
Neutrino, 9

Neutrinos, 20, 43
Newness, 83
Newspaper, 211
Nicodemus, 167, 202, 207, 233
Nine, 100, 141, 225
Ninth, 57, 86, 91, 99-100, 102, 125,
    137, 142, 147-149, 167, 170,
    201, 208-209, 227, 232, 234,
    238
Ninth Circle, 125, 142
Ninth Sphere, 57, 86, 91, 99-100,
    102, 137, 142, 148-149, 167,
    170, 201, 208-209, 227, 232,
    234, 238
Nirvana, 5, 192, 197-198, 203, 232-
    233, 237
Nirvanic, 197, 232
Nirvi-Kalpa-Samadhi, 56, 106
Nitrogen, 20, 57
Nocturnal, 4, 115
Nordic, 13, 35, 163
North, 5, 49, 79, 162, 195, 225
Noumenon, 34
Nuclear, 45
Nuclei, 20, 43
Nucleons, 19
Nucleus, 31, 33-34
Number, 7-8, 62, 231
Numbers, 20, 227-228
Nuncio, 158
Nuptial, 86, 88
Nymphs, 5, 107, 169-172
Observation, 19-20, 45, 70, 82, 96
Observe, 21, 70, 81, 84, 89, 117, 144,
    181
Observed, 64, 87, 174
Occidental, 157, 207
Occult, 9, 57, 62, 78, 111-112, 148,
    170, 198, 211, 227-228, 236
Occult Science, 57, 62, 111
Occultism, 27, 170
Ocean, 5, 36, 38-39, 44, 70, 72-73,
    94, 106, 119, 161, 170, 172,
    199, 220
Odyssey, 109
Oenotrians, 38
Oeta, 52, 156

Offering, 59, 95, 99
Offerings, 24, 35, 60, 87
Ogre, 71
Olin, 116-117
Olympus, 16, 151
Omega, 205
Omen, 23, 112, 160
Omnipotence, 197
Omnipotent, 6
Omnipresent, 34
Omniscience, 197, 199
Omphale, 52, 156
Open Sesame, 39
Ophite, 74
Opposite, 43, 45, 111, 120-121, 210
Opposites, 69-70
Oracle, 12, 35-38, 73-74
Orange, 107
Orco, 158
Orcus, 100, 155, 158
Ordeal, 90, 102, 138, 147, 232
Ordeals, 47, 138, 147
Order of Melchizedek, 76, 78-79
Orestes, 59
Organ, 111-112, 122-123, 126, 145,
    227-228, 235
Organic, 55, 94, 227
Organism, 14, 20, 38, 79, 112, 142,
    189-190, 217, 219, 228, 231-
    232, 235
Organisms, 8, 25, 175, 207, 218, 235
Organized, 44, 101
Organs, 86, 116, 184, 195, 222, 232
Oriental, 64, 106, 157, 190, 197, 223
Origin, 21, 28, 34, 36-37, 81-82, 119,
    121, 123, 126, 167, 209, 224,
    232
Original, 31, 41, 45, 52, 62, 128, 207,
    217, 229, 235
Orpheus, 74, 99, 159
Os, 115-118
Ovid, 112
Owl, 87
Oxen, 48
Oxygen, 20, 57
Pacific Ocean, 72, 119
Palm Sunday, 68

Pan, 11
Paracelsus, 116
Paralda, 164
Parallel Universes, 7-9, 12-13, 18, 21,
        32, 34, 57, 139, 163, 193
Paranirvanic, 91
Paranishpanna, 57
Paris, 16
Parricide, 153
Parsifal, 182-183, 185-187
Particle, 8, 19, 224
Particles, 8-9, 19-21, 44-45
Parvati, 111, 135
Pascal Lamb, 187, 238
Passion, 6, 16, 85-88, 102, 105, 107,
        153, 185, 222, 234, 236
Passions, 4, 85, 159, 184, 236
Patala, 205
Patar, 41, 194-195
Patience, 105, 165, 173, 211
Patrick, 161
Paul of Tarsus, 79
Pausanias, 12
Peacocks, 129
Pearl, 86
Pentalpha, 51
Pentecost 12-13, 161-162, 217, 224
Per Aspera Ad Astra, 79
Percent, 40, 187
Perception, 83, 93, 108, 218
Perfect, 70, 81-82, 86, 91, 111, 149,
        157, 177, 194, 196, 211, 213,
        215, 217, 221-222, 224-226,
        229, 231-234, 236-237
Perfection, 194, 198-199, 203, 235-
        236
Pergamum, 36-37, 159
Personalities, 144, 177, 215, 223
Personality, 55, 165, 223, 225
Peter, 41, 78, 91, 194-195, 209
Phallic, 187
Phallus, 51, 104, 148, 219
Phallus-uterus, 189
Phantom, 7, 53
Pharaohs, 61, 117, 131, 147-148,
        164, 192
Pharisees, 53, 103, 165, 210, 233

Philae, 156
Philoctetes, 41
Philosophical, 11, 41, 51, 215
Philosophical Stone, 41, 51, 215
Philosophy, 62, 207, 233
Phoebus, 36, 38, 48, 85-86
Phoenix, 186, 195
Physical, 6, 12, 38, 41, 49, 55, 57, 62,
        64-65, 72, 95, 112, 131, 137,
        157, 174, 178, 190, 193, 217,
        219, 223-224, 231-232, 236
Physicist, 8, 19, 206, 208
Physics, 11, 20-21, 43, 45
Piglets, 159-160
Pilate, 125
Pillar, 152
Pine, 170
Pineal, 12, 56, 121, 221
Pines, 72, 169-171
Pingala, 118
Pisces, 78
Pituitary, 121
Planck, 8
Planes, 7, 9
Planet, 9, 89-91, 148, 157-158, 176
Planetary, 79, 142
Plant, 26, 67, 170, 226
Plants, 26, 89, 170, 225, 235
Plasma, 45
Plato, 170, 214, 232
Pleroma, 12, 187
Pliny, 62, 75, 174
Pluralized, 55, 62, 65, 119-121, 123,
        126, 136, 139, 151, 178, 187,
        203-204, 211, 223
Pluto, 52-53, 98-99, 102, 192
Poem, 63, 74, 157
Poems, 39
Poet, 160, 219
Poetry, 155
Polar, 79, 119, 157
Polarities, 111, 120
Polarization, 189-190
Police, 130
Polidorus, 25
Pollute, 23, 47
Polluted, 15, 37, 47-48

Polluting, 47
Pollution, 115
Polybotes, 102
Polydorus, 24, 35
Polyphemus, 71, 73, 75
Pomponio Mela, 62
Pontecorvo, 9
Popocatepetl, 64
Pornographic, 115
Porsenna, 144
POSCLA, 199
Posture, 13-14, 29
Potencies, 59, 200, 209
Potency, 4, 13, 221
Potion, 109
Poverty, 100
Power, 1, 4, 6, 34, 53, 77, 94, 111-
    112, 116, 122, 133, 139, 174,
    177-179, 190-191, 193, 195,
    214, 221, 227-228, 230, 235
Powers, 6, 12, 27, 89, 91, 137, 145,
    170, 172, 177, 189-190, 198,
    211, 215, 224, 228-229, 236,
    239
Practical, 211, 238
Practice, 13-14, 30, 42, 54, 66, 80,
    82, 92-93, 104, 115, 117, 133,
    145, 148, 163, 180, 196, 204,
    211, 219, 236, 239
Practiced, 62, 83, 104, 148, 179, 239
Practices, 12, 66, 103, 117-118, 166,
    180, 209, 216, 235-236, 238
Practicing, 192, 227
Prajna, 94, 233
Prakriti, 27-28, 49, 85, 92, 111, 192,
    219
Pralaya, 57, 91, 197
Prana, 116, 118, 135, 180, 227
Pranayama, 13, 180
Pray, 3, 23, 38, 92, 98, 118, 138, 227
Prayed, 14, 94, 98, 138, 177, 227
Prayer, 13-14, 17, 92, 172, 184, 191-
    192
Prayers, 3, 60, 98, 122, 160, 192, 209,
    238
Praying, 14, 30, 107
Priam, 15, 23, 59, 87, 141

Pride, 53, 152, 212, 215, 225, 236-
    237
Priest, 56, 145, 215, 224, 235
Priestess, 51, 60, 88, 97-98, 130, 142,
    145, 148, 235
Priestesses, 61-62, 76, 78, 148
Priesthood, 95, 215, 235
Priests, 62, 76-78, 144, 207
Projecting, 166-167
Prophecies, 38, 98, 144-145
Prophesies, 15, 59, 204
Prophesy, 38, 159
Prophesying, 203
Prophet, 60, 126
Prophetess, 15, 38, 60, 174
Prophetic, 60, 143
Prophets, 165
Proserpine, 28, 49, 97-99, 111
Protect, 36, 236
Protected, 121, 186, 235-236
Protection, 4, 179, 230
Protective, 6
Protector, 18, 109, 142, 224
Protector Spirit, 18
Proton, 8, 43, 45
Protoplasmic Root Race, 119
Protoplasmic, 72, 119, 202, 207, 218,
    223
Prudent, 77
Pseudo-esoteric, 138
Pseudo-learned, 112
Pseudo-occultism, 7, 116, 207
Pseudo-occultist, 21, 138
Pseudo-occultists, 27-28, 132, 168
Psuchikon, 209
Psyche, 13, 218, 226, 234
Psychic, 25, 198, 201, 220, 226, 230
Psychoanalysis, 81
Psychological, 55, 81-82, 123, 138,
    154, 218, 220, 225, 229-230
Ptah-ra, 12
Puncta, 19-21, 34
Purgatorial, 151-154, 165, 167, 178
Purgatorial Region, 151-154, 165,
    167, 178
Purgatory, 150, 152-154, 165, 229
Purifications, 154

Purify, 152, 229
Purifying, 17, 236
Purity, 4, 117, 214, 217, 230, 235-236, 238
Purple, 145
Purple Race, 145
Purplish, 15, 171
Purusha, 199
Putrefaction, 37
Pygmalion, 153
Pygmies, 116, 205
Pyre, 52, 88, 156
Pyrrhus, 15, 59
Pythagoras, 24, 232
Pythagoreans, 1
Python, 122
Pythoness, 97
Qabbalah, 156
Queen, 3-5, 28, 60, 85-88, 98-100, 102, 105, 121, 127, 219
Queens, 76, 78
Quetzalcoatl, 102, 222, 225
Quietude, 70, 83-84, 198
Ra, 41, 133
Ram IO, 92
Race, 18, 36, 38, 72-73, 78-79, 119-121, 145, 157, 159-160, 174, 215, 225, 234, 238
Races, 73, 90, 119-120, 213, 221
Radiation, 31
Radio, 7
Rain, 164, 195
Rainbows, 113
Rajeswari, 135
Ram, 135
Rams, 98
Ravens, 47
Ray, 37, 54, 217, 220
Rays, 13, 39-40, 43, 109, 152, 221
Razor, 149, 179, 189
Reality, 51, 55, 67, 69-71, 84, 106, 108, 191, 199, 202, 213, 216, 225, 227, 233, 238
Realization, 84, 97, 141, 175, 197, 206-207, 234, 239
Realize, 69
Reason, 60, 82, 132, 220

Reasoning, 70, 226
Rebel, 16
Rebellion, 79, 127, 219, 228
Reborn, 24, 33, 130, 151, 195
Recapitulate, 147
Rector, 18, 149
Recurrence, 79, 130
Red, 15, 87, 107, 112, 147, 157, 162, 171, 183, 219
Redeemer, 183, 192
Reed, 163
Reflect, 8, 70, 84, 202
Reflected, 194
Reflecting, 101, 152
Reflection, 70, 82-83
Reflections, 49
Reflective, 70, 90
Regenerated, 187
Reincarnate, 21, 65, 91, 94, 198
Reincarnating, 65, 215, 225
Reincarnation, 51, 65, 129, 177
Reincorporate, 22, 24-25, 65, 77
Relativity, 31
Relaxation, 30, 82-83, 150, 180
Religion, 1, 53, 91, 132, 214, 216, 222, 238
Religions, 122, 218, 222-224, 226, 230
Religious, 160-161, 205, 217, 235
Remorse, 40, 133, 183, 185, 187
Remus, 143-144
Renounce, 94, 168, 175, 197-199, 222, 234, 237
Renounced, 176, 192, 203
Repeat, 118, 169
Repeated, 28, 33, 79, 96, 122, 130, 166
Repeating, 209
Repeats, 152, 155, 166
Repentance, 152
Repentant, 40, 94
Repetition, 26, 51, 132, 162
Reproduction, 121
Reptiles, 107, 122
Republic of Mexico, 173
Resentment, 81
Respiratory, 12, 238

Resurrection, 116, 161-162, 164
Retrospectively, 33
Return, 23-26, 51, 65, 103-105, 113,
    129, 147, 162, 164, 166-167,
    218, 225
Returned, 41, 117, 160, 162
Returning, 24-25
Returns, 65, 152
Reveille, 184
Revelation, 82, 126, 128, 195, 217,
    234
Revolution, 9, 28, 175, 204, 211, 215,
    220, 222, 225-226, 228-229,
    231, 233, 239
Revolutionary, 7, 9, 30, 119, 204, 221
Revolutions, 200
Rhea, 135, 141, 219
Rhoeteum, 36
Rhu, 91
Ri, 42, 133
Rich, 36, 47, 160-161
Riches, 109
Rig Veda, 43, 221
Right, 13, 15, 18, 54, 57, 78-79, 104,
    107, 125, 130, 132, 152, 163,
    178-181, 186, 197-198, 205,
    216
Rita, 129, 131-133, 149
Rites, 59, 109, 220
Ritual, 4, 59, 187, 214, 229
River, 7, 35, 50, 100, 120, 122, 139,
    159-160, 162, 165, 167, 228
River Jordan, 165
River Lethe, 165, 167, 228
Rivers, 28, 98, 120, 178, 191, 195,
    229
Ro, 133
Robber, 153
Robes, 18
Rock, 35, 38-39, 41, 73, 82, 91, 97,
    156, 163, 171, 194
Rocks, 5, 26, 73, 75, 87, 90, 172
Rocky, 121, 156, 162, 167
Roman, 62, 132, 144, 163
Romulus, 143-144
Root, 4-5, 21, 27-28, 33, 62, 72-73,
    79, 81, 90, 119-121, 126, 157,

160, 174, 215, 220-221, 225,
    230, 235, 237-238
Root Race, 72-73, 79, 119-121, 157,
    160, 174, 225
Root Races, 73, 90, 119-120
Roots, 24-25, 90, 111, 116, 215, 223
Rose, 23, 52, 63, 94-95, 105, 160,
    172, 228
Rosicrucian-Gnostics, 12
Rosicrucians, 1, 228
Ru, 133
Rune, 10-11, 13-14, 27, 29-30, 39,
    41-42, 51-54, 63, 65-66, 77,
    79-80, 89, 91-92, 103-104,
    114-118, 129, 131-133, 145-
    149, 159, 161, 163-164, 173,
    175, 177, 179-181, 193, 195-
    196, 205-207, 209, 211
Rune Ar, 39, 41-42
Rune Bar, 77, 79-80
Rune D, 133
Rune Dorn, 118
Rune F, 133
Rune Fa, 10, 14, 117
Rune Fah, 11, 13
Rune Gebo, 206
Rune Gibur, 205, 207, 209
Rune Hagal, 159, 161, 163-164
Rune Is, 27, 29-30, 209
Rune K, 148
Rune Kaum, 145-149
Rune Laf, 193, 195
Rune Not, 173, 175, 177, 179-181
Rune O, 133
Rune of Mercury, 13
Rune Olin, 116-117
Rune Os, 115-118
Rune Rita, 129, 131-133, 149
Rune Sig, 51-54
Rune Thorn, 103-104, 116
Rune Tyr, 63, 65-66, 80
Rune U, 133
Rune Ur, 89, 91-92
Runes, 80, 101, 103, 118, 163, 204,
    211
Runic, 13-14, 41, 90-91, 118, 133,
    157, 209, 211

Runic Letters, 133
Runic Ur, 90-91
Rye, 171
S. O. S., 179
Sabbaths, 47
Sabines, 143
Sacrament, 121, 229
Sacred Order of Tibet, 79
Sacrifice, 23, 47-48, 88, 99, 176
Sacrificed, 71, 86, 98, 163, 176, 187
Sacrifices, 164, 184
Sacrificing, 48, 87, 176
Sadducees, 165
Sadhaka, 4
Sadhu, 49
Sadness, 82
Sage, 40, 45
Sahaja Maithuna, 114-115, 233
Sahasrara, 56, 228
Sail, 23, 37-38, 48, 109
Sailboat, 171
Sailed, 36, 48, 162
Sailing, 35, 109
Sailors, 37
Sails, 60, 109
Saint, 11, 161-162, 184, 203, 215,
    222, 238
Saint Ailbeo, 161
Saint Brendan, 162
Saint Malo, 161
Saint Patrick, 161
Saints, 51, 53, 84, 158, 160, 162
Sais, 61
Salamanders, 116
Salt, 152
Salvation, 3, 79, 199
Samadhi, 56, 82-84, 94, 106, 108,
    173, 231, 233, 238
Samoans, 1
Samothrace, 61
Samsara, 65, 218
Samson, 52, 156
Sanctity, 103
Sanctuaries, 156, 170
Sanctuary, 38-39, 41, 65, 97-98, 101,
    155-156, 177
Sanctuary of Hercules, 155

Sanctum Regnum, 207
Sannyasi, 30
Sarcasm, 113
Sarira, 209
Satan, 51, 104, 106, 112, 123, 146,
    214-215, 227, 233
Satanic, 112, 123, 178, 187, 210
Satori, 83-84, 173, 233
Saturn, 73, 128, 157
Saturnian, 191
Saturnine of Antioch, 145
Savior, 183, 195
Saviors, 156
Scandinavian, 163
School, 55, 84, 129, 201, 212-215,
    233
Schools, 207, 216, 219, 235-238
Science, 13, 44, 52, 57, 62, 73, 93,
    107, 111-112, 156, 163, 170,
    192, 211, 215, 222, 226, 228,
    231, 235
Scientific, 7, 9, 13, 19, 81-83
Scientist, 9
Scientists, 8-9, 34, 45
Scorpion, 116
Scots, 74, 195
Scribes, 77
Scriptures, 35, 109, 146, 229, 236
Scylla, 5, 60
Scyros, 151
Sea, 4-5, 16, 35, 37-38, 47-49, 52,
    106, 109, 131, 153, 170-171,
    191-192, 220
Seas, 107, 109
Seashells, 66
Second, 21, 26, 28, 36, 40, 55, 72, 79,
    82, 93, 98-99, 101, 118-119,
    125, 138, 149, 155, 157, 163,
    167-168, 184, 192, 199-200,
    202-203, 207-209, 212, 215,
    225-226, 229, 233-234, 236
Second Birth, 99, 101, 138, 149, 163,
    167-168, 184, 192, 199, 202-
    203, 207-209, 233-234
Second Death, 26, 212, 226, 234
Second Logos, 155, 168, 184, 229
Secrecy, 28, 138, 166, 185, 230, 238

Secret, 1, 7, 11, 18, 20-21, 30, 41, 44,
    51, 64, 72-75, 112, 118, 138,
    142, 148-149, 156, 184, 191,
    215, 217, 219, 221-222, 231,
    235
Secret Doctrine, 1, 11, 72-75, 217,
    221-222
Secret Enemy, 112
Sect, 49, 219-220
Seduce, 52, 186, 211
Seduced, 52, 185
Seduction, 183, 227
Seductive, 79, 186, 216
Seed, 4, 90, 99, 118, 121, 197, 221-
    222, 235
Seed-atoms, 57-58
Seeds, 90, 127, 151, 154, 168, 178,
    187, 214, 229, 235
Seers, 44, 74, 201, 221
Seity, 4
Selene, 49, 90-91
Self, 12-13, 29, 40, 69, 82, 84, 92,
    96-97, 99, 141, 175, 177, 197,
    206-207, 234-235
Self-conscious, 56
Self-consideration, 202, 212
Self-consolation, 202
Self-justification, 202, 212
Self-realization, 149, 158, 210, 225,
    234, 239
Self-realize, 28, 116, 149, 204, 232
Self-realized, 56-57, 65, 197-198, 220
Selfish, 103
Semen, 121, 189, 206, 216, 221, 235
Semi-liquid, 189
Seminal, 104, 142, 189, 227, 235
Seminis, 145, 148, 189, 206
Sensation, 52, 81, 218
Sensation of Contemplation, 81
Sense, 19, 29, 40, 64, 70, 80, 89, 93,
    121, 157, 217, 237-238
Sentimentalism, 52
Sentiments, 3
Septenary, 51, 142, 217
Septentrion, 119
Septuple, 174
Sepulchre, 50-53

Seraphim, 59, 200, 236
Serenity, 70, 81-83, 96, 211
Serpent, 4, 12, 28, 111, 122, 137,
    145, 155, 190, 192, 205, 214,
    224, 227-228
Serpentine, 100, 148, 190, 227
Serpents, 102, 122, 125, 158, 166,
    214
Serpent-stones, 74
Sethenos, 119
Seven, 19-21, 25, 33-34, 67, 73, 89-
    90, 152, 154, 156-157, 189,
    191, 205, 214, 216-218, 220,
    225, 227-228, 231-232, 238
Seventeen, 161
Seventh, 1, 20, 161, 197, 231, 233
Severity, 137
Sex, 28-29, 41, 51, 90-91, 115, 123,
    136, 141-142, 147-149, 156,
    167-168, 176, 187, 189, 194-
    195, 201, 206, 208, 210, 215,
    217, 230, 232, 234, 236, 239
Sex Yoga, 28-29, 51, 115, 148-149,
    167, 189, 194, 201, 206, 210
Sexes, 120-121, 238
Sexto, 25
Sexual Alchemy, 27, 207, 210, 216
Sexual Magic, 104, 115, 145, 158,
    206, 216, 227, 235-236,
    238-239
Sexual Mysteries, 187, 209
Sexually, 121, 229, 235
Shambhala, 79
Sheep, 71, 161
Shekelmesha, 205
Shells, 80, 122
Shield, 142-145
Shiva, 89, 111, 189, 219, 229
Sibyl, 60-61, 98, 100, 163
Sibyls, 36, 61-62
Sick, 63
Sickening, 47
Sickly, 37
Sickness, 94, 126, 176
Sicknesses, 89
Sidereal Gods, 39
Sidereal Light, 12

Siderites, 74
Sig, 51-54
Sigberto of Gemblours, 162
Sigel, 51
Sight, 4, 16, 160, 175-176, 221
Signs, 86, 229
Silence, 37, 63, 70, 83-84, 94, 105,
    133, 213, 231
Silent, 5, 93, 152, 184
Silver, 39, 109, 174, 193
Silvery, 157
Simoniacs, 53
Sin, 167, 183, 222, 230
Sinful, 167
Sing, 6, 30, 73, 104, 183, 215
Singing, 63, 80, 101, 161, 167
Single, 115-116, 166-167, 232
Sings, 7, 85
Sinned, 186, 227
Sinning, 108, 139, 152-153
Sins, 79, 176, 183, 220, 234
Sion, 41, 194
Siren, 153
Sister, 86, 88, 101, 129-132, 154,
    204, 220
Sisters, 79, 90-92, 100, 103, 108, 117,
    125, 137, 171, 198, 211
Sivananda, 4, 28-30, 217, 228, 230,
    235-236, 238
Six, 111, 148, 161, 228
Sixth, 43, 90, 95, 111, 121, 233
Sixth Arcanum, 111
Skepticism, 160
Slander, 68, 90, 203-204
Slave, 69, 87, 165
Slaves, 68, 144, 191
Sleep, 65, 201, 203, 233
Sleeping, 64-65, 71, 201-203, 227-
    228
Sleeplessness, 52-53
Sleeps, 38, 108, 136
Sleepy, 202-204, 211
Slug, 126, 152
Snake, 123, 155, 227
Sodomites, 210

Solar Bodies, 28, 57, 101, 142, 148-
    149, 158, 168, 196, 202, 208-
    209, 223, 234, 236-237
Solar Fire, 11, 221
Solar Logos, 4, 77
Solar Man, 12, 166, 207, 238
Solar Mind, 208
Solar Race, 78
Solar Vehicles, 209
Soma, 166-167, 207, 209, 236, 238
Soma Psuchikon, 209
Son, 2-5, 15-18, 49, 53, 59, 77-79, 87,
    97, 127, 129-132, 137, 141,
    146, 160, 167-169, 177-178,
    186, 224, 229, 234
Son of God, 146
Son of Man, 77-79, 167-168
Song, 64, 87
Sons, 15, 34, 36, 48, 80, 110, 141
Sons of Men, 80, 110
Sophia, 85, 135, 220, 229-230
Sophia Achamoth, 85, 135
Sophia Prunikos, 85
Soul, 4, 25, 38-39, 56, 69, 77, 83-84,
    89, 91, 105, 108, 131-133,
    142, 144, 149, 151, 153-154,
    158, 165-167, 170, 193, 196,
    204, 207-209, 212, 221-222,
    226, 230-233, 237
Souls, 26, 49, 100, 105, 153-154,
    158, 165, 170, 174, 193, 198-
    199, 202, 214-215, 229, 231,
    234, 238
Sound, 30, 42-43, 51, 54, 66, 74, 93,
    99, 105, 118, 147, 184, 206,
    213, 230
Soviet Union, 175
Sow, 127, 159-160, 235
Sowed, 90, 225-226
Sower, 90
Space, 4, 8-9, 18-21, 27, 31, 33-34,
    43, 45, 49, 55-56, 69, 85,
    88-92, 98, 103, 111, 122, 135,
    163, 187, 193, 197, 213
Spain, 186
Spanish, 49
Spark, 41, 104, 226

Sparks, 11, 13, 159, 162, 164, 168
Spartan, 5, 16
Spear, 184-187
Species, 121, 123, 176
Spell, 48
Spermatic, 97, 191
Sphere, 34, 57, 86, 91, 99-100, 102,
    137, 142, 148-149, 151, 167,
    170, 201, 208-209, 227, 232,
    234, 238
Sphinx, 117, 146, 164
Spill, 97, 189, 191, 121, 210, 216,
    222
Spinal, 99, 188, 217-218, 228
Spine, 12, 189-190, 217
Spirit, 12-13, 15, 18, 27-28, 52, 91,
    120, 142-143, 151, 173, 177,
    183-184, 186, 189, 199, 205,
    208, 213-214, 217, 224-226,
    228-229, 231, 233, 238
Spirits, 3, 126, 158
Spiritual, 9, 18, 39, 55, 57, 64, 73, 89,
    119, 137, 189, 193, 221, 227-
    229, 235-236, 238
Spirituality, 206
Spouse, 115, 130, 142, 145, 191
Spring, 3, 62, 143
Squires, 183-184
Stables, 155 165-166
Star, 17, 51, 55-56, 211
Starless, 47
Starry, 14, 21, 34, 113, 193
Stars, 4-5, 20, 39, 43, 45, 51, 56-57,
    60, 63, 116, 130, 160, 192,
    213-214
Statue, 72-73, 156
Steel, 16, 48, 103-104, 140, 142, 147
Step, 40, 152, 171, 198, 231
Steps, 7, 64, 99, 101, 151, 156
Stone, 1, 41, 51, 64, 72-75, 79, 83,
    90-91, 103, 117, 125, 146-
    147, 156, 194-195, 209, 214-
    215, 224
Stone of Jacob, 1, 195
Stonehenge, 73, 75
Stones, 41, 73-75, 121, 146, 162, 195,
    214

Strawberry, 171
Strength, 98, 104, 150, 230
Strophades Islands, 47, 49
Styx, 100, 191
Subconscious, 70, 83-84, 155
Subconsciousness, 13, 115, 153, 190,
    211
Subject, 75, 238
Subjective, 7, 25, 108, 115, 226
Subplanes, 9, 232-233
Subrace, 90
Subterranean, 26, 44, 49, 156
Suidas, 75
Sukra, 157
Sulu-Sigi-Sig, 51
Summer, 7, 57
Sun, 13-14, 31, 51, 78-79, 88, 90, 92,
    97, 103-104, 109, 157-158,
    165, 191-192, 196, 217,
    225-226
Sun Christ, 13-14, 196, 217
Sun-King, 27
Sun-Lady, 149
Sunday, 68
Sunlight, 102
Sunny, 27, 48, 120, 145-146
Sunrise, 104, 196
Suns, 67
Super-efforts, 90, 152
Superior Worlds, 18, 38, 145, 178,
    217, 226, 234, 239
Super-soul, 89, 214
Supper, 95, 178, 187
Swan, 163, 186
Swastika, 205-210
Sweatborn, 72
Swines, 111-112, 154
Sword, 39, 52, 54, 88, 110, 122, 132,
    140, 142, 145, 147-148, 152,
    191
Swords, 16, 52, 132, 141
Sychaeus, 6, 85, 102
Sylphs, 116, 163
Symbol, 49, 97, 99, 116, 178-179,
    183, 186-187, 205, 219, 224
Symbolic, 48, 52, 103, 145, 215,
    228-229

Sympathetic, 118, 217-218
Synthesis, 1, 20, 55, 112, 196, 214, 223, 231
Synthesis Religion, 1
Syria, 62, 77
Szechuan, 94
Tail, 112, 123, 214, 227, 233
Talaveranean, 171
Tara, 62
Tarot, 111, 213, 216-217, 224, 226-227, 229, 232, 238-239
Tartarus, 103-104, 139, 166
Tau, 41, 66, 147, 183
Tau Cross, 147, 183
Tea, 14, 30, 93
Tehuantepec, 113
Teiwaz, 63
Telemachus, 49, 53, 170
Tempest, 38, 47, 70, 225
Tempests, 11, 85, 205
Templar Knights, 183
Templars, 1
Temple, 11, 17, 39-41, 56, 65, 83, 97-98, 101, 103, 120-122, 127-128, 131, 137-138, 146-147, 155-158, 166, 168, 186, 189, 193, 195, 206, 222, 234
Temple of Apollo, 11
Temple of Ceres, 17
Temple of Chapultepec, 101
Temple of Delphi, 83
Temple of Hercules, 155-158
Temple of Jagrenat, 155
Temple of Janus, 127-128
Temple of Kali, 122
Temple of Karma, 131
Temple of Montserrat, 186
Temple of Philae, 156
Temple of Vesta, 11
Temples, 27, 88, 121, 125, 148
Tempt, 146, 197
Temptation, 146, 198
Tempted, 146, 182
Tempter, 5, 126
Tempting, 111, 122, 125, 155, 197
Ten, 42, 81-83, 159, 180, 218
Teocali, 156

Teotihuacan, 156
Termites, 175
Terrestrial, 90, 176, 225
Testament of Learning, 27
Thebes, 25, 61
Thelema, 103-104, 118, 142, 149
Theologies, 49
Theories, 9, 67, 90, 149, 195, 208, 216
Theory, 19, 31, 33, 222
Theory of Relativity, 31
Theosophists, 89, 228, 233
Theosophy, 27
Thersilochus, 102
Theseus, 97, 99, 125, 153
Thetis, 141
Third, 21, 28, 37, 43, 55, 59, 72, 77, 79, 88, 91, 97-98, 111, 119-121, 125, 142-143, 155, 157, 167-168, 179, 183-184, 186, 191, 200, 208, 210, 214, 221, 224, 229, 231, 233
Third Degree, 179
Third Logos, 111, 142-143, 155, 167-168, 183-184, 186, 191, 210, 224, 229
Thirty, 159-160
Thirty-fold, 90
Thirty-two, 93
Thor, 205
Thorn, 101, 103-104, 116, 118
Thorns, 90, 94, 103, 166
Thought, 20, 30, 38, 44, 63, 70, 81-82, 113, 121, 129-130, 138, 163, 166, 184, 208, 213, 221, 229, 235
Thoughts, 82, 88, 231, 239
Thousand, 56, 78, 103, 127, 171, 183, 205, 223
Thousands, 16, 120, 139, 198, 208, 223, 230, 236
Thrace, 23, 99
Three, 5, 8, 28, 41-42, 45, 47, 49, 53-55, 57, 76, 79, 93-94, 102-103, 111, 124-127, 135, 142, 151-152, 159, 162, 190, 192,

194, 197, 200, 204-205, 211, 213, 220, 229, 237-238
Three Furies, 5, 103, 124-127
Threshold, 15, 17, 83, 126, 137, 147, 215
Thurisaz, 101
Thybris, 160
Tiber, 159-160
Tibet, 79, 174, 216, 219, 236
Tigers, 87
Tijitlis, 199
Timeaus, 170
Tin, 157
Tir, 66, 78, 80
Tisiphone, 125
Titans, 65, 72, 103, 120, 157, 174
Titurel, 183-184
Tlaloc, 164
To Soma Heliakon, 166-167, 207, 236, 238
Tonatzin, 135
Tower, 63-64
Towers, 15-16
Traitor, 88, 125, 144, 153
Traitors, 53, 103, 125
Tranquil, 81-82, 214
Tranquility, 70, 178
Transcendental, 7, 34, 39, 79, 112, 205, 219, 233
Transcendental Church, 39
Transfiguration, 165
Transform, 49, 229, 231
Transformation, 43, 119, 216
Transformative, 142
Transformed, 16, 23, 43, 47-48, 82, 87, 90, 111, 165, 185, 193
Transforming, 13, 236
Transforms, 33, 69, 84, 93, 106, 111-112, 192, 222
Transmigration, 23, 25-26
Transmutation, 115, 208
Transmute, 149, 214
Transmuted, 104, 140, 142, 208
Transubstantiation, 187
Tree, 23-24, 32, 52, 58, 60, 99, 102, 120, 173, 220, 223, 231-232

Tree of Life, 32, 52, 58, 102, 220, 231-232
Trees, 25, 107, 159-160, 162, 169-170
Tribunal of Karma, 132
Tribunals, 130
Trident, 4, 16
Tridimensional, 34, 55
Tripurusndari, 135
Triumphal, 40, 68
Triumphant, 77, 79
Triumphant Church, 79
Triveni, 189
Trojan, 4-5, 15-18, 23, 35-38, 47, 59-60, 71, 85-88, 97-98, 126, 155, 169-170, 191
Trojans, 4, 15, 23, 47-48, 59-60, 71, 109, 169
Troubadour, 12
Troy, 15-18, 23, 36, 38, 59, 74, 98-99, 102, 127, 141, 159, 169, 205
Truth, 19, 33, 51, 53, 57, 67, 69, 77, 84, 93, 98, 108, 125, 167, 170, 174, 190, 197, 201
Tui Keng, 96
Tunic, 147-148, 156, 174
Tunics, 183, 197
Turnus, 127-128, 142, 169-170, 191
Twelve, 45, 93, 121, 156, 174, 180
Twentieth, 112, 130
Twenty, 75, 93
Twice, 160, 234
Twin, 143-144, 156, 204, 220
Two, 7, 28, 30, 35-36, 43, 45, 49, 64, 72, 77, 80, 85, 99, 111, 117-118, 120, 135, 144, 147, 157-158, 171-172, 179-180, 184, 187, 189-190, 192, 195-196, 204, 209-210, 218, 220-221, 223, 228, 235-236
Twofold, 153
Tyndareus, 16
Tyr, 63, 65-66, 78, 80
Tyranny, 175
Uhr, 91
Ulysses, 18, 49, 53, 71, 109, 112, 153
Uma, 111, 135

Unconscious, 70, 84, 191, 224
Uncreated, 69, 91
Uncreated Light, 91
Understand, 20, 60, 96, 137, 144, 170, 178, 201, 213, 215, 218, 226, 238
Understanding, 138, 175, 216, 233
Understood, 70, 117, 131, 138, 154, 178, 221, 224
Underworld, 98, 228
Union, 175, 228-230, 233-234, 238
United, 8, 121, 130, 218, 228-230
United States, 8
Unity, 34, 120, 163, 231
Unity of Life, 163
Universal Spirit of Life, 91, 199
Universal Womb, 49
Universe, 3, 7-9, 20-21, 24, 28, 31, 33, 43-45, 80, 83, 89, 92, 103, 131, 137, 163-165, 193, 198-199, 214, 222, 227
Universes, 7-9, 12-13, 18, 20-21, 32-34, 57, 139, 163, 193
Unknown, 20, 43, 49, 61, 72, 84, 91, 163, 165, 231
Unknown Darkness, 91
Unmanifested, 28, 192, 219
Upadhis, 126
Upper Egypt, 156
Ur, 89-92
Urania, 14, 63, 106, 193
Uriel, 157
Uruz, 89
Urwala, 163
Usanas, 157
Utica, 165
Valkyries, 163
Valley, 24, 37, 65, 72, 234
Varuna, 164
Veda, 43, 221
Vedantic, 190
Vehicle, 58, 64, 66, 69, 119, 173-174, 217, 231
Vehicles, 207, 209, 236
Veil, 1, 4, 28, 79, 168, 218
Veil of Isis, 1, 79, 168
Veiled, 1, 44

Veils, 16
Venus, 4-6, 15, 49, 85, 134-135, 141-144, 148, 157
Veronica, 103
Vertebrae, 189
Vertical, 99, 112, 187
Vertically, 209
Vessels, 66
Vesta, 11
Vestal, 148, 192
Vesture, 122
Vestures, 120, 207
Vice, 111, 180, 202
Vigil, 87
Vigilant, 5, 204
Violet, 13
Violets, 171
Viper, 51, 122, 155
Virgil, 160
Virgin, 2-3, 60, 98, 111, 126
Virgin-Mother, 49
Virginal, 119-120
Virgins, 35
Virile, 29
Virtue, 3, 53, 111, 167, 233, 235
Virtues, 59, 112, 167, 178, 191, 198, 200, 236
Virtutis, 189
Vishnu, 205, 221, 229
Vision, 3, 16, 59, 89, 160
Visions, 53, 160
Vital, 34, 78, 91, 115, 136, 167, 180, 190, 209, 216, 218-219, 221, 232, 236
Void, 9, 106, 214, 233
Volcanic, 121
Volcano, 31, 128
Volcanoes, 64, 120
Vowels, 14, 192
Vows, 60, 94, 98, 160
Vrittis, 82
Vulcan, 25, 28, 57, 141-145, 155-156, 166-167, 169, 183, 187, 191, 227
Wagner, 183
Walnut, 171
Wan Shan, 93, 96

Wand, 110, 158
War, 25, 48, 85, 98, 100, 126-128,
    141, 143-144, 157, 159, 169,
    204
Warrior, 16-17, 24, 35, 59, 71, 98,
    109, 144-145, 169
Warriors, 16, 24, 48, 121, 155, 169-
    170
Wars, 169, 191
Watchers, 81
Watchman, 204
Water, 17, 43, 50, 78-79, 87, 96,
    120, 147, 163-164, 173, 191,
    206, 209, 214, 218, 220-221,
    232-233
Water of Life, 120, 206
Waters, 5, 18, 82, 100, 128, 139, 142,
    159-160, 167-168, 171, 184,
    186-187, 191, 224-226, 229
Wave, 96, 199
Waves, 4-5, 43, 49, 82-84, 91, 171
Wax, 97
Ways, 127, 165, 189
Wedding, 88, 149, 158, 166-167, 170,
    196, 202, 207-209, 236-238
Wedding Feast, 207
Wedding Garment, 149, 158, 166-
    167, 196, 202, 207-209,
    236-238
Wednesday, 105
Westminster, 75
Whale, 161
Wheat, 171
White, 23-24, 30, 49, 109, 111, 114,
    120, 131, 145-149, 157, 159-
    160, 174-176, 183, 194-195,
    204, 209, 214-216, 223-225,
    227, 229, 232, 234, 236-238
White Brotherhood, 131, 145, 195,
    229, 238
White Initiation, 209, 225, 232
White Lodge, 149, 194, 215, 236
White Moon, 109, 111
Whitened, 53
Whiteness, 186, 194
Whore, 111
Widow, 129, 179

Wife, 16-18, 51, 59, 99, 141, 148,
    152, 204, 210, 224, 227-230
Wild, 16, 86, 109, 127
Wilderness, 11-12, 51, 146, 165
Willpower, 83, 103-104, 117-118,
    121, 142, 149
Wilson, 31
Wind, 4-5, 23, 37-38, 60, 63-64, 116,
    164, 225
Windmill, 206-207
Winds, 4, 37, 48, 109, 142, 144, 147-
    148, 161, 216
Wine, 24, 71, 85-87, 107, 183, 187
Wings, 3, 47, 97, 107, 176, 190
Wisdom, 1, 16, 24, 71, 107, 120, 144,
    158, 168, 177-178, 202, 212,
    216-217, 222, 225, 233
Witches, 47-48, 100, 227
Wives, 15, 53, 111, 222
Wizards, 74
Wolf, 71, 143, 158, 160
Woman, 16, 38, 52, 59, 86-87, 107,
    127, 129, 148-149, 185-186,
    195, 221, 229-230, 238
Womb, 3, 15, 49, 65, 91-92, 100, 121,
    131-132, 141, 230, 233-234
Women, 7, 15, 35, 52, 64, 86-87, 111,
    115-116, 142, 145, 148, 169,
    185, 211, 230
Word, 1, 29-30, 34, 40, 49, 62, 70, 77,
    94, 113, 125, 146, 152, 165-
    166, 172, 193, 199, 213-214,
    217, 219-223, 228-230, 232,
    235-238
Worlds, 18, 21-22, 24, 26, 33-34, 38,
    49, 53, 64, 92, 100, 103, 145,
    178, 185, 192, 209, 211, 217,
    223, 225-226, 232, 234, 239
Wu, 8, 93-95
Xanthus, 98
Xochipilli, 164
Xuanzang, 72
Year, 1, 43, 94-95, 115, 161, 174, 211
Years, 17, 41, 57, 91, 120, 157, 159,
    171, 173, 195, 205, 211, 214,
    223, 226, 229-230, 236, 238
Yellow, 95, 148, 239

Yellow Dragon, 95
Yesod, 195, 223, 232
Yoga, 28-29, 51, 115, 121, 148-149,
        167, 189, 194, 201, 206, 210,
        217, 228, 230, 234, 236,
        238-239
Yogi, 28-29, 64, 225, 235, 239
Yogis, 12, 151, 239
Yoni, 41, 206
Youth, 107, 171, 225
Yucatecan, 205
Yuga, 111
Zeal, 160
Zen, 55, 173, 207
Zen Buddhism, 55, 173, 207
Zen Philosophy, 207
Zero, 31, 33, 212
Zeus, 12
Zigzag, 51-52, 54
Zodiacal, 78, 156, 228-229, 232, 234
Zombie, 64-65
Zoroaster, 11, 232
Zoroastrians, 89

Glorian Publishing is a non-profit publisher dedicated to spreading the sacred universal doctrine to suffering humanity. All of our works are made possible by the kindness and generosity of sponsors. If you would like to make a tax-deductible donation, you may send it to the address below, or visit our website for other alternatives. If you would like to sponsor the publication of a book, please contact us at help@gnosticteachings.org.

Glorian Publishing
PO Box 110225
Brooklyn, NY 11211 US

VISIT US ONLINE AT:
gnosticteachings.org